Interrogating and Innovating Comparative and International Education Research

New Research – New Voices

Series Editor

Halla B. Holmarsdottir
(*Oslo Metropolitan University, Norway*)

International Advisory Board

Karen Biraimah (*University of Central Florida, USA*)
Heidi Biseth (*Buskerud University College, Norway*)
Joan DeJaeghere (*University of Minnesota, USA*)
Zubeida Desai (*University of the Western Cape, South Africa*)
Alawia Farag (*Ahfad University for Women, Sudan*)
Fatma Gok (*Bogazici University, Turkey*)
Lihong Huang (*Norwegian Social Research (NOVA) Institute, Norway*)
Suzanne Majhanovich (*University of Western Ontario, Canada*)
Diane Napier (*University of Georgia, USA*)
Vuyokazi Nomlomo (*University of the Western Cape, South Africa*)
Gerald Ouma (*University of Pretoria, South Africa*)
Adila Pašalić-Kreso (*University of Sarajevo, Bosnia and Herzegovina*)
Yusuf Sayed (*University of Sussex, UK*)

VOLUME 9

The titles published in this series are listed at *brill.com/nrnv*

Interrogating and Innovating Comparative and International Education Research

Edited by

Caroline Manion, Emily Anderson, Supriya Baily,
Meagan Call-Cummings, Radhika Iyengar,
Payal P. Shah and Matthew A. Witenstein

BRILL
SENSE

LEIDEN | BOSTON

Cover illustration: Artwork by Nishaad S. Lorengo.

All chapters in this book have undergone peer review.

The Library of Congress Cataloging-in-Publication Data is available online at http://catalog.loc.gov

Typeface for the Latin, Greek, and Cyrillic scripts: "Brill". See and download: brill.com/brill-typeface.

ISSN 2542-9221
ISBN 978-90-04-41145-6 (paperback)
ISBN 978-90-04-41146-3 (hardback)
ISBN 978-90-04-41147-0 (e-book)

Copyright 2020 by Koninklijke Brill NV, Leiden, The Netherlands.
Koninklijke Brill NV incorporates the imprints Brill, Brill Hes & De Graaf, Brill Nijhoff, Brill Rodopi, Brill Sense, Hotei Publishing, mentis Verlag, Verlag Ferdinand Schöningh and Wilhelm Fink Verlag.
All rights reserved. No part of this publication may be reproduced, translated, stored in a retrieval system, or transmitted in any form or by any means, electronic, mechanical, photocopying, recording or otherwise, without prior written permission from the publisher.
Authorization to photocopy items for internal or personal use is granted by Koninklijke Brill NV provided that the appropriate fees are paid directly to The Copyright Clearance Center, 222 Rosewood Drive, Suite 910, Danvers, MA 01923, USA. Fees are subject to change.

This book is printed on acid-free paper and produced in a sustainable manner.

Contents

Foreword IX
    Halla B. Holmarsdottir
Preface XII
Acknowledgements XV
About the Cover XVI
List of Figures and Tables XVII
List of Acronyms XVIII
Notes on Contributors XIX

1 Interrogating and Innovating CIE Research: Setting the Stage 1
    Meagan Call-Cummings, Caroline Manion and Payal P. Shah

PART 1
Interrogating and Innovating CIE Research

2 Onto-Epistemological Frontiers in CIE Research: Exploring the Problematic 17
    Caroline Manion

3 Before Reconciliation, There Must Be Truth 29
    Leigh Patel

4 Beauty and Comparative Education Research Methods: A Consideration for Aesthetic Cognitivism 34
    Derrick Tu

5 Interrogating Impact: Whose Knowledge Counts in Assessment of Comparative and International Education Interventions? 49
    Karen Ross

PART 2
Decolonizing Methodology by Invoking Local Voices

6 Decolonializing Voice and Localizing Method in Comparative Education 67
    Gerardo L. Blanco

7 Amplifying Indian Women's Voices and Experiences to Advance Their Access to Technical and Vocational Education Training   72
   Radhika Iyengar and Matthew A. Witenstein

8 Contemporary Traditions of State-Madrassa Relationships in India   86
   Huma Kidwai

9 'I Walk Each Village': Transforming Knowledge through Citizen-Led Assessments   109
   Erik Jon Byker

PART 3
Destabilizing Power and Authority: Taking Intersectionality Seriously

10 Destabilizing Power and Authority: Taking Intersectionality Seriously   129
    Payal P. Shah and Emily Anderson

11 Notes on Intersectionality and Decolonizing Knowledge Production   140
    Patricia S. Parker

12 Knowledge Hierarchies and Interviewing Methods in Cambodia: Strategies for Collaborative Interpretation   148
    Kelly Grace and Sothy Eng

13 Amplifying the Voices of People with Disabilities in Comparative and International Education Research with PhotoVoice Methodology   166
    Alisha M. Braun

PART 4
Implications for Methodology: Towards More Equitable Futures

14 Implications for Methodology: Towards More Equitable Futures   187
    Supriya Baily, Betsy M. Scotto-Lavino and Meagan Call-Cummings

15 CIE Methodology and Possibilities of Other Futures   195
    Ameena Ghaffar-Kucher

16 The "Significance" of Epistemicide: Unpacking the Problematic
Statistical Foundations of Knowledge Production in Global Education
Governance   206
   D. Brent Edwards Jr.

17 Continuing the Conversation: Towards a Model of Collective Critical
Reflection in CIE Research   225
   *Lê Minh Hằng, Brendan DeCoster, Jeremy R. Gombin-Sperling and
   Timothy D. Reedy*

18 New Directions for Consideration: Looking Forward and Ahead   241
   *Emily Anderson, Supriya Baily, Radhika Iyengar and
   Matthew A. Witenstein*

   Index   251

Foreword

Over the past fifty years, the field of Comparative and International Education (CIE) has moved from a sole focus on measurement, through the application of nomothetic research aimed at improving evidence-based findings, to recognizing the importance of qualitative inquiry with the goal of understanding context and meaning. The inclusion of qualitative research has brought with it concerns over issues such as hegemonic power, limited understanding of cultures and peoples and a desire to decolonize the field of CIE. Such questions have also begun to be applied in the context of quantitative and mixed-methods approaches as well. As the series editor for *New Research – New Voices*, I was delighted that the seven editors have chosen this series for the publication of a collection of papers from the second CIES Symposium, held from October 26–27, 2017, at the Arlington campus of George Mason University (GMU). The symposium was hosted by members of the Gender and Education Committee, the South Asia SIG and faculty at GMU, with the theme "Interrogating and innovating CIE research".

To some degree the symposium aimed to problematize and challenge us to move beyond the "what works" agenda, founded on the belief that "education should be or become an evidence-based practice and that teaching should be or become an evidence-based profession" (Biesta, 2007, p. 1). For Phillips this agenda is closely linked to the concept of evidence and necessitates an understanding of empirical research. Phillips (2005) argues that empirical educational research faces a number of challenges:

> On the one hand, there are influential figures who countenance only rigorous scientific research; they use as their model of science the randomised controlled experiment or field trial, and they point to experimentation in medicine as the ideal model for educational research. The existence of this group of hardliners fills many other members of the research community with feelings of despair and utter hopelessness … at the other extreme pole of opinion – there are those who see the members of the first group as advocating 'their father's paradigm' (here Phillips borrows the expression from Patti Lather, 2004) – [this] … paradigm … is hopelessly modernist, positivistic and imperialistic; those clustering at this second pole want to see an educational research that (again in Lather's words) moves 'toward a Nietzschean sort of "unnatural science" that leads to greater health by fostering ways of knowing that escape normativity' (Lather, 2004, p. 27). This second position is so murky and fraught with danger that it is regarded by the advocates of scientific rigour as

leading to the total extinction of the empirical research enterprise ... Let us pray we have the wisdom to choose correctly! Or rather, let us have the wisdom to reject both poles – for neither point the way to the development of an empirical educational research that can illuminate educational phenomena and that can be useful to practitioners or policymakers as they hone their practice or shape their policies. (Phillips, 2005, p. 579)

In order to justify educational investment and assure trust in educational policymaking this volume points to the need for careful scrutiny of the epistemological, ontological and ideological basis of educational research findings. Equally, the volume attempts to challenge the epistemological basis and the narrow idea of what counts as research and in doing so points to the need for discussion and dialogue amongst CIE scholars who are committed to fostering a deeper understanding of methods and methodological issues. This goal corresponds well to the two strands of the *New Research – New Voices* series:

Strand 1: New Voices and New Knowledge in Research Methodology
This strand is dedicated to producing cutting-edge titles focusing on Research Methodology and intends to contribute to the knowledge foundation in educational research by specifically seeking out those who work both across disciplines and inter-disciplinary in terms of their methodological approaches.

Strand 2: New Voices and New Knowledge in Educational Research
This strand focuses on theoretical and empirical contributions that are unique and will provide important insights into the field of educational research across a range of contexts globally. This part of the series will collectively communicate new voices, new insights and new possibilities within the field of educational research.

The book has new voices who otherwise would not be heard without the CIES support for the symposium. This symposium served as a platform for the seven editors to locate voices that seek to challenge the narrow idea of what counts in educational research and in doing so suggestion alternative directions for the CIE field. The dedication and commitment of the seven editors to undertake the responsibility for the realization of the volume means that important and new voices are included in how we can understand and approach educational research.

This volume serves to share a collection of papers from the symposium that aim achieve the overall goal of offering a platform for discussion and dialogue amongst CIE scholars, while making a significant contribution to both strands in the book series. The volume is divided into four parts with each focusing on distinct aspects from the four symposium plenaries: Plenary I: Interrogating and Innovating CIE Research; Plenary II: Decolonizing methodology by invoking local voices; Plenary III: Destabilizing power and authority: Taking intersectionality seriously; Plenary IV: Implications for methodology: Towards more equitable futures.

The volume and the voices in it reflect not only on moving us beyond what works in educational research, but moreover takes up the challenges we face in relation to larger philosophical questions and how we can know what we know. Questions this volume attempts to tackle are: who has power over knowledge production and its dissemination, to whom access is granted, while also questioning the role of researcher identity and what researchers and practitioners can do to displace entrenched power relations in and through the production and use of CIE knowledge. The last part in this volume takes up the future of CIE research and reminds us of the need "to move beyond the more narrow definitions of empiricism and science and the pursuit of objectivity and neutrality as the Gold Standard to embrace new onto-epistemological approaches, fresh methodological designs, and innovative and increasingly technology-savvy tools".

I applaud both CIES for supporting this important symposium and to the seven editors for taking up the challenge to move the field forward and to questions the future of CIE research.

References

Biesta, G. (2007). Why "what works" wont' work: Evidence-based practice and the democratic deficit in educational research. *Educational Theory, 57*(1), 1–22.

Lather, P. (2004). This IS your father's paradigm: Government intrusion and the case of qualitative research in education. *Qualitative Quarterly, 10*(1), 15–34.

Phillips, D. C. (2005). The contested nature of empirical research (and why Philosophy of Education offers little help). *Journal of Philosophy of Education, 39*(4), 577–597.

Halla B. Holmarsdottir
Series Editor
Oslo Metropolitan University

Preface

In October 2017, over 150 people involved in the field of comparative and international education (CIE) came together to discuss the work of interrogation and innovation within the context of CIE. The symposium, funded by the Comparative and International Education Society (CIES) and other partners, was organized in collaboration with the Center for International Education, George Mason University, the Gender and Education Standing Committee of CIES, and the South Asia Special Interest Group also of CIES. This book is the culminating product of a powerful two-day event with conversations related to epistemology and methodology present within the context of international comparative education.

How comparative and international education phenomenon are studied, the questions we ask, the tools we use and the epistemological, ontological, and ideological orientations they reflect, shape the nature of the knowledge produced, the value placed on that knowledge, and of critical importance, its pedagogy and implications for practice in diverse societies globally. Yet, from both within and outside of the field of Comparative and International Education (CIE), scholars and practitioners have raised concerns about the colonial and neo-colonial practices and dynamics that have been reproduced and/or have characterized (in part) the history of CIE. This was the focus of both the symposium and of this book.

"Historically, within ICE [International Comparative Education] there has been a sense that the goals of research are to furnish reliable information about educational systems, ideals, problems and activities" (Carey, 1966, p. 418). Over time, this idea has consistently changed and with that evolution comes an effort to deconstruct systems and subsystems towards sharing and utilizing "theories and concepts … in cooperatively developing strategies for educational development (p. 419). In the intervening years, discussions addressing concerns of hegemonic power, insular understanding of cultures and peoples and increased awareness of the colonizers and the colonized have grown (Marginson & Mollis, 2001; Benhabib, 2002). Nóvoa and Yariv-Mashal (2003) provide a timeline of the past century that demonstrates shifts in understanding. Understanding the fluctuations of how we know what we know provides some context and the changing nature of ontology and epistemology among comparativists. Nóvoa and Yariv-Mashal's (2003) timeline explores the early forms of documenting knowledge in the 1880s as a time of knowing the *other*; the 1920s as an effort to understand the *other*; the 1960s as a time of constructing the *other*; and finally, the 2000s where the focus has been on measuring the *other*. Their contention lies within the notion that comparative research has been used primarily to suggest comparison as a mode of governance (Baily, Shah, & Call-Cummings, 2016).

The emergence of measurement as the foundation of comparison in the 2000s would certainly suggest that the need for metrics supports the overall continued push for evidence-based findings and emphasis on positivist models of research. This affects comparative education in a unique fashion where, due to the scope of work, the impacts can affect policy, projects, and programs on a wider dimension as mandated by global frameworks such as Education for All, the Millennium Development Goals and others. Nóvoa and Yariv-Mashal (2003) argue that knowing the historical journey of a geographic space might be a more appropriate use of comparative research. This focus on qualitative understanding of context and meaning draws attention to the debate over the last fifty years on the role, function and use of research and the larger philosophical questions that are both explicit and implicit, as well as overt and covert. Questions relate to-how we know what we know; and, how do our experiences color what and how we know? Other questions emerging from this discussion include: addressing who has power over knowledge production and its dissemination (Quinn, 1998), to whom access is granted, and interrogating the role of researcher identity.

Recent efforts to contest larger epistemological issues include drawing attention to the importance of reflexivity and interrogating the role of the researcher (i.e., subjectivity and positionality), focusing on epistemological issues of what can be known and how, challenging dominant and hegemonic discourses and presenting alternative perspectives/knowledge. Critical questions concerning the dominant application of "Western" epistemologies and research paradigms in the field of CIE draw our attention to problems of exclusion and the reproduction of rigidly unjust hierarchies (of diverse peoples, knowledges and practices).

Simply put, failing to recognize and meaningfully learn from and apply critical and alternative methodologies (i.e., Indigenous, anti- and post-colonial, participatory, feminist, etc.), means that CIE may not necessarily be experienced as a safe and/or inclusive space.

Some regional efforts and certain fields of study have been characterized by both change and continuity in terms of the research paradigms and methodologies embraced. We believe that the influence of South Asian scholars and feminist writers in the field of gender and education have sought to break traditional and dominant notions of how knowledge is created, studied, and formalized. While much work has relied on dominant positivist research approaches in the social sciences, innovative currents in South Asia and in gender and education research have developed and used critical, participatory, decolonizing, postcolonial, and feminist methodologies. This has offered fresh insights in terms of how our work can challenge global hierarchies of knowledge while promoting gender equality in education as a matter of global social justice (Unterhalter, 2007; Takayama, 2011).

For this symposium and this book, we invited paper proposals that interrogate existing practices of knowledge production, dissemination and application in the field of gender and education and/or present examples of CIE research implemented using epistemologically and methodologically innovative approaches. Our vision is to synthesize some of these discussions and offer CIE scholars who are committed to methodology, a platform for dialogue and discussion. In a landscape that appears to lack clear focus of the underlying methodological and epistemological roots of methods as a central and guiding theme of inquiry, we hope to provide an explicit outlet for dialogue to promote engaged and deep conversations on comparative methodology.

Our goal for both the symposium and the book is to provide a foundation through which those conducting and consuming research in CIE can engage in further dialogue about their practices and learn from each other. We hope this book continues the conversations begun at the symposium, allows those who were not able to attend to see the power of these discussions and offer us all a chance to continue to have these conversations in our work, our classrooms, our writing and in our professional associations. We have been humbled by these experiences over the past eighteen months and we look forward to continuing to interrogate and innovate with the field of comparative and international education.

Acknowledgements

A book such as this requires a number of acknowledgements for the support and help along the way. We extend our gratitude to:

1. CIES Past President Dr. Noah Sobe, and the entire Board of Directors of CIES for their support of this endeavor;
2. Our stalwart group of plenary speakers who came ready to challenge and be challenged and engage in a rather innovative format of discussion and debate. These speakers include: Anjali Adukia, Lesley Bartlett, Emily Bent, Peter Demerath, Barbara Dennis, Ameena Ghaffar-Kucher, Shenila Khoja-Moolji, Huma Kidwai, Patricia Parker, Leigh Patel, Oren Pizmony-Levy, Gerardo Blanco Ramírez, Lilliana Patricia Saldaña, Riyad Shahjahan, Fran Vavrus and Dan Wagner;
3. Dr. Halla B. Holmarsdottir for both her championing of this book and for representing Oslo Metropolitan University as a partner in this effort;
4. George Mason University, Dr. Beverly D. Shaklee and the Center for International Education for their tireless work to make this symposium a success;
5. All of the symposium attendees who came to learn, unlearn and relearn over the course of the two-days;
6. The team at Arizona State University who hosted the first CIES Symposium in 2016 and shared their knowledge and lessons learned generously;
7. Dr. Will Brehm and his team at FreshEd who hosted four plenary speakers for deeper conversation about their speaker statements in his cutting edge podcast; and
8. Betsy Scotto-Lavino a graduate student at GMU, who supported our work in collecting information and formatting chapters.

About the Cover

Nishaad S. Lorengo is an artist studying Fine Arts at Virginia Commonwealth University. His work has been exhibited in galleries in Reston, Virginia, Richmond, Virginia and New York City. He has received a national gold medal for his work from the National Scholastic Art and Writing Awards. The cover is inspired by a series of words and phrases the editors of this volume shared with him including 'interrogate, create, change, disrupt, voice, amplify, deconstruct, reconstruct, valuing/honoring voice, imagine/imagination, liberate/emancipate, involvement and engagement and participation'.

Figures and Tables

Figures

10.1 Meta collage.   132
12.1 Decolonizing concepts between researchers and interpreters.   163
13.1 Distribution of comparative education articles on disability published by year.   171
13.2 "I am not a car". Turn stall campus entrance gate in use.   178

Tables

8.1 Government officials' perceived reasons for parents choosing madrassas (based on 29 semi-structured interviews conducted first-hand by the author).   93
9.1 In what area did you grow up?   116
9.2 Citizenship and identity.   116
17.1 Potential themes and questions for reflection sessions.   235

List of Acronyms

ABER	Arts-Based Educational Research
APC	Association of Cuban Educators
ASDP	Aajeevika Skill Development Programme
ASER	Annual Status of Education Report
BCP	Building a Culture of Peace
CE	Comparative Education
CiA	Community in Action
CIE	Comparative and International Education
CIES	Comparative and International Education Society
CRPD	Convention on the Rights of Persons with Disabilities
DIET	District Institutions of Education and Training
EFA	Education For All
HBCU(s)	Historically Black Colleges and Universities
ICT	Information Communication and Technology
IED	International Educational Development
ILSA(s)	International Large-Scale Assessment(s)
MDG(s)	Millennium Development Goal(s)
MoRD	Ministry of Rural Development
MSK	Mahashakti Seva Kendra
NGO(s)	Non-Governmental Organizations
NRLM	National Rural Livelihood Mission
NSDC	National Skill Development Corporation
NSS	National Service Scheme
PAR	Participatory Action Research
PISA	Programme for International Student Assessment
RCT	Randomized Control Trial
SDG(s)	Sustainable Development Goal(s)
SSLC	Secondary School Leaving Certificate
TIG	Topical Interest Group
TVET	Technical and Vocational Education and Training
UN	United Nations
UNESCO	United Nations Educational, Scientific and Cultural Organization
UP	Uttar Pradesh
USAID	United States Agency for International Development
YYC	Yes Youth Can!

Notes on Contributors

Emily Anderson
is a Visiting Assistant Professor of International and Intercultural Education at Florida International University and, currently, a Visiting Scholar with the Al Qasimi Foundation for Policy Research. Her research investigates the construction, diffusion, and complex negotiation of girls' education policy discourses through qualitative, network, and participatory approaches. She is a former (2017–2019) Co-Chairperson of the Gender & Education Standing Committee of the Comparative and International Education Society, and has over a decade of experience working in the areas of girls' education policy and international development, teacher education and training, and school-community engagement. Dr. Anderson was a founding co-editor of the *Annual Review of Comparative and International Education* (Emerald Press) and her work appears in peer-reviewed journals and edited collections.

Supriya Baily
is Associate Professor at George Mason University where she teaches international and comparative education, qualitative research methods and teacher education courses. She is also the Associate Director for the Center for International Education. Her research interests focus on gender, education and empowerment, the role of teacher agency towards social justice, and theorizing qualitative research methods. She is the co-editor of *Experiments in Agency: A Global Partnership to Transform Teacher Research* (Sense Publishers, 2017); *Educating Adolescent Girls Around the Globe: Challenges and Opportunities* (Routledge, 2015); and *Internationalizing Teacher Education in the US* (Rowman and Littlefield, 2012) and author of numerous journal articles and book chapters.

Gerardo L. Blanco
is an assistant professor at the Neag School of Education, University of Connecticut. His research explores the intersections of quality, branding and position taking in the context of global competition in higher education. This analysis incorporates critical perspectives of globalization and internationalization. Gerardo is an internationally engaged scholar; his research and teaching span across four continents. His work has been published in the *Comparative Education Review*, *Higher Education*, and *Studies in Higher Education*.

Alisha M. Braun
is an Assistant Professor of Social Foundations in the Department of Educational and Psychological Studies at the University of South Florida. Her research examines policy and practice related to access to quality education for marginalized children. Her current research focuses on inclusive education for students with disabilities in sub-Saharan Africa. She completed her PhD in Educational Policy from Michigan State University with graduate specializations in International Development and African Studies and has a background in psychology with an MA in School Psychology from Michigan State University and BA in Psychology from the University of Calgary.

Erik Jon Byker
is an Assistant Professor in the Department of Elementary Education at Stephen F. Austin State University. He has a PhD in Curriculum, Teaching, and Educational Policy from Michigan State University and holds a MEd Degree from the University of Virginia. Erik's research is international and comparative in scope as he has conducted ethnographic field studies in England, Cuba, India, South Korea, and across the United States on how students and teachers use and construct meaning for computer technology. Over the 2010-2011 academic year, he lived in Bangalore, India, and collected dissertation data on how an economic cross-section of Bangalore's elementary schools were using computer technology in their schools. Erik is the Secretary for the South Asia Special Interest Group at the Comparative and International Education Society.

Meagan Call-Cummings
is an Assistant Professor of Qualitative Methodology at George Mason University in Fairfax, Virginia, USA. Dr. Call-Cummings focuses on critical, feminist, and participatory forms of inquiry. That work most often takes participatory action research (PAR) and youth participatory action research (YPAR) forms. Dr. Call-Cummings is particularly interested in how university-based researchers can work with community members and various stakeholders to make the research (knowledge production) process more equitable and deeply rooted in intersubjective understanding. Her writing often takes up themes around the ethics and validity of knowledge creation.

Brendan DeCoster
is a PhD candidate in International Education Policy at the University of Maryland. His dissertation focuses on how academic integrity policies and plagiarism detection services disproportionally affect international students, and how this same is understood and perceived by stakeholders in institutes of higher education. His additional research interests include language policies

NOTES ON CONTRIBUTORS   XXI

in education and development, the ongoing commodification and essentialization of higher education, the role of intensive English programs in higher education, the establishment and dissemination of authoritative knowledge in education and development, and the nature of research and knowledge extraction across international borders.

D. Brent Edwards Jr.
is an Assistant Professor of Theory and Methodology in the Study of Education at the University of Hawaii, Manoa. His work focuses on the global governance of education, methodological critiques of best practice research, and the political economy of education reform. Geographically, these three areas of focus have lead to research in Latin America (Mexico, Colombia, El Salvador, Honduras), Southeast Asia (Cambodia, Indonesia, the Philippines), and Africa (Zambia).

Sothy Eng
is Assistant Professor of Human Development and Family Studies at the University of Hawaii at Manoa. Dr. Eng's area of expertise includes Cambodian education including access and equity, program development and evaluation, child and adolescent learning and development, family and community development, social capital, remarried families, gender-based violence, and international development

Ameena Ghaffar-Kucher
is a Senior Lecturer in the Literacy, Culture, and International Education Division at the University of Pennsylvania's Graduate School of Education, where she is also the Co-Director of the International Educational Development Program. Her research has focused on the socialization, academic engagement, and civic commitments of migrant children and youth. Her practitioner work has been around teacher education, curriculum development and school climate issues (particularly related to bias-based bullying and Islamophobia). Her work has been published in the *American Education Research Journal*; *Harvard Educational Review*; *International Journal of Intercultural Relations*; *Race, Ethnicity & Education*, *International Journal of Qualitative Studies in Education*; and *The Urban Review*.

Jeremy R. Gombin-Sperling
(he, him, his) is a 3rd year PhD Student in the International Education Policy program, and a Research Associate with a focus on diversity and inclusion in the Education Abroad office at the University of Maryland-College Park. He received his BA in Religious Studies and Psychology from New York University,

and a MA in the same program where he is earning his PhD. Jeremy's current research interests revolve around studying the implementation and impact of critical pedagogical practices into the teaching and management of study abroad and global service-learning programs throughout all stages of the experience.

Kelly Grace
earned her PhD from Lehigh University in the Department of Comparative and International Education. Her research focuses on gender and education in Cambodia and specifically on the everyday experiences of girls and women related to their academic achievement. She is also a consultant and freelance researcher.

Radhika Iyengar
has a PhD (with distinction) in Economics of Education from Teachers College at Columbia University in 2011. She holds an Associate Research Scholar's position at the Center for Sustainable Development at the Earth Institute, Columbia University. With her team of experts, she leads education and gender projects in multiple Sub-Saharan countries as well as in South Asia. Dr. Iyengar also oversees multi-country research projects on language literacy, promoting and implementing the Sustainable Development Goals for Education and Gender. She also teaches graduate level courses on Evaluation Research Methods, Development Economics and Data Analysis for Developing Countries at Teachers College and at the School of Public Affairs at Columbia University.

Huma Kidwai
is working as an Education Specialist in the East Africa education unit of the World Bank. Currently she is focusing on early learning and basic education programs and research in Rwanda, South Sudan, Tanzania, and Ethiopia. Huma has a doctoral degree from Teachers College – Columbia University; her research focused on the relationship between the State and madrassas in India. Her other professional experiences include projects with the Poverty Reduction Group of the World Bank; projects related to health and social equity at the Praxis Institute for Participatory Practices in New Delhi; and education programs and research at the Earth Institute's Global Center in Mumbai on their Model District Education Project.

Lê Minh Hằng
is a current PhD student in the International Education Policy program at the University of Maryland – College Park. Her research critically examines the global mobilities of educational policies, practice, and normative ideas of

'best practices' from a decolonial stance. Her current project examines race as a global ontological grammar underpinning post-socialist South-South international development. Originally from Hanoi, Vietnam, she holds a BA in Educational Studies and Political Science from Swarthmore College, PA, and an MA in International Education Policy from the University of Maryland – College Park.

Caroline Manion
is a Lecturer at OISE, University of Toronto. She is an active member of the comparative and international education community, with her research interests including, equity and social justice, decolonization, gender and education, teacher development, educational multilateralism, and the governance of education. Caroline's research has been supported by a variety of agencies and organizations, including the Social Sciences and Humanities Research Council of Canada, the International Development Research Centre of Canada, the Canadian International Development Agency (now Global Affairs Canada), and she has provided contract services, including educational program development and evaluation for such groups as the Aga Khan Foundation, Canada, British Council, Hewlett Foundation, Ontario Ministry of Education, and the United Nations Girls' Education Initiative.

Patricia S. Parker
is chair of the Department of Communication at the University of North Carolina at Chapel Hill, where she is also an associate professor of critical organizational communication studies and director of the Graduate Certificate in Participatory Research. Parker is co-editor (with Larry Frey) of the new book series at the University of California Press, "Communication and Social Justice Activism." She is finishing a book for the series, which documents a multiyear participatory research study with African American girls in under-resourced communities leading social justice activist campaigns.

Leigh Patel
is an interdisciplinary researcher, educator, and writer. Her work addresses the narratives that facilitate societal structures. With a background in sociology, she researches and teaches about education as a site of social reproduction and as a potential site for transformation. She works extensively with societally marginalized youth and teacher activists. Prior to working in the academy, Professor Patel was a journalist, a teacher, and a state-level policymaker. Across all of these experiences, her focus has been on the ways that education structures opportunities in society and the stories that are told about those opportunities.

Timothy D. Reedy

is a PhD student in the International Education Policy program at the University of Maryland-College Park. His research focus operates at the intersection of education for sustainability and socioscientific approaches to teaching and learning. He is particularly interested in how embedding moral and ethical issues in science curricula can be a means of fostering character formation and epistemological sophistication in pursuit of a scientifically literate citizenry. Tim currently teaches a robotics service learning practicum for engineering students enrolled in College Park Scholars: Science, Technology, and Society program.

Karen Ross

is an assistant professor in the Department of Conflict Resolution, Human Security, and Global Governance at UMASS Boston, where her work focuses on conceptual and methodological issues at the nexus of education, peace building, and socio-political activism. She is also a dialogue practitioner and trainer.

Betsy M. Scotto-Lavino

is a PhD student in International Education at George Mason University. Her research interests include gender equity in education, the relationship of power and ethics within educational contexts and knowledge production, and epistemological and ontological inclusion within methodology. She serves as the Fairfax Campus Vice-President for the George Mason Graduate and Professional Student Association. Betsy holds a bachelor of arts degree in Politics and Government from Ohio Wesleyan University and a Master of Arts in Teaching E.S.O.L. from American University.

Payal P. Shah

is an Assistant Professor of Educational Foundations and Qualitative Inquiry in the Department of Educational Studies at the University of South Carolina. She conducts critical ethnographic research on gender, education, and development in India and has published across the fields of international and comparative education, qualitative inquiry, and women's and gender studies. Her current projects include a book manuscript based on an 8-year longitudinal ethnographic project examining the relational and intergenerational processes of female empowerment in rural Gujarat; and research on the ways educated women in South Asia navigate the discourses of modernity and tradition embedded in processes of globalization and international development.

Derrick Tu

is a PhD candidate in the Faculty of Education at York University. His current research interests include undergraduate music education, international education, and East Asian studies. He is an oboist and has taught music for over ten years. As a researcher, he uses the arts to examine issues in education.

Matthew A. Witenstein
is an Assistant Professor in the Department of Educational Administration at the University of Dayton. His US work focuses on immigrants in higher education and international student experiences while his international/comparative education research focuses on higher educational quality, organization and governance issues. He is co-editor of the Palgrave Macmillan book series "South Asian Education Policy, Research and Practice" and author of numerous peer reviewed articles and book chapters. He has been an invited speaker at higher education institutions, ministry and government agencies throughout the US and South Asia.

CHAPTER 1

Interrogating and Innovating CIE Research: Setting the Stage

Meagan Call-Cummings, Caroline Manion and Payal P. Shah

Abstract

The purpose of this introductory chapter is to identify and situate the key questions and issues taken up in the volume and its constitutive essays, as well as presenting an overview of the main lines of theoretical debate and development reflected in the contributions: coloniality/decolonization; power; voice and re-presentation; and intersectionality. The authors highlight the volume's central premise: that radical, inclusive and decolonizing change is imperative for the field of comparative and international education (CIE) research and practice. After first framing the volume as part of a continuing conversation begun at the 2017 CIES Symposium of the same name ("Interrogating and Innovating CIE Research"), the authors then identify and discuss some of the key theoretical debates and questions emergent from the Symposium activities and conversations and extended by the volume contributors, including issues related to identifying and understanding the problem(s), ideas for change, as well as assessing the opportunities and challenges for affecting meaningful and sustained changes in the way CIE researchers think about and do their work. Following this, the chapter presents the organization of the book and shares highlights from each of the contributing chapters, showing how the different pieces respond to, build on and extend the Symposium dialogue and calls to action.

Keywords

theory – decolonization – intersectionality – change – inclusivity – power – voice – feminist

We begin this volume by highlighting its central premise: that radical, inclusive and decolonizing change is imperative for the field of comparative and international education (CIE) research and practice. We want to use this collection of critical and change-oriented essays to continue the at times difficult conversations begun at the 2017 CIES Symposium, focused on what an inclusive CIE would look like and how we might get there. We argue that the changes necessary are ones that will work to bring about greater inclusivity and equity in terms of how, who and the purposes to which CIE research is designed, implemented and applied in different contexts around the world (see for example, Odora Hoppers, 2000). In doing so, we recognize that critical conversations related to epistemology and methodology have been present in the field since its inception (see for example, Epstein, 2008; Masemann, 1990; Novoa & Yariv-Mashall, 2003). How comparative and international education phenomena are studied, the questions asked, the tools used and the epistemological, ontological, and ideological orientations they reflect, shape the nature of the knowledge produced, the value placed on that knowledge, and its pedagogy and implications for practice in diverse societies. Yet, from within and outside the field, scholars and practitioners have raised concerns about ongoing coloniality in CIE research and practice, and the ways that neocolonial practices and dynamics have been legitimated and reproduced throughout much of the history of CIE (see for example, the 2017 special issue of *Comparative Education Review*, edited by Takayama, Sriprakash & Connell). Thus, we as the co-editors of this book see ourselves and our chapter authors as joining in emergent and ongoing dialogue with others who are also deeply concerned with the reification of Eurocentric onto-epistemologies in CIE research, and the implications of neocolonialism in terms of the field's complicity and/or active participation in the silencing, marginalization, and exploitation of non-dominant Others, as researchers and research subjects (see for example, de Sousa Santos, 2005).

The purpose of this introductory chapter is to identify and situate the key questions and issues taken up in the volume and its constitutive essays, as well as presenting an overview of the main lines of theoretical debate and development reflected in the contributions: coloniality/decolonization; power; voice and re-presentation; and intersectionality. In turn, the authors engage and apply insights from these three broad theoretical fields to their own research to interrogate and critique CIE research orthodoxy and/or to the development and exploration of epistemological and methodological innovations that can be helpfully applied towards transformative and socially just CIE research and practice.

We first step back in time and provide a series of reflections on the process through which we "dreamed into existence" (Patel, Chapter 3, this volume) the 2017 CIES Symposium and its theme, "Interrogating and Innovating CIE

Research". Next, we identify and discuss some of the key theoretical debates and questions emergent from the Symposium activities and conversations and extended by the volume contributors, including issues related to identifying and understanding the problem(s), ideas for change, as well as assessing the opportunities and challenges for affecting meaningful and sustained changes in the way CIE researchers think about and do their work. In the concluding part, we present the organization of the book and share highlights from each of the contributing chapters, showing how the different pieces respond to, build on and extend the Symposium dialogue and calls to action.

1   Building the Conversation: From Ideas to Action

From October 26–27, 2017, a group of renowned scholars, researchers, students and practitioners convened for a two-day symposium on *Interrogating and Innovating CIE Research*, at George Mason University, Arlington, VA, campus. The symposium, sponsored[1] by the Comparative and International Education Society (CIES) was co-organized by the Center for International Education at George Mason University, the CIES Gender and Education Standing Committee, and the CIES South Asia Special Interest Group.

In the lead-up to our team coming together in July 2016 to propose and ultimately plan the 2017 CIES Symposium (hereafter, "the symposium"), we had all been engaging in scholarship (see for example, Baily, Shah & Call-Cummings, 2015; Shah & Manion, 2019) and dialogue about the state of the field, and in particular, problematizing the way standardized practices of CIE research have functioned to maintain problematic hierarchies, silences and exclusions in the production and use of research-based educational knowledge. Thus, we were excited when in May 2017, Comparative Education Review published an issue focused on postcolonialism in the field of CIE, as this collection of essays provided us with a strong and critical foundation to reflect on and discuss questions and strategies that we wanted to explore further, and what we wanted to accomplish with the symposium more broadly: In short, our goal was to provide a space to continue and extend the conversation about how CIE research needs to be, and can be done, differently (see for example, Takayama, Sriprakash, & Connell, 2017).

As we put together the symposium program, we spent considerable time discussing who should be invited to participate as plenary panel speakers. As organizers, we decided that these individuals would be intentionally selected and structured so that they approach the symposium theme (Interrogating and Innovating CIE Research) from different perspectives.[2] And we agreed that in addition to CIE scholars engaging in critical conversations and work in the field, we wanted to include researchers from outside the field, that in their scholarship and practice, talk about and do ethically-grounded and justice-oriented social science research. We believed that through listening to and learning from researchers working within and outside of our professional community, important new ideas would be injected, debated and built-upon to extend and deepen the conversation about change in the field of CIE research.

The symposium was organized around four plenary sessions: (1) interrogating and innovating CIE research; (2) decolonizing methodology by invoking local voices; (3) destabilizing power and authority: taking intersectionality seriously; and (4) implications for methodology – towards more equitable futures. The goal of these plenary sessions was to anchor conversations around these themes by inviting a variety of scholars and practitioners to engage in a dialectical discussion with symposium members to inspire inquiry into the methodological and epistemological roots of research in the field of CIE. Leading up to the symposium, we worked with Will Brehm and his FreshEd podcast to create a series of episodes featuring the comments of one plenary speaker from each panel. Each speaker shared their thoughts on issues related to epistemology and methodology that might decenter current practices within and outside CIE. The FreshEd episodes were another way that we sought to disseminate information about the core issues addressed in the symposium and enable broader engagement with these issues leading up to and in addition to the symposium. We sought to use the symposium and its related activities as spaces for the generation of new knowledge concerning comparative methodology in a more equitable and democratic manner (Smith, 2012), and for the engagement of disparate voices in moments of, perhaps, uncomfortable reflexivity (Pillow, 2003) about the realities of our onto-epistemological commitments and related practices.

For the symposium, we also invited paper proposals that interrogated existing practices of knowledge production, dissemination and application in CIE research and/or otherwise represented a critical departure from the status quo in CIE research. Our vision was to offer platforms for discussion and dialogue amongst CIE scholars who are committed to fostering a deeper understanding of methods and methodological issues. We also wanted to ensure as diverse a group of presenters as possible at the symposium, as well as in the context of the contributors to this volume. Diversity here included consideration of gender, ethnicity, socio-economic status, geographic location, disciplinary background, and professional roles and affiliations (e.g., practitioners, researchers, policymakers, and junior and more senior faculty). To assist in generating relevant paper contributions, we encouraged authors to submit proposals in which

they responded to one or more thematic questions. These thematic questions were developed in conversation with critical, feminist, decolonial, and other transformation- and social justice-oriented theories, and were intended to drive engaged and deep conversations on comparative methodology in the context of the symposium. The questions were,
- How might questions concerning the dominant application of positivist epistemologies and research paradigms in the field of CIE draw our attention to problems of exclusion and the reproduction of rigidly unjust hierarchies?
- What sorts of regional efforts have characterized both change and continuity in terms of the research paradigms and methodologies embraced in CIE?
- How might we conceptualize and account for intersectionality in research, policy and practice?
- What are the linkages between research and international education agendas?
- What are the research and policy trends in the area of educational equity?
- How can we better acknowledge and address value pluralism in the context of research, policy and advocacy?
- How can local epistemologies and positionalities (particularly those of women and other marginalized populations) be leveraged to improve educational contexts in post-colonial societies?
- How do existing power and authority dynamics shape CIE research and practice? How can the field of CIE confront internal and external power and authority dynamics?
- How can the field destabilize and transform knowledge hierarchies through research and practice?

Based on participant feedback and our own observations, we believe that the concurrent paper sessions at the symposium offered deep engagement with a diverse range of topics, methods, and geographic regions, and encouraged participants' productive engagement, learning and reflection on the implications of the presentations' intersections with the symposium theme.

Ultimately, through intentionally dialectical engagements across distinguished plenary speakers, breakout sessions, concurrent paper sessions, and workshops, the symposium provided spaces and resources for students, junior and senior scholars, practitioners and policymakers to not only interrogate and challenge existing practice, but to learn and develop new ways of thinking about and doing CIE research. Participant feedback after the symposium suggested that this was largely experienced as a provocative and generative event that worked toward the goal of supporting greater inclusivity and safety in the knowledge production processes and application practices of the CIE community. It is to continue, extend and deepen these critical conversations and prompt concrete action that we have put together this volume. In the next section, we briefly identify and discuss some of the key ideas and concerns that emerged at the symposium and which are reflected and built upon in this volume.

2   2017 CIES Symposium: Emergent Debates, Issues and Questions

During and after the two-day symposium, some key debates, issues, and questions emerged as particularly salient. Across methodological divides, identity differences, and geographical borders, those who attended and presented at the symposium seemed to agree on a few points. Anjali Adukia (2017) articulated one simple yet profound point in her plenary statement. She implored us to, "Look, listen, learn", and then shared the following:

> When working with communities, whether they be households or schools, beginning by spending non-contingent time with people and in their environments allows me as a researcher to better understand the local context and to build relationships and trust. I observe my surroundings and how people live their lives, I listen to words and to body language. This helps to shape my research questions and ensure that they are relevant to people's lives (and not just for academic discourse). I have also found that people are more likely to open up to me if they feel like I care: people don't care how much you know until they know how much you care. As researchers, we must remember that "human subjects" are first and foremost humans, and therefore we must always respect and consider one's humanity when approaching work that involves others' lives. (Adukia, 2017)

This sentiment was shared by many in attendance who spoke of the epistemological, methodological, and ethical importance of first paying attention to what is happening in local contexts and simultaneously building relationships of trust and mutual recognition.

Another key question that was addressed in many ways at the symposium centered on how CIE can destabilize and transform knowledge hierarchies through research and practice. Plenary speakers, presenters, and audience members addressed this in a myriad of ways. One particularly timely approach to thinking about how to destabilize knowledge hierarchies was a naming or outing of white supremacy as structuring and resourcing ofttimes violent onto-epistemological approaches to research in CIE. Barbara Dennis called for comparative and international education researchers to center white supremacy and racism in our work:

> As we know, knowledge is not neutral and does not exist outside of us. If my research and activism are not pushing against my privilege and working to dismantle white supremacy, I am failing women of color. And I am failing feminism. I am failing academia. White supremacy and racism must be moved from the margins to the middle of our work in comparative and international education. (Dennis, 2017)

In relation to her work in (de)colonization, Leigh Patel named the duty of CIE "to contend with the roots, logics, and material realities of stratification and exploitation", and "to rigorously question and address what are the assumptions of the classificatory system, what are the tacit referents, and how do those foment coloniality and the elevation of some by the lowering of others" (Patel, 2017).

Conversations continually returned to a central question of responsibility. We pushed ourselves and each other to imagine the ways in which the CIE community can foster inclusive and creative methodological spaces for practitioners and researchers that more clearly make meaning of educational contexts other than the dominant Western ones. Gerardo Blanco responded to this question not in terms of steps we could take but by issuing an apt warning: "I want to be very careful with the language of empowering and giving voice. These approaches are laudable but often lead to undesired outcomes. What I would argue is an ethics of engagement"(Blanco, 2017). In discussing this theme of engagement, Lesley Bartlett said that she is – and CIE should be – "skeptical of research that seems too certain of its emancipatory stance or contributions" (Bartlett, 2017). Overall, these discussions treated the question of ethical engagement as both necessary and rife with potential unintended negative consequences. We, the co-editors, as well as symposium participants, were left with a sense of increasing urgency to act, but a warning to act – and engage – responsibly, ethically, and reflexively.

3   Theoretical Resources Engaged and Developed in This Volume

There is no single theoretical framework guiding the contributions to this volume, and this was intentional given our purpose to interrogate and open up CIE research as a site for scholarly and practical contestation as well as innovation. Thus, authors draw on an eclectic, but always critical, range of theories that thematically can be grouped into four main areas: coloniality/decolonization; voice and representation; critical theory/power; and feminist intersectionality. We provide brief synopses of these theoretical resources below, followed in the next and final section by a more detailed look at the organization and nature of the chapters in the volume.

3.1   Coloniality/Decolonization

The concepts of coloniality and decolonization are used by some of our authors in their efforts to name and explore CIE research structures and processes that reflect and reinforce Eurocentric ways of knowing and being. While colonialism and decolonization are often associated with geographically-based political and socio-economic changes, as applied in this volume, the focus is primarily on the onto-epistemic hegemony and ongoing coloniality represented in and carried by dominant CIE research praxis (Mignolo, 2013; Patel, 2016). For example, decolonial theory is used by some of our contributors to problematize the positioning (read: subjugation) of Others as passive objects from which data is "extracted" or "mined", and resulting in a product that most benefits the researcher and their career. More broadly, decolonial theory is used as a resource to explore and demonstrate how dominant onto-epistemological, methodological and axiological dimensions of CIE research work to reproduce (unearned) privilege for some, and epistemic injustice and violence for Others.

3.2   Voice and Representation

Some of the contributors to this volume both critically explore and challenge the concept of voice and practices of re-presentation that are central to comparative and international education inquiry praxis. Much of these contributions are informed by poststructural and non-representational theories (for example Lather, 2009), which "have implied a profound reconceptualization of voice, bringing to the fore the ambiguities, complexities, and historicity of voice that was hitherto erased or marginalized" (Dussel & Dahia, 2017, p. 2). As we work toward this reconceptualization, we lay bare our discomfort with unquestioned and normed colonial(izing) practices and seek to complicate simplistic narratives of "giving voice" to an Other, neocolonial ideals of re-presentation, and paternalistic goals of empowerment and transformation.

3.3   Critical Theory/Power

Critical theory, especially as it relates to questions of power, informs much of the writing included in this volume. Throughout each part of the volume, contributors acknowledge and critique the structures that both produce and constrain comparative and international education as a field. We highlight the clear linkages between power and knowledge in an effort to disrupt the reproduction and both implicit and explicit support of systems of hegemony, marginalization, injustice, and violence.

3.4   *Feminist Intersectionality*

In this volume, we engage with intersectionality theoretically, methodologically, and in praxis to critique and transform relationships that both privilege and oppress individuals, groups, and institutions. Drawing from feminist theory and praxis, many chapters within engage a postcolonial, global, Third World feminist vision to deeply examine intersections between race, class, gender, language, place, immigration, and citizenship status and their relationship with education, broadly (Anzaldua, 1987; Mohanty 1984).

4   Reflections on the Process of Editing This Volume

Over the course of more than one year, the editors of this volume have grappled with and reflected on both our initial goals for the symposium as well as our evolving understanding of what CIE scholars and practitioners might need in order to call for and create necessary change in our field. This process has been difficult and has challenged us in unexpected but important ways. Many of our initial discussions about this volume were idealistic. We wanted to push ourselves and the volume's contributors to model the kind of open, decolonized, and democratic spaces we were discussing in the book. For example, we thought of creating non-text-based work, such as an accompanying website or arts-based product, that could be disseminated and accessed more broadly. This simply became too difficult given time and resource constraints. We wanted to highlight the work of contributors that were not university-based researchers, or whose language of writing was not English, but again, this proved difficult. Despite such difficulties, however, we have been able, within limitations, to include and honor voices in this volume that are representative of the many experiences, knowledges, and identities in CIE.

5   Organization of the Book

The book is structured by four parts that map on to the four plenary panel discussions at the symposium. The same symposium co-organizers that programmed the plenary sessions have also provided editorial leadership for their respective parts. Each part is structured similarly, involving leading with an introductory chapter, followed by a conceptual essay by one of the distinguished plenary panelists at the symposium, and then the presentation of two longer empirical or conceptual chapters.

The theme of the first part, led by Caroline Manion, is interrogating and innovating CIE research. Here, the focus is on critical questioning and exploration of the epistemological, ontological, methodological, and axiological boundaries reflected in the production, organization, and use of CIE research – issues that are introduced in this part and taken up within it and the other three parts as well. In the introductory chapter and in the contribution by symposium plenary speaker, Leigh Patel, attention is paid to defining and theorizing coloniality and neo-colonial influences and structural relations present in the field of CIE. In the conceptual chapter that follows, Derrick Tu takes on the epistemological dominance and rigidity seen as characterizing much of CIE research. He uses the lens of aesthetic cognitivism to explore the epistemological foundations of the Arts-Based Educational Research (ABER) approach, and to "speculate on how it can be effectively used to address inequalities arising from (neo-)colonial forces in CIE research". The part concludes with a reflective chapter by Karen Ross, in which she problematizes the dominance of outsider perspectives closely connected with donors and funding agencies, in defining legitimate knowledge – its form and content – in evaluative inquiry and CIE research more broadly. Ross critiques the dominant approach to evaluation research that defines success in terms of the priorities and beliefs of outsiders, and instead argues the importance of aligning impact evaluation criteria to locally defined goals and values.

The theme of the second part, led by Radhika Iyengar and Matthew Witenstein, is decolonizing methodology by invoking local voices, guided by the central question of how the field of CIE can be a vehicle for making the un-heard voice(s) heard? Gerardo Lu Blanco begins the part by pushing on the notions of giving and finding voice. He highlights how the chapters in the part demonstrate ways in which research and methods are pushing boundaries instead of treating local methods and knowledge as fragile. He concludes by arguing that researchers and practitioners can and should consider abandoning familiarity to make space for "difference". Radhika Iyengar and Matthew Witenstein's empirical chapter questions gender biases that are entrenched in culture and traditions as they examine women's participation in non-formal technical and vocational education and training programs in South Asia. The authors urge policy makers to reform vocational education by incorporating the reality that many women face. Through participatory action research, Iyengar and Witenstein elicit the cultural, religious, and intergenerational practices that tend to thwart basic human rights for women. The next chapter, by Huma Kidwai, pushes readers to question commonly held assumptions concerning the function and processes of formal schooling as she narrates the resistance of the Madrassa teachers and leaders against the State in India, while at the same time highlighting the inherent biases of the Indian State against the Madrassas. Overall, the chapter presents insightful findings on how culture and religion are entangled with politics and bureaucracy as they shape education policy. Finally, Erik Byker's empirical chapter takes readers to Punjab, India, as he writes about the motivated volunteers who use data to energize common citizens. Byker helps us understand the motivation of these foot soldiers, the volunteers, who walk village after village to build awareness of the learning levels and needs of different students.

The theme of the third part, led by Emily Anderson and Payal Shah, is on destabilizing power and authority, and taking intersectionality seriously. The plenary session grounding this part sought to interrogate the legitimization of knowledge in scholarship, funding and evidence-based practices in CIE. After a brief introduction, the part moves into plenary panelist Patricia Parker's chapter where she examines how CIE can productively engage in conversations about the ideas, problematics, and opportunities for creating academic and community spaces that challenge existing power-knowledge dynamics in research. In the next chapter, Kelly Grace and Sothy Eng seek to problematize hierarchies within the knowledge production process, focusing on the role of interpreters in CIE. By providing a reflective treatise on the development of a collaborative method to include the worldviews of the Cambodian interviewers, the authors offer a concrete way to broaden the knowledge production process and decolonize the research process using interviews and focus groups themselves. They argue that transformation of knowledge hierarchies requires a collaborative relationship between researcher and interpreter. In the final chapter in this part, Alisha Braun uses photovoice as a way to bring the voices of people with disabilities more centrally into CIE research. Her chapter details her use of photovoice in a recent study on access to higher education for students with mobility disability in Ghana. Braun's chapter provides an excellent illustration of how broadening the breadth of intersectional research in CIE can be productive in transforming knowledge hierarchies as well as investigating power and authority dynamics related to whose experiences are excluded from mainstream CIE policy and research.

The theme of the fourth part, led by Supriya Baily and Meagan Call-Cummings, focuses on the future of CIE research. The introductory chapter is used in part to highlight the debates that emerged at the symposium concerning the inherent complexity represented in understandings and practices associated with research quality, rigor, impact, and ethics. The authors also use the shifts CIE has experienced in terms of methodological approaches that attempt to move beyond the more narrow definitions of empiricism, science, and the pursuit of objectivity and neutrality as the gold standard, to embrace new onto-epistemological approaches, fresh methodological designs, and innovative and increasingly technology-savvy tools. In the next chapter, symposium plenary speaker, Ameena Ghaffar-Kucher challenges researchers to ask themselves if they are ready to give up their power to make changes, and discusses opportunities and barriers that need to be recognized and understood in order that transformative and transformed methodological practices can be realized. The part continues with a chapter by Brent Edwards, whose work deconstructs and pushes on specific research methods with a vision toward prying open the field of CIE to alternative methods, politics, epistemologies and ontologies. The last chapter in this part is written by Lê Minh Hằng, Brendan DeCoster, Jeremy Gombin-Sperling and Timothy Reedy, who outline what collaboration and reflexivity look like among novice scholars. They hope that by outlining their own process of collaboration they can disabuse other junior scholars of the idea that collaboration must be or always is harmonious or free of tensions. Overall, the part aims to provide a window into the arguments of change, the uncertainty of the future, and the issues of power and hegemony that exist within.

Rounding out the volume is a concluding chapter that re-visits the issues, critiques, and ideas for change animating the conversations and research presented by the various contributors, and links these to a series of recommendations. With these recommendations, we aim to keep this critical work of interrogating and innovating CIE research moving forward, and to bring more people on board to build and sustain the transformative change that we argue is demanded of CIE research.

Notes

1 The following organizations also provided financial support for the 2017 CIES Symposium: Center for Sustainable Development, Earth Institute, Columbia University; OISE, University of Toronto; Oslo and Akershus College University; University of Redlands; University of South Carolina.
2 We were honored to have the following plenary panel speakers participate at the symposium: Anjali Adukia; Lesley Barlett; Emily Bent; Gerardo Lu Blanco; Barbara Dennis; Peter Demerath; Ameena Ghaffar-Kucher; Shenila Khoja-Moolji; Huma

Kidwai; Patricia Parker; Leigh Patel; Oren Pizmony-Levy Drezner; Lilliana Saldaña; Riyad Shahjahan; Fran Vavrus; Dan Wagner.

References

Adukia, A. (2017). Remarks. In *Proceedings of the 2nd Comparative and International Education Symposium: Interrogating and Innovating CIE Research*. George Mason University. Arlington, VA: GMU.

Anzaldua, G. (1987). *Borderlands – La fontera: The new mestiza*. San Francisco, CA: Aunt Lute.

Baily, S., Shah, P., & Call-Cummings, M. (2015). Reframing the center: New directions in qualitative methodology in international comparative education. *Annual Review of Comparative and International Education, 2015*, 139–164.

Barlett, L. (2017). Remarks. In *Proceedings of the 2nd Comparative and International Education Symposium: Interrogating and Innovating CIE Research*. George Mason University. Arlington, VA: GMU.

Blanco, G. (2017). Remarks. In *Proceedings of the 2nd Comparative and International Education Symposium: Interrogating and Innovating CIE Research*. George Mason University. Arlington, VA: GMU.

Dennis, B. (2017). Remarks. In *Proceedings of the 2nd Comparative and International Education Symposium: Interrogating and Innovating CIE Research*. George Mason University. Arlington, VA: GMU.

de Sousa Santos, B. (2015). *Epistemologies of the South: Justice against Epistemicide*. New York, NY: Routledge.

Dussel, I., & Dahya, N. (2017). Introduction: Problematizing voice and representations in youth media production. *Learning, Media and Technology, 42*(1), 1–7.

Epstein, E. H. (2008). Setting the normative boundaries: Crucial epistemological benchmarks in comparative education. *Comparative Education, 44*(4), 373–386.

Lather, P. (2009). Against empathy, voice and authenticity. In A. Y. Jackson & L. A. Mazzei (Eds.), *Voice in qualitative inquiry. Challenging conventional, interpretative and critical conceptions in qualitative research* (pp. 19–26). London: Routledge.

Masemann, V. (1990). Ways of knowing: Implications for comparative education. *Comparative Education Review, 34*(4), 465–473.

Mignolo, W. (2013). Imperial/Colonial metamorphosis: A decolonial narrative, from the Ottoman Sultanate and Spanish Empire to the US and the EU. In G. Huggan (Ed.), *The Oxford handbook of postcolonial studies*. Oxford: Oxford University Press. Retrieved from http://www.oxfordhandbooks.com/view/10.1093/oxfordhb/9780199588251.001.0001/oxfordhb-9780199588251-e-013

Mohanty, C. (1984). Under western eyes: Feminist scholarship and colonial discourses. *Boundary, 12*(3) (Spring-Autumn).

Odora Hoppers, C. A. (2000). The centre-periphery in knowledge production in the twenty-first century. *Compare, 30*(3), 283–291.

Patel, L. (2016). *Decolonizing educational research: From ownership to answerability*. New York, NY: Routledge.

Patel, L. (2017). Remarks. In *Proceedings of the 2nd Comparative and International Education Symposium: Interrogating and Innovating CIE Research*. George Mason University. Arlington, VA: GMU.

Shah, P., & Manion, C. (2019). Decolonizing gender and education research: Unsettling and recasting feminist knowledges, power and research practices. *Guest Themed Issue, Gender and Education, 31*(4).

Smith, L. (2012). *Decolonizing methodologies: research and indigenous peoples*. London: Zed Books.

Takayama, K., Sriprakash, A., & Connell, R. (2017). Toward a postcolonial comparative and international education. *Comparative Education Review, 61*(S1), S1–S24.

PART 1

Interrogating and Innovating CIE Research

∴

CHAPTER 2

Onto-Epistemological Frontiers in CIE Research: Exploring the Problematic

Caroline Manion

Abstract

The purpose of this chapter is to introduce and frame the three essays comprising the first part of the volume, as they connect with the first plenary panel at the 2017 CIES Symposium. The author first revisits the Symposium plenary to identify some of the key issues, critical questions and calls for change animating the conversation. Next, an overview of the topics and arguments represented in the chapters by Leigh Patel, Derrick Tu, and Karen Ross is presented, discussing their relevance to a core theme from the symposium panel discussion: interrogating and challenging the exclusionary onto-epistemic frontiers in CIE research and the implications for research practice.

Keywords

onto-epistemology – axiology – coloniality – decolonization – exclusion – knowledge – socialization – methods

1   Introduction

The purpose of this chapter is to introduce and frame the three essays comprising this part of the volume as they connect with the first plenary panel at the 2017 CIES Symposium. I will first take us back to the Symposium plenary to identify some of the key issues, critical questions and calls for change animating the conversation. Next, I overview the topics and arguments represented in the chapters by Leigh Patel, Derrick Tu, and Karen Ross, discussing their relevance to a core theme from the symposium panel discussion: interrogating and challenging the exclusionary onto-epistemic frontiers in CIE research and the implications for research practice.

Before proceeding though, it is my responsibility to first locate myself as a White settler on Turtle Island (North America). Like many in the field of comparative and international education (CIE), I often travel and work in societies with histories of colonization. When not, I live and work on the unceded territories of indigenous peoples in southern Ontario, Canada. My office at the University of Toronto and my house that I often work from, are located in the homes/land of First Nations peoples. Acknowledging that I am inextricably bound up, professionally, personally and spiritually, with ongoing coloniality and its attendant (neo)colonial logics and dynamics, therefore, is non-negotiable. A further imperative is to acknowledge, as I later discuss in this chapter, that the broad field of comparative and international education itself, in all its diversity and complexity, is also inextricably bound up with colonial histories and (neo)colonial realities that continue to have deep and troubling consequences for societies and people around the world.

If we accept the reality that CIE has been and continues to be practiced and applied as part of colonial and (neo)colonial systems and agendas, it seems reasonable to frame the solution as one involving decolonization. But what does this mean for us in the field of CIE, if we accept Tuck and Yang's (2012) argument that "decolonization is not a metaphor" (p. 1)? For Tuck and Yang, "decolonization brings about the repatriation of Indigenous land and life", and moreover, that,

> Because settler colonialism is built upon an entangled triad structure of settler-native-slave, the decolonial desires of white, nonwhite, immigrant, postcolonial, and oppressed people can similarly be entangled in resettlement, reoccupation, and reinhabitation that actually further settler colonialism. The metaphorization of decolonization makes possible a set of evasions, or 'settler moves to innocence', that problematically attempt to reconcile settler guilt and complicity, and rescue settler futurity. (p. 1)

So, how ought we talk about and do decolonization work in CIE in meaningful and tangible ways? Ways that avoid the metaphorization of what must necessarily be anything but a metaphor? As an initial response, I suggest that knowledge and knowledge creation processes, as these relate to land and life, are a necessary starting point for a decolonization project in CIE. Dominant onto-epistemologies and methodologies in CIE need to be unsettled, decolonized, and it is our responsibility to figure out what repatriation, or what Māori performance artist Victoria Hunt refers to as *rematriation,* entails in the context of CIE research and knowledge production, dissemination, and application processes. This discussion will continue below.

2 Organizing the Plenary Panel Discussion: Interrogating and Innovating CIE Research

The first plenary panel was framed as a space for an initial opening up for the symposium conversations focused on problems of exclusion in CIE research. As the organizer of this panel, I wanted the panelists to identify and discuss their points of critique with respect to the CIE status quo, and to suggest possibilities for change. To help guide the discussion, I developed a visioning statement and a series of accompanying questions that were shared with the featured speakers: Leigh Patel, Riyad Shahjahan, Fran Vavrus, and Dan Wagner.[1] At the time, I wrote that reflecting on the role, function, and use of research, CIE now attends to larger philosophical questions that are explicit, implicit, overt, and covert. In the background essays that they prepared for the Symposium and during the plenary discussion, the panelists focused on the following questions:

– How might questions and critiques concerning the dominant application of positivist epistemologies and research paradigms in the field of CIE draw our attention to problems of exclusion and the reproduction of rigidly unjust hierarchies?
– What are the linkages between research and international education agendas? And what are some of the implications and/or challenges and opportunities suggested by these linkages?
– What challenges and opportunities are associated with the policy uptake and broader use of findings from non-dominant, innovative and social justice-oriented education research approaches?

Centering these questions are issues related to how we know what we know, and, how our experiences colour what and how we know. I suggested that critical issues of representation, recognition, knowledge production and values in the design and application of CIE research demand that we ask tough questions of ourselves and our work; questions that require careful reflection and thought, to navigate through and towards a better future for CIE research and educational change and development more broadly.

The unfolding panel discussion centred on various 'ologies': epistemology (the study of knowledge), ontology (the study of existence), methodology (the study of research methods), and axiology (the study of ethics and values). The assumption argued by Vavrus is that interrogation and innovation are inextricably connected and that, "we, as researchers, practitioners and/or activists must ask different questions – ontological, epistemological, methodological, and axiological – to effect a different research ethos in CIE" (Vavrus, 2017a, p. 1). To help set the stage for reading the contributions in this part, in what follows I identify and discuss the key questions and insights raised by the panelists with respect to these different 'ologies', focusing more on the epistemological and ontological dimensions, with methodological and axiological questions taken up further in other parts of this volume.

3   Justice and Inclusivity: The Philosophical and Practical Limits of Dominant 'Ologies' in CIE Research

3.1   *Knowers, Knowing, and Being Known in CIE Research*
It is important at the outset to specify that the activities and debates concerning interrogating and innovating CIE, in the context of the symposium, were not about re-visiting the longstanding tensions and debates concerning the relative merits of quantitative and qualitative research. As was noted by several plenary speakers as well as symposium participants, examples of ethical and/or justice-oriented research exist in both designs, as well as mixed-methods studies. Thus, rather than re-hash old discussions, the conversation at hand is about questioning the onto-epistemological assumptions reflected in CIE research broadly, concerning who is conferred the label of "knower" (i.e., the researcher), and what is deemed legitimate knowledge, by whom/what and how.

The dominant, Euro-centric onto-epistemological orientation that has long influenced and been reflected in much of CIE research practice, was centrally problematized by the plenary panelists, with the discussion connecting with similar critiques from scholars across a variety of social science disciplines (see for example, Mignolo, 2002, 2014; Romm, 2018; Savanskry, 2017; Strega & Brown, 2015; Sundberg, 2014). Speaking of "Western" (read: dominant) knowledge, Stein (2017) asserts,

> Western knowledge is characterized as much by its particular content as it is by its organizing principles of progress, possession, universalism, certainty, and neutralization of difference (either through incorporation, erasure, or elimination; Silva, 2007, 2013). Uncertainty, contradiction, and unassimilable difference are then treated as a problem. (p. S29)

Of particular significance is the matter of ongoing coloniality in the way CIE researchers, practitioners and policymakers see and seek to produce knowledge. We are all familiar with research metaphors that speak of data "mining" and "extraction", and the concept of "mastery" is frequently applied as a goal and achievement scholars should strive for in relation to their respective knowledge domains. But we have to recognize that the power and ubiquitousness of such concepts is not an accident: mining, extraction, and mastery are all laden with colonial and imperialist onto-epistemological understandings that position some people (read: Euro-descended) as knowers and Others (read: non-Euro-descended) as objects of knowledge (Stein, 2017, p. S28). As Stein (2017) suggests, "much of what is now claimed as "Western thought" was stolen or adapted from others without due acknowledgement", and moreover, that,

> This colonial politics of knowledge may be summarized as an imperial effort (always incomplete) to capture and contain the threat that other knowledges and ways of knowing pose to the modern Western episteme and its ordering of the world, given that these other knowledges both signal the limits of mastery and continue to hold possibilities for worlds otherwise. (Stein, 2017, p. S28)

In his background paper, Riyad Shahjahan argued that "how we know" cannot be separated from questions of ontology, temporality, and affective economies: that we need to challenge our ways of knowing and being in the world in order to recognize and effectively address problems of exclusion in dominant onto-epistemological formations (Shahjahan, 2017a). Introducing and paraphrasing de Sousa Santos' (2007) arguments with respect to the concept of "epistemic blindness", Shahjahan suggested, like Stein quoted above, that "dominant knowledge systems simply make other knowledge systems invisible, or they try to appropriate it to something instrumental, or simply negate it" (Shahjahan, 2017b). Critiqued is the ongoing and persistent coloniality in social science research, including CIE, driven by a colonial "erase to replace" imperative (Patel, 2017a).

Critical scholars have used concepts such as "epistemic domination" (Stein, 2017), "epistemic violence" (Spivak, 1988) and "epistemic injustice" (Fricker, 2007; Ramos, 2017) to problematize the Othering (Said, 1978) work that is accomplished and constantly reaffirmed as part and parcel of the ongoing coloniality that organizes the dominant onto-epistemological imaginary in CIE. The concept of epistemic injustice refers to the,

> systematic harm done to a person regarding their capacities as a knower, based on their belonging of a certain group. This means that we consider epistemic injustice as prejudice toward the epistemic abilities possessed by an individual, such as the capacity for epistemic agency, or developed epistemic resources, based on their appearance, language, social group,

or any other external factor putting them in a weakened position in the face of their supposed listener or listeners. (Fricker, 2007, as cited in Ramos, 2017, p. 5)

I would suggest that epistemic injustice has actually been foundational to the colonial and neo-colonial project of CIE. Here it is important for me to acknowledge that few in the field consciously intend to inflict such harm in their work, but is that not a large part of the problem? That is, in the absence of critical reflexivity concerning the onto-epistemologies that inform our research, colonial and neo-colonial views and assumptions have become normalized, and thus ongoing coloniality in our approaches, processes, and products is rendered invisible.

3.2 Seeing and Being in the World as Part of the CIE Research Problematic

During the plenary panel, it was argued that largely unexamined ontological questions and issues must be foregrounded as part of interrogating CIE research.

The ways in which we see, hear, and experience life and our relationships with other humans, are all shaped by how we are socialized. Social psychologists point to the socialization processes we experience from infancy and how through these, cognitive frames are built that we then use to engage with and understand the world and others around us. Schools are spaces of institutionalized socialization of a particular kind, where dominant ways of being and seeing are reproduced, with further implications for the nature and potential blind spots of our cognitive frames. Other research has alerted us to the socialization that is experienced as part of earning a degree in a particular discipline, for example. Socialization has been framed as necessary for survival – of the individual, group (society), or discipline – yet depending on how we have been socialized, by who and how, we can "over hear" (Rosa & Flores, 2017) some things and not hear other things. Put more simply, it is difficult to hear things that our socialization makes less discernible to us (Patel, 2017b).

To help us think more critically about our responsibilities as producers and users of CIE research, and drawing on the work of Bakhtin (1990), Patel raised the ontological idea of "answerability" (Patel, 2017a). Who are we as researchers (and practitioners) answerable (responsible) to? Patel notes that among other things, within the notion of answerability and in the context of a broader discussion of dialogism, the principle of stewardship of ideas, and not ownership is, pivotal (Patel, 2017a).

Like in the constructivist paradigm, multiple realities may be acknowledged in an Indigenous ontology; however, the difference is that, rather than the truth being something that is 'out there' or external, reality is the relationship that one has to the truth. Thus, an object or thing is not as important as one's relationships to it ... reality *is* relationships or sets of relationships. Thus, there is no definite reality but different sets of relationships that make up an Indigenous ontology. Therefore, reality is not an object but a process of relationships, and an Indigenous ontology is actually the equivalent of an Indigenous epistemology. (Wilson, 2008, p. 73)

Linking back to the idea of answerability, yes it is an ontological issue; however, I suggest that it also is an important axiological one, that speaks to the values underpinning our interactions and relationships with other humans and the world around us (including plants, animals, water, soil, the cosmos, etc.). Central to an Indigenous axiology is the concept of relational accountability:

Right or wrong; validity; statistically significant; worthy or unworthy: value judgements lose their meaning. What is more important and meaningful is fulfilling a role and obligations in the research relationship – that is, being accountable to your relations. The researcher is therefore a part of [their] research and inseparable from the subject of that research. (Wilson, 2000, cited in Wilson, 2008, p. 77)

Seeing ourselves and being seen/experienced as researchers who work *with* and not *on* diverse subjects, demands that we make central and ensure that the values of respect, reciprocity and responsibility guide our CIE research processes. Here, Patel reminds us of the importance of considering social location:

I don't have an easy answer to how to reconcile the fundamental nature of knowledge and ideas with the longstanding material realities of global capitalism and colonization, but I do know being mindful, humble and respectful of social locations has to be in there somewhere. All things are not equal. Our present moment will more than likely echo and refresh previous colonizing moments if left unchecked. Appropriating and even improving on an idea is possible but it is insufficient and harmful if it does little to rupture the thin slice judgments that reproduce associations of talent, intelligence, ownership with some and backstage, service, and labor for others. (Patel, 2017a, n.p.)

Vavrus, drawing on Johannes Fabian's notion of "coevalness" (1983) and Richa Nagar's (2014) notion of "situated solidarities", suggests that, "In the context of affective relationships, our metaphors change from those of mining other people's lives to receiving other people's opinions and ideas and viewpoints as gifts, and to be respectful and humble in the presence of such gifts" (Vavrus, 2017b).

With respect to the preceding critical discussions of onto-epistemological and axiological issues in CIE research, and responding to the question of "what next?", Vavrus continued,

> Rather than seek one methodology, I'd like us to consider a different orientation, one that is far more respectful than what we often see. It's about a way of being with other people whenever we are engaged in a collective effort of knowledge-making. (2017b, n.p.)

3.3 Changing Our CIE Research Orientations and Practices: Risks and Opportunities

Challenging the status quo of something is always difficult, and realizing change in CIE research and its various epistemological, ontological, methodological and axiological underpinnings is no exception. Indeed, conflict and resistance was observable and experienced during the first symposium plenary panel, as Patel takes up in the next chapter. As one example, panelist Dan Wagner critiqued the very premise of interrogating and innovating CIE research on the basis that this conversation is not really new, and moreover, he remained skeptical of the possibilities opened up by post and anti-colonial analyses. He also suggested that the field of CIE is already involved in the "post-colonial enterprise" (Wagner, 2017), though implied was the assumption that "post-colonial" refers simply to the time after colonialism. The other panelists did not share this perspective. In response to the implied nihilism in Wagner's critique of post-colonial theory and research, Patel responded, "The challenge is to be able to hear what is proffered as possibility and not have it be heard as leaving the conversation at interrogation" (Patel, 2017a).

Pointing to a central and unavoidable challenge, Vavrus suggested that degrees of risk and risk-taking depends on one's position in the organization, including the academy (Vavrus, 2017b). For example, it is far riskier for graduate students to do radically different research than it is for tenured faculty to do the same. But at the same time, it was also recognized that for tenure-track faculty, the risks of doing radically different research can be similar to those faced by graduate students.[2] As tenured academic positions are steadily become a thing of the past, what does this mean for realizing the types of changes in CIE research orientations and practices that we are calling for?

Continuing the discussion, Vavrus argued that we cannot "ever escape the risks posed by the unanticipated consequences of our research", and that it is dangerously misguided to search for a "single ethical, egalitarian way of doing research that can be used in every case" (Vavrus, 2017b). It is much more complicated than that and we, as CIE actors (researchers, students, practitioners, policymakers, funders) need to nurture within ourselves (and students, as applicable) a different, relational orientation to CIE research and practice (Vavrus, 2017b). As an example of the desired relational orientation Vavrus advocates, we can look to the work of Tariq Jazeel, a postcolonial geographer who talks about "slow immersive research". When applied to school-based research, we are forced "into a slow uncertain immersion in a school's ordinary dimensions, wherein the political effects of the ordinary can be revealed" (Vavrus, 2017b).

Considerations of the feasibility of doing CIE research differently were asked, connecting the discussion with the practical implications of historical and contemporary research funding processes. The discussion pointed to the fact that beyond the very real individual-level risks and opportunities for doing CIE research differently, lie entrenched, and more troublesome structural features of the research funding architecture and research publication process. I believe it fair to say that the bulk of CIE research is made possible by funding received from external agencies and organizations. Without these external funds, little research would (or could) happen. Thus, it seems clear that a key component of meaningful and sustained decolonization processes must necessarily involve advocacy and efforts to educate and transform – perhaps "re-socialize" might be appropriate here – research funders, in accordance with the decolonizing agenda discussed in this book.

4   Organization of Part 1

Leading the part is a contribution by CIES 2017 symposium plenary panelist Leigh Patel, entitled, "Before Reconciliation, There Must Be Truth". The focus of the chapter is on colonialism and coloniality as ongoing and ubiquitous features of the historical and contemporary contexts within which CIE researchers and practitioners work. She directly engages with the concept of "inclusive, safe spaces" (the subtitle of this volume), to discuss the challenges of having the difficult conversations that are needed about CIE research, and particularly the way such spaces and conversations can be taken over and derailed by defensive responses by those unwilling to consider their role(s) in reproducing and legitimizing an unequal status quo. She calls CIE scholars to concerted action and to "consider deeply how coloniality, the ranking of some as more human than others, has been a consistent logic, precisely so that other logics and practices can be dreamed into existence" (Patel, Chapter 3, this volume). In short, we must first have these difficult conversations about our ongoing ways of being and knowing in CIE so that we may generate new, inclusive, equitable and non-violent ones.

In the next chapter, entitled, "Beauty and Comparative Education Research Methods: A Consideration for Aesthetic Cognitivism", Derrick Tu takes on the epistemological dominance and rigidity seen as characterizing much of CIE research. He uses the lens of aesthetic cognitivism to explore the epistemological foundations of the Arts-Based Educational Research (ABER) approach, and to suggest its possibilities for challenging and transforming the ongoing coloniality evident in the different 'ologies' underpinning and driving the production and dissemination of CIE research. Though importantly, Tu cautions readers that ABER (or arts in research more generally) is not inherently decolonizing, and that care needs to be given to ensuring that such arts-based approaches do not replicate, legitimate, and maintain colonial and (neo-)colonial mentalities.

The part concludes with a chapter by Karen Ross, entitled, "Interrogating Impact: Whose Knowledge Counts in Assessment of Comparative and International Education Interventions?". Here, Ross problematizes the dominance of outsider perspectives closely connected with donors and funding agencies, in defining legitimate knowledge – its form and content – in evaluative inquiry and CIE research more broadly. The purpose of the chapter is to question who decides, and on what grounds, what "success" or "impact" is (and is not) in educational interventions, and importantly, what this bodes for ensuring that interventions meet local needs. Ross' arguments center on the possibilities and value of thinking about impact in terms of organizational learning as well as the impacts that can be realized through sustained academic research partnerships. Ultimately, she critiques the dominant approach to evaluation research that defines success in terms of the priorities and beliefs of outsiders, and instead argues the importance of aligning impact evaluation criteria to locally defined goals and values.

Notes

1 Leigh Patel is an educator and sociologist, but her professional home is not CIE. Riyad Shahjahan, Francis Vavrus and Dan Wagner will likely be familiar names to those in CIE community.
2 An example shared by Vavrus involved an academic colleague in South Africa who presented her with "the list" of journals that would count in her tenure review.

References

Bakhtin, M. M. (1990). *Art and answerability: Early philosophical essays.* Austin, TX: University of Texas Press.

de Sousa Santos, B. (2007). Beyond abyssal thinking: From global lines to ecologies of knowledges. *Review (Fernand Braudel Center), 30*(1), 45–89.

Fabian, J. (1983). *Time and the other: How anthropology makes its object.* New York, NY: Columbia University Press.

Fricker, M. (2007). *Epistemic injustice: Power and the ethics of knowing.* Oxford: Oxford University Press.

Hunt, V. (2019). *Copper promises: Hinemihi Haka* (live performance). Peterborough, Ontario, Canada.

Mignolo, W. D. (2014). Spirit out of bounds returns to the east: The closing of the social sciences and the opening of independent thoughts. *Current Sociology, 62*(4), 584–602.

Mignolo, W. (2002). The geo-politics of knowledge and colonial difference. *South Atlantic Quarterly, 101*(1), 57–96.

Nagar, R. (2014). *Muddying the waters: Coauthoring feminisms across scholarship and activism.* Urbana, CL & Springfield: University of Illinois Press.

Patel, L. (2017a). Remarks. In *Proceedings of the 2nd Comparative and International Education Symposium: Interrogating and Innovating CIE Research.* George Mason University. Arlington, VA: GMU.

Patel, L. (2017b). Symposium statement. In *Proceedings of the 2nd Comparative and International Education Symposium: Interrogating and Innovating CIE Research.* George Mason University. Arlington, VA: GMU. Retrieved from https://cehd.gmu.edu/2017symposium/speaker-statements

Ramos, A. C. (2017). *Denial of coevalness as an epistemic injustice* (Unpublished thesis). University of Tartu, Institute of Philosophy and Semiotics, Department of Philosophy, Tartu, Estonia.

Romm, N. R. (2018). *Responsible research practice: Revisiting transformative paradigm for social research.* New York, NY: Springer.

Rosa, J., & Flores, N. (2017). Unsettling race and language: Toward a raciolinguistic perspective. *Language in Society, 46*(5), 621–647.

Said, E. W. (1978). *Orientalism.* New York, NY: Pantheon Books.

Savransky, M. (2017). A decolonial imagination: Sociology, anthropology and politics of reality. *Sociology, 51*(1), 11–26.

Shahjahan, R. (2017a). Symposium statement. In *Proceedings of the 2nd Comparative and International Education Symposium: Interrogating and Innovating CIE Research.* George Mason University. Arlington, VA: GMU. Retrieved from https://cehd.gmu.edu/2017symposium/speaker-statements

Spivak, G. C. (1988). Can the subaltern speak? In C. Nelson & L. Grossberg (Eds.), *Marxism and the interpretation of culture*. Champaign, IL: University of Illinois Press.

Stein, S. (2017). The persistent challenges of addressing epistemic dominance in higher education: Considering the case of curriculum internationalization. *Comparative Education Review, 61*(S1), S25–S50.

Strega, S., & Brown, L. (2015). *Research as resistance: Revisiting critical, indigenous, and anti-oppressive approaches*. Toronto: Canadian Scholars' Press; Women's Press.

Sundberg, J. (2014). Decolonizing posthumanist geographies. *Cultural Geographies, 21*(1), 33–47.

Tuck, E., & Yang, K. W. (2012). Decolonization is not a metaphor. *Decolonization: Indigeneity, Education and Society, 1*(1), 1–40.

Vavrus, F. (2017a). Symposium statement. In *Proceedings of the 2nd Comparative and International Education Symposium: Interrogating and Innovating CIE Research*. Arlington, VA: George Mason University. Retrieved from https://cehd.gmu.edu/2017symposium/speaker-statements

Vavrus, F. (2017b). Remarks. In *Proceedings of the 2nd Comparative and International Education Symposium: Interrogating and Innovating CIE Research*. Arlington, VA: George Mason University.

Wagner, D. (2017). Remarks. In *Proceedings of the 2nd Comparative and International Education Symposium: Interrogating and Innovating CIE Research*. Arlington, VA: George Mason University.

Wilson, J. (2000). *King Trapper of the north: An ethnographic life history of a traditional aboriginal sporting king* (Unpublished master's thesis). University of Alberta, Edmonton, Alberta.

Wilson, S. (2008). *Research is ceremony: Indigenous research methods*. Black Point, NS: Fernwood Publishing.

CHAPTER 3

Before Reconciliation, There Must Be Truth

Leigh Patel

Abstract

In this chapter, I situate the call for interrogation and innovating comparative and international education research from a lens of the ongoing logics and practices of colonization. In doing so, I necessarily point out the narratives about colonization and decolonization that are told that work to perpetuate the accumulation of wealth and well-being for a few and vulnerability and suffering for millions more. This chapter recants a pointed example of these narratives that unfolded within the opening panel of the 2017 CIES symposium. I close with a call for the truth-telling about the ongoing reality of colonization and reference to past and ongoing quests for freedom that reach far beyond achievement and well-being based on the colonizer's standards.

Keywords

decolonization – truth – developing countries – research ethics – freedom – borders

In the fall of 2017, the *Third World Quarterly* published an article entitled, The Case for Colonialism, by Bruce Gilley. In essence, the article argued that colonialism really should not have such a bad name, because, look at all the development and good things that have taken place because of, more specifically, Western colonization. Outrage ensued, the internet responded, retractions were demanded. In response to the reaction more than the article itself, Eve Tuck (2017) tweeted the following remarks:

> I know that there is much deserved outrage about that article, but much of social science is a tacit endorsement of colonialism. This is not 'new', it is the past and the future of many disciplinary fields. Those which do work on people and not with them. Those which make the external research and not the person or community the expert. Research that is

obsessed with "development", or closing gaps, catching up, even sometimes reconciliation. All of this can naturalize the (ongoing) violence as a starting point of colonization and thereby posit that good things can from colonialism.[1]

Tuck's comments are, in essence, calling attention the fact that colonialism has always had a place in Westernized social science. For example, Lozenski (2017) points out that the continued references to crises about the education of Black boys is anathema to the fact the United States was formed out of and grew its wealth through the intertwined subjugation of Black peoples. Tuck's comments makes this same point, but on a larger scale, noting that the majority of social science assumes a colonizing stances in which expert outsiders identify and then create interventions for populations who have, for centuries, purposefully been relegated as less than human. Her points are crucial for helping us to contend with the fact that colonialism is ubiquitous, as are its referents, figurations, and justifications. Outrage is appropriate to such a poorly researched and even worse ethics-based article, but where is our outrage for research articles published by outsiders to communities who then enjoy wide celebration in part because of their subject positions and credentials gained through, in part, social connections and economic capital that ease the pathways through admissions, matriculation, and degree conferment by historically and still male and Eurocentric institutions of higher education? Put another way, colonialism is ongoing, and its primary products of stratification and exploitation are justified and refreshed on a daily basis for the benefit of a few and the dispossession of many. To be even more specific, each week brings news in which Black death remains both spectacle and normalized, the government continues to contain bodies in holding facilities that mushroom in type, and Black, migrant, and Indigenous children continue to be torn from their families.

It is from this basic fact of historical and contemporary contexts that I cautiously take up the question of this volume, decolonizing practices for inclusive, safe spaces. The comparative study of different social, political, and cultural geographies offers much to be learned about the contours, affordances, and productive limitations in different contexts. However, too often comparative educational research has been taken up in such a way that implicitly, or more sadly, explicitly holds up Western, "developed" countries as those that have pursed and anointed preferred knowledge to then offer to the darker nations. Inclusion to such a context begs the question of who needs inclusion and what sorts of assimilation are expected as the implicit terms of that inclusion. Within such interactions, that may take place in service trips, non-government organizations developing community preferred knowledge, as well as the intimate spaces of classrooms, the idea of who is 'safe' in these interactions is, minimally, fraught.

Additionally, as Sara Ahmed (2015) so brilliantly put it, when it comes to safe spaces,

> The assumption that safe spaces are themselves about deflecting attention from difficult issues is another *working assumption*. Safe spaces are another technique for dealing with the consequences of histories that are not over (a response to a history that is not over is necessarily inadequate because that history is not over). The real purpose of these mechanisms is to enable conversations about difficult issues to happen. So often those conversations do not happen because the difficulties people wish to talk about end up being reenacted within discussion spaces, which is how they are not talked about. For example, conversations about racism are very hard to have when white people become defensive about racism. Those conversations end up being about those *defences* (sic) *rather than about racism*. (n.p., para. 22)

This dynamic plays out in real time in myriad places, and it did so during a plenary opening session at the CIES symposium, the ideas from which are built upon and extended in this volume. My critique about colonialism that day, on a panel with others, as a few other panelists did, addressed the complexities of decolonizing knowledge and material relations that have been, purposefully, colonial for hundreds of years. I closed my comments with the fact, though, that as long as colonization has been, for hundreds of years, trying to collapse Black people into chattel property, brown peoples into coolie laborers, and altogether erase Indigenous peoples, it has failed. Myriad examples exist of life being bigger than colonization's quest for stratification and dominant for a few. There is the bare fact that Indigenous peoples have lived, survived, and sustain not just cultures and languages in the face of extermination, but also sovereignty and stewardship of the land. There is also the fact that in Turtle Island, weeks after formerly enslaved peoples had been only considered property, they dreamed into existence what we now know as Historically Black Colleges and Universities (HBCUs). But for HBCUs, the nation's statistics in terms of Black middle-class professionals would be drastically different, and not for the good. And yet, HBCUs and Indigenous actions for sovereignty are not established out of desire to be at the top of the empire, but rather to build strength from within.

All too typically, strong critique and analysis of today's coloniality is dismissed as fatalistic and conflated with inaction. That is precisely what happened at the symposium, and while it may have been a productive moment of contestation for beginners to the field, it also held us, collectively at bay from digging deeper into questions that don't reify the center and see its demise as anarchy. My critique then, and now, in this essay, is not meant to suggest inaction. On the contrary, I suggest that this field of research consider deeply how coloniality, the ranking of some as more human than others, has been a consistent logic, precisely so that other logics and practices can be dreamed into existence. I would expect scholars who study international relations have a deep analysis about borders, how they are created, moved, and protected, and all too often sites of violence, as one example.

I also suggest that to learn about decolonization, one must study how it has been practiced as an agentic act of refusal of colonial logics, racist capitalism, and heteropatriarchy. In her recent book, *The Lost Education of Horace Tate* (2018), Siddle Walker artfully traces the literal provocative activities that Horace Tate and dozens of Black educators, lawyers, and organizers in the South undertook, under the knowledge of the law, to create conduits and sidestreets (both literal and figurative) to combat the racist effects of segregation. These are the places where fields can learn what freedom is, what agency looks like, and from there, where coloniality has insisted upon stratification of who, literally, can know and write about others.

I entitled this essay using the word reconciliation, as that might be an appropriate goal for this field, but truly, what I seek for so many "developing" nations is different than reconciliation, which would undoubtedly require more labor on the part of those who have been colonized. Instead, I find it imperative to think about freedom. About Autonomy. About collective and individual self-determination.

I close with this quote from Stefano Harney and Fred Moten's book, *The Undercommons* (2013):

> There will be a jubilee when the Global South does not get credit for discounted contributions to world civilization and commerce but keeps its debts, changes them only for the debt of others, a swap among those who never intend to pay, who will never be allowed to pay, in a bar in Penang, in Port of Spain, in Bandung, where your credit is no good. (p. 63)

Note

1 Retrieved September 16, 2017, from https://twitter.com/tuckeve/status/917389967931985921

References

Ahmed, S. (2015, June 5). Against students. *The New Inquiry*. Retrieved August 11, 2018, from https://thenewinquiry.com/against-students/

Harney, S., & Moten, F. (2013). *The Undercommons: Fugitive planning and Black Study*. New York, NY: The New Press.

Lozenski, B. D. (2017). Beyond mediocrity: The dialectics of crisis in the continuing miseducation of Black youth. *Harvard Education Review, 87*(2), 161–185.

Siddle Walker, V. (2018). *The lost education of Horace Tate: Uncovering the hidden heroes who fought for justice in schools*. New York, NY: The New Press.

CHAPTER 4

Beauty and Comparative Education Research Methods: A Consideration for Aesthetic Cognitivism

Derrick Tu

Abstract

Comparative and international education (CIE) researchers have used education as a mirror to understand practices in countries for educational planning (Bereday, 1964). Although there is a belief that "…there are many schools of thought, and none have dominance…" (Altbach, 1991, p. 493), CIE research is still based on a hegemonic (neo)colonial mindset that can create unjust hierarchies in education (Tikly & Bond, 2013). As a research methodology, Arts-Based Educational Research (ABER) (Cahnmann-Taylor, 2008; Eisner, 2008) is considered to be emancipatory or anti-colonial, but does this approach automatically make educational and research practices more equitable? The purpose of this chapter is to examine epistemological foundations of ABER, and to consider how it can address inequalities in the field of CIE. Specifically, how do researchers know what they know through the aesthetics of an artwork? This chapter explores theoretical issues of aesthetic knowledge in CIE through the lens of aesthetic cognitivism (Kieran, 2011). Aesthetic knowledge is important for addressing inequalities in CIE research because it highlights ephemeral qualities that question positivistic paradigms and scientism within the field (Manzon, 2011). However, using ABER in CIE research does not automatically resist a (neo-) colonial mindset because it can also be reproduced in the arts.

Keywords

arts-based educational research – aesthetics – comparative and international education – research methodology – social justice – colonialism – creative writing

1. Introduction

Historically, comparative and international education (CIE) researchers have used education as a mirror to understand precedents in countries for educational planning (Bereday, 1964). Research in the field has evolved through the phases of borrowing, prediction, analysis, and is currently in a period of multiplicity of theories (Altbach, 1991). The shifts in CIE research methodology have been heavily informed by the social sciences from developed countries and international organizations. The push towards systematization and standardization of methods in comparative education is partly influenced by empirical scientific inquiry as a major paradigm in CIE theory and research. However, the research community should avoid prescribing what comparative education must do, as well as scientism (Altbach, 1991; Manzon, 2011; Mitter, 1997; Ruscoe & Nelson, 1964; Torres, 2013). Rather, the future of comparative education lies in greater academic independence, less dogmatism about methodology, and recognition of limits as researchers in the field (Halls, 1977; Manzon, 2011; Torres, 2013). As such, increased interest in qualitative research was a product of epistemological critiques of positivism in social and educational research based on models developed in the natural sciences and medical models (Vulliamy, 2004).

Despite the belief that "... there are many schools of thought, and none have dominance ..." (Altbach, 1991, p. 493), CIE research is still based on hegemonic power and a (neo-)colonial mindset and unjust hierarchies in education (Marginson & Mollis, 2001, Tikly & Bond, 2013). One methodological approach that is argued to be emancipatory or anti-colonial is Arts-Based Educational Research (ABER) (Cahnmann-Taylor, 2008; Eisner, 2008). Part of the purpose of developing ABER was to liberate research from traditional, hegemonic perspectives of the natural sciences and scientific practice in the social sciences, and to bring awareness to different epistemologies and research methods through the arts (Eisner, 2006). However, is it enough to simply conduct research with an arts-based methodology and assume that educational practice will automatically become more socially just and equitable? Critics of ABER have claimed that it is either a weak form of research that merely acts as political legitimization of the arts in the social sciences, or that they reproduce colonial and scientific mindsets that they seek to disrupt (Bourdieu, 1993; Finley, 2005; Mienczakowski, 2006; Pariser, 2009). Despite its criticisms and limitations, ABER can address some issues related to hegemonic power, (neo-)colonial forces, and inequalities in CIE.

The purpose of this chapter is to conceptually reflect on the epistemological foundations of aesthetic knowledge in ABER and to speculate on how it can be effectively used to address inequalities arising from (neo-)colonial forces in CIE research. Specifically, I address the following question: how do researchers know what they know through the aesthetics of an artwork? By situating ABER within discussions about social sciences research methods and comparative education, I explore theoretical issues in understanding aesthetic knowledge through the lens of aesthetic cognitivism. The first section of this chapter defines ABER and situates it within the development of research methods and paradigm shifts in CIE research (Bereday, 1964; Cahnmann-Taylor, 2008; Eisner, 2006). The next section provides a general overview of debates about aesthetic cognitivism (Aumann, 2012; Gaut, 2003). I examine what is aesthetic knowledge, how it is unique compared to scientific knowledge, and the importance of aesthetic knowledge when dealing with values and the evaluation of qualities.

Poetic reflection from my own contemplations about music and beauty is weaved throughout the chapter (Bray, 2012; Miller & Paloa, 2005). While the academic portions discuss controversies in ABER and reframe the benefits of ABER through aesthetic cognitivism, the work of creative writing reflects upon the nature of beauty in music. It opens with a question of what is beauty and where does it exist. Answers to the question make flash references to piano fugues by J.S. Bach, *The Hebrides* by Mendelssohn, Haydn's *Farewell Symphony*, Stravinsky's *Rite of Spring*, and Bizet's *Carmen*. Through these references, I attempt to reveal the ephemerality of beauty through its personification as a phantom with a will of its own. The piece of creative writing concludes with the point that there is a need to reflect more about beauty as an example of an aesthetic quality.

In the discussion section, I suggest that aesthetic knowledge is important for CIE research when addressing inequalities and marginalization because it can allow scholars to understand ephemeral qualities and values through aesthetic cognitivism (Kieran, 2011). The arts can be a means to challenge inequalities from (neo-)colonial forces because it reveals and questions assumptions of positivistic paradigms that have been a foundation to CIE research (Manzon, 2011). However, scholars and educators need to be mindful that using the arts in research does not automatically resist a (neo-)colonial mindset because it can also be reproduced in and through the arts.

2 Arts-Based Educational Research and Comparative Education

Arts-based research methods is a qualitative approach that uses the arts to collect data and represent results in the social sciences (Eisner, 2008). Some projects are based in social sciences methodologies and incorporate the arts in parts of the research project while others result in a work that acts as a piece of art and research (Cahnmann-Taylor, 2008). This type of emancipatory or anti-colonial research lets people engage in an issue by connecting with the human condition or seeing the unexpected (Barone, 2006, 2008; Denzin, 2005; Eisner, 2006; Finley, 2005; Mienczakowski, 2006). To access knowledge, both researchers and audience have to immerse themselves in the work and engage with its aesthetic qualities (Blumefeld-Jones, 2008; Eisner, 2008).

Eisner's (2006) interest in arts-based research was initially driven by a tension that he felt as a scholar trained in social sciences research but immersed in the arts. From this tension, he tried to imagine how the arts might be used to more imaginatively and emotionally understand problems and practices in schools. Eisner explains that the arts are means to emotionally access knowledge and experiences that are more difficult to secure through other more traditional forms of research and representation. In order to develop arts-based research, it was important to understand how research is conceptualized in universities. Research in the arts and sciences are not identical and should not be treated as such. Eisner conceptualized research as a broad umbrella process that can be broaden human experience and foster understanding through knowledge creation or the processes of knowing through the arts and sciences. Since part of the purpose of engaging in ABER is to liberate research from traditional, hegemonic perspectives of the natural sciences and scientific practice in the social sciences, and to bring awareness to different epistemologies and research methods (Eisner, 2006), this approach to research may be important in CIE research because of the history of its methodological developments.

> What is beauty? A deceivingly simple question that may not have a very simple answer. Who knows where it can be found, but I think it was in Europe one time. I heard it in Leipzig, Germany. It was a Baroque fugue spiraling out from a piano. Another time, it was in a group of island just west of Scotland. There were powerful waves crashing on the shore near Fingal's Cave stirred up by solemn farewells. It was even in Russia in the spring. It radiated from the *Ballets Russes*. These were some of the sounds that beauty made. Apparently, Bach, Mendelssohn, Haydn, and Stravinsky knew what it was, but I continue to search for it.

A major purpose of comparative education is to understand education systems in different countries while trying to ethically implement education reform (Bereday, 1964). The uses of quantitative, qualitative, and mixed methods in comparative education are based on developments in methodologies in the social sciences where paradigms and paradigm shifts reflect ontological, epistemological, and axiological assumptions of a research community (Creswell, 1998; Guba & Lincoln, 1994; Teddlie & Tashakkori, 2009; Zha & Tu, 2016). In the second half of the 20th century, the questioning of a unified social science and the nature of knowledge challenged positivistic norms in the natural sciences partly by showing limitations from viewing reality as independent from unbiased researchers. Postpositivism tries to address the limitations of positivism by acknowledging that value-systems play a role in research while still trying to maintain the use of quantitative methods in science (Phillips, 1987).

The increase of alternative world views of knowledge led to a renewed interest in qualitative research in the 1980s and the paradigm of constructivism. In the constructivist paradigm, knowledge is derived from the interaction between the observer/researcher and the environment through a construction of meaning of phenomena and empathic understanding (Guba & Lincoln, 1994).

During this time, dogmatic attachments to quantitative and qualitative methods led to a conflict between paradigms in the social sciences where one method was viewed as superior to the other (Guba & Lincoln, 1994; Teddlie & Tashakkori, 2009). In the 1990s, pragmatism and mixed research methods attempted to address this problem by offering a middle ground between quantitative and qualitative approaches through philosophical pluralism to ask research questions and interpret data (Johnson, Onwuegbuzie, & Turner, 2004; Teddlie & Tashakkori, 2009). Despite addressing the paradigm wars, pragmatism failed to address who benefits from "pragmatic" solutions in research (Mertens, 2007). The transformative paradigm addresses this limitation by explicitly recognizing power relations in social contexts. Researchers who use a transformative paradigm may employ mixed methods in their research to challenge social injustices and promote social equity (Mertens, 2007; Teddlie & Tashakkori, 2009).

> What is beauty? Is there an answer to be found? Whatever it is, I know it exists.

Although ABER emerged from paradigm shifts in the social sciences is the use of the arts as part of their research methods (Eisner, 2006), one challenge in the development of arts-based research methods is the definition of research and its related epistemological foundations. Pariser (2009) also acknowledges that artistic and scientific research are different, but believes that calling both

> Sometimes it just needs to be found, or drawn out from hiding.

works research is misleading and inappropriate. He states that Eisner's original intent in promoting the arts-based research model was an attempt to legitimize the work of arts practitioners and educators in the academy, but arts-based research has become a political act of legitimizing itself in the natural and social sciences. The foundation of Pariser's critique about arts-based methods is based on the definition of research where it is a normative science based on positivistic epistemology. In this context, science is cumulative and tentative, but must always persuade its audience with demonstrable evidence through rigorous methods.

In addition to the tension between Eisner (2006) and Pariser (2009), a romanticization of the arts does not make research more accessible or representation more ethical (Alexander, 2005; Denzin, 2005). The integration of production, dissemination, and analysis with the increased use of visual arts and theatre to engage with social materials can allow for various forms of dialogic, social, public art (Bishop, 2006). This type of constructivist, critical, and participatory ontological foundation seems to support post-modern constructivist paradigms in social sciences research. However, arts may also reproduce ontologies and epistemologies that they want to challenge because they were developed with the philosophical basis of Western science. Additionally, the historical lineage of the arts in Western civilization can reproduce notions of class distinction (Bourdieu, 1993; Finley, 2005; Mienczakowski, 2006). For example, theatrical performances that feature characters are still viewed by an audience in an auditorium which may reproduce a position similar to the rational, logical scientist (Denzin, 2005; Mienczakowski, 2006). As a result, dominant performance practices used in scholarly research may inadvertently reproduce positivistic paradigms that the arts are supposed to challenge or disrupt. This again leads to issues around access to knowledge, representation, the impossibility of neutrality, authenticity and the demand for self-reflexivity coupled in activist research (Denzin, 2005; Mienczakowski, 2006). To address these issues and criticisms, the next section focuses on issues in aesthetic knowledge through aesthetic cognitivism.

Art does that.

3   Aesthetic Knowledge and Aesthetic Cognitivism

Aesthetics is a branch of philosophy that examines conceptual and theoretical concepts in art and aesthetic experience (Levinson, 2003). Three major foci of aesthetics are: practice; features or qualities; and attitude or mindset. Generally speaking, art and artistic practice are a means for contemplation, expression, and representation or mimesis of the external world. Aesthetic properties are directly observable characteristics that are relevant to the aesthetics of an object (Levinson, 2003). They are qualities such as beauty, ugliness, happiness, sadness, peacefulness, or liveliness. Attitude or mindset refers to a unique experience through a particular state of mind or perception that sets an aesthetic experience apart from a non-aesthetic one. It is characterized by disinterested detachment from desires, non-practical use, contemplative for its own sake, appreciation of aesthetic qualities, and an interest in the relationship between a work's form, content, and character. Similar to paradigm shifts in the social sciences, there are numerous debates about aesthetic knowledge because of notions of expression and emotions (Kieran, 2011). These debates are situated within a larger discussion on whether or not art can provide knowledge to its audience (Aumann, 2014; Gaut, 2003; Radman, 2012). Can art provide substantive knowledge and does this capacity to impart meaningful knowledge determine its own value?

> It was there in Germany, off the coast in Scotland, and in Russia, but it is a phantom that disappears the moment that someone approaches it.

One important discussion about art and knowledge is based on aesthetic cognitivism: the claim that aesthetic appreciation is a rational act that provides conceptual knowledge, possibilities, knowledge of that which is real, practical knowledge, the importance of events, experiential or phenomenal knowledge, and ethical values (Aumann, 2012; Gaut, 2003). However, it is also possible to challenge this stance on the basis that what is learned is not easily articulated, that it is merely learning from metaphor, that there are no unique differences between scientific and artistic truths, that truths are not possible in art because it lacks reference to facts in the real world, and that any truth is not justifiable because it is usually only based on knowledge of an artwork (Aumann, 2012; Gaut, 2003). Although aesthetic cognitivism requires further elaboration and development, Gaut (2003) claims that it is supported through:

> ... an instance of a more general phenomenon in epistemology, that of testimony: while experience is a ground for our *a posteriori* knowledge, it is also true that much of our knowledge is derived from relying on what others, who we believe to be in a position to know about the relevant area, tell us .... (p. 442)

In fact, the differences between fiction and academic works, for example, highlight different epistemic foundations between the two forms of writing (Mikkonen, 2015).

As for the claim that the value of art rests in the fact that it can impart knowledge, aesthetic cognitivists suggest that the value results from insight and profundity arising from new concepts developed in artworks that deepen our understanding of a subject (Aumann, 2014; Gaut, 2003; Radman, 2012). The critics of aesthetic cognitivism criticize it for valuing aesthetic judgement over facts to the point where truth claims are irrelevant to aesthetic values. Themes such as fate and free will can be explored through literature, while debates of truth claims are the core of philosophical works (Gaut, 2003). However, artistic works not only provide new insights to meaningful themes, but also scholars, critics, and audiences do debate truths of artistic claims. In other words, the difference between artistic criticism and other forms of criticism is exaggerated. Gaut (2003) states:

> It has a will of its own. It's not a slave to form or fashion. It becomes visible by shedding its many guises. Even in opera, it roams the stage.

> ... we celebrate the insight and profundity of artworks, and think these features are aesthetically relevant. And we deride works for their shallowness and sentimentality and think them thereby aesthetically flawed. Here we are making *bona fide* aesthetic evaluations that seem also to be cognitive evaluations ... It is the way that a work conveys its cognitive merits – the mode by which it conveys its insights – that makes them of aesthetic relevance ... The cognitive merits of a novel typically are aesthetically relevant when they are displayed in the particular detailed descriptions of characters, the narrative events, and the feelings prescribed by works ... For example, Austen's insights into human nature artistically enhance her novel when they are displayed in her construction of Emma's character and what is internally related to it, in what Emma does and how she responds to others. In Emma, Austen has in effect constructed a new concept, one that bundles together a set of characteristics, and we can learn to see real people in these terms: we can see a young woman as an Emma, and by application of this concept can learn more about the real person. (pp. 445–446)

From this statement, it is evident that judgements and evaluations are part of evaluating artistic works for excellence based on features that are aesthetically relevant. Cognitive evaluations of art are related to aesthetic evaluations where the mode of conveying knowledge makes aspects aesthetically relevant. In the example of a novel, aesthetically relevant characteristics include (but are not limited to) detailed character descriptions, plot, and emotions evoked. Truth claims may be general, but it is their aesthetic stylization of particulars that warrants merit. Not only does Jane Austen create a new concept of understanding people through the constructed archetype of Emma, but also the aesthetic qualities of the novel add depth to the character. The aesthetic cognitivist position not only suggests that truth claims are relevant to artistic works, but also that there are differences in evaluation of scientific an artistic works. In science, the ultimate standard of evaluation is explanatory truth, while perceived falsehoods do not automatically discredit the aesthetic qualities of a work of fiction. "... To agree that truth in art does not have the final authority it possesses in science is a long way from agreeing that truth is never relevant to aesthetic evaluation" (Gaut, 2005, p. 450).

> I went to see one in Paris one time with a woman from Spain. She worked in a cigarette factory in Seville, I think. She said that love is a rebellious bird that can't be tamed.

The points raised by Gaut (2005) about aesthetically relevant qualities revealing insights from new concepts are also present in ABER. As an example, Jenoure's (2008) *Hearing Jesusa's Laugh* can help ground aesthetic cognitivism in practice. *Hearing Jesusa's Laugh* (Jenoure, 2008) is a musical performance that presented findings from educational research in South Africa. Data from music, dance, poetry, journal entries, taped interviews, and visual imagery created by students and Jenoure addressed how to arts-based pedagogy in different cultural contexts. What emerged from her research was a continuous questioning of her teaching practice, family history, and her own identity. Through the documentation of journeys between New York, Puerto Rico, and South Africa in prose, poetry, and stories, she discovered that ultimately, "... everything is connected" (Jenoure, 2008, p. 176). Her artistic exploration of "otherness" helped broaden her understanding of culture and artistic practice through art itself. Aesthetic cognitivism is a useful lens to understand Jenoure's work because it was not about debate over a truth claim, such as what are the lived experiences of students in South Africa, but rather using the combination of sensual, aesthetic qualities and cognitive evaluations of those qualities to question social relations for "... the sole purpose of creating a more equitable society" (Jenoure, 2008, p. 177). In other words, cognition and sensation are connected to engage with aesthetic qualities to gain a deeper understanding of our world.

> One of the soldiers in Seville didn't believe her though and just ignored her.

4 Discussion and Conclusion

Based on my previous survey of debates about aesthetic cognitivism, it is evident that the tensions that exist between Eisner (2006) and Pariser (2009) stem from a conflict between proving truth claims through logical argument and evaluating excellence of relevant aesthetic qualities that bring new insights to the human condition (Aumann, 2014; Gaut, 2005; Radman, 2012). By making a shift from thinking sociologically to thinking philosophically, the previous section revealed

> Later on, she found out that the soldier was seeing someone else and it drove her mad.

that Eisner's (2006) and Pariser's (2009) debate can be understood as a discussion of issues related to aesthetic cognitivism (Aumann, 2012; Gaut, 2003). Additionally, the combination of academic and creative writing not only reveals unique differences between the two genres of writing, but also concretizes issues raised by academic discussions about ABER and aesthetic cognitivism (Aumann, 2014; Eisner, 2006; Gaut, 2005; Pariser, 2009; Radman, 2012). What does all of this mean for research methods in comparative education? I am not suggesting that all scholars suddenly have to become artists. However, rather than dismissing the arts as something that is merely subjective, mystical, or arbitrary, I want to raise an awareness of aesthetic qualities. It combines knowledge from logic, emotion, and embodied experience to evoke different ways of knowing and to provoke questions that deepen our understanding of ourselves (Aumann, 2014; Barone, 2008; Cahnmann-Taylor, 2008; Cole & Knowles, 2008; Dewey, 1958; Greene, 2002; Neilsen, 2004; Radman, 2012). I highlight the aesthetic dimension because it reveals knowledge that is different from – but just as important as – scientific knowledge, but different from dogmatic scientism (Eisner, 2008; Manzon, 2011; Torres, 2013). Through this awareness, CIE scholars can consider different ways to transform epistemological norms of research in the field.

The juxtaposition of academic and creative writing provides examples of issues about the epistemological foundations of art and controversies surrounding ABER. Researchers need to recognize aesthetic qualities in the arts to access knowledge in ABER (Blumefeld-Jones, 2008; Eisner, 2008). Through a simple comparison of texts in this chapter, it is clear that there are differences in the way that language is used. The poetic prose makes use of metaphors, personification, and imaginative storytelling as a means to search for beauty in music – an elusive quality. It summons beauty through creative writing and artistic practice. The academic text uses language to develop an argument using logic. The juxtaposition and comparison of the two genres of writing highlight not only different uses of language to achieve different goals, but also how aesthetic qualities emerge from creative writing. It is these qualities that are important to ABER, and researchers need to be aware of these qualities. In addition to recognizing aesthetic qualities, it is important to note that aesthetic qualities are not merely emotional (Eisner, 2008). The positivist stance views the arts as primarily emotional, but it is the synthesis of the cognitive dimension with emotion and embodied experience that gives ABER its unique qualities (Aumann, 2012; Blumefeld-Jones, 2008; Eisner, 2008; Gaut, 2003).

Additionally, the field of comparative and international education should create spaces and opportunities for dialogue that not only support multiple theories from different perspectives (Altbach, 1991), but also different epistemological stances. In fact, the continuous iterations of creative writing in this chapter co-exist with academic writing. The fragments of poetic prose not only shift to create their own space in the field, but can also shift academic research that may be normalized in CIE through a (neo-)colonial mindset and positivistic assumptions (Manzon, 2011; Marginson & Mollis, 2001; Tikly & Bond, 2013). Aesthetic knowledge is not just a theoretical consideration, but is also grounded in artistic practice (Blumefeld-Jones, 2008; Levinson, 2003; Radman, 2012). It is the shifting of academic research through artistic practices that can potentially destabilize knowledge hierarchies in CIE research that have been based on colonial epistemologies (Blumefeld-Jones, 2008; Eisner, 2008; Manzon, 2011; Marginson & Mollis, 2001; Tikly & Bond, 2013). Although more refinement is needed between the theory and practice of ABER to truly highlight the importance of the aesthetic dimension in addressing inequalities in CIE research, I hope that this reflection on aesthetic cognitivism has provoked thoughts and ideas on possibilities of using ABER to address inequalities in comparative and international education through a combination of reason, aesthetics, and embodied experience (Dewey, 1958; Eisner, 2008; Gaut, 2003; Kieran, 2011; Morris, 2012).

> Maybe if she listened to her own words, she might have understood more about passion and desire.

Having stated the importance of aesthetic cognitivism, there are also examples of its limitations in this chapter. First of all, using the arts and ABER does not automatically make research anti-colonial or emancipatory. This chapter demonstrates this point because it is a reflection and discussion about European philosophy and Western art music. In fact, using the arts can reproduce a colonial mindset (Bourdieu, 1993; Finley, 2005; Mienczakowski, 2006). However, this limitation is an important starting point to investigate epistemological foundations and artistic practices because the field of CIE research evolved from European thought and positivistic assumptions (Bereday, 1964; Manzon, 2011). It highlights the need to continue questioning research and education, where Eurocentrism still exists in subject disciplines and CIE research (Bourdieu, 1993; Finley, 2005; Manzon, 2011; Mienczakowski, 2006). Secondly, publications of written texts limit the artistic practices when using ABER in CIE research. Although music is a performing art, I reflected on the nature of beauty in written text using literary techniques such as metaphors and personification. This does not mean that it is ineffective to reflect on beauty in music through creative writing. It can be an effective means to reflect upon an art form that does not use words. However, it means that readers are removed from art forms that do not use written text, and researchers can only make limited (or no) use of media in publications. This is also evident in Jenoure's (2008) work that was originally a musical performance, but we can only access poetry and narratives from the written text.

Despite its limitations, ABER is a possible methodological approach to challenge positivistic paradigms in CIE research (Eisner, 2008; Manzon, 2011). Throughout this chapter, poetic prose weaves in and out of traditionally accepted academic writing. At the moment, it is not completely clear as to how ABER is situated within the larger CIE research community. Is ABER a passing trend? Is it something that will grow in the field? Despite this uncertainty, ABER does expand the epistemological boundaries in social sciences research (Eisner, 2008) and CIE can benefit from this. In fact, raising awareness of ABER can provoke CIE researchers to not only talk about aesthetics and art, but to also consider what are aesthetics, beauty, and the arts in different countries to challenge inequities in education. If the field of CIE research is going to embrace a multiple theoretical frameworks (Altbach, 1991), then it would inevitably have to embrace a multiplicity of research methods and epistemologies. Aesthetic cognitivism not only provides a language for researchers to talk about aesthetic qualities, but it also creates opportunities for robust academic conversations about education, the arts, social justice, and global issues in education.

> Or beauty.

In this chapter, I reflected on aesthetic knowledge and ABER to consider on how it can be used to address inequalities arising from (neo-)colonial forces in CIE research. Through a theoretical consideration on aesthetic cognitivism using academic and creative writing, I contemplated how researchers know what they know through aesthetics of an artwork. By situating ABER within discussions about social sciences research methods and comparative education, I suggested that researchers can gain a deeper understanding of the world from aesthetic qualities through epistemological holism. Further scholarship in the field of comparative and international education should continue to foster a space that embraces different theoretical perspectives and epistemological stances to avoid prescriptive scientism (Altbach, 1991; Mitter, 1997).

References

Alexander, B. (2005). Performance ethnography, the re-enacting and inciting of culture. In N. Denzin & Y. Lincoln (Eds.), *The Sage handbook of qualitative research* (3rd ed., pp. 411–443). Thousand Oaks, CA: Sage.

Altbach, P. G. (1991). Trends in comparative education. *Comparative Education Review, 35*(3), 491–507.

Arnove, R. (2013). Introduction: Reframing comparative education: The dialectic of the global and local. In R. Arnove, C. A. Torres, & S. Franz (Eds.), *Comparative education: The dialectic of the global and local* (4th ed., pp. 1–25). Lanham, MD: Rowman & Littlefield.

Aumann, A. (2014). The relationship between aesthetic value and cognitive value. *The Journal of Aesthetics and Art Criticism, 72*(2), 117–127.

Barone, T. (2006). Arts-based educational research then, now, and later. *Studies in Art Education, 48*(1), 4–8.

Barone, T. (2008). How arts-based research can change minds. In M. Cahnmann-Taylor & R. Siegesmund (Eds.), *Arts-based research in education: Foundations for practice* (pp. 31–46). New York, NY: Routledge.

Bereday, G. (1964). *Comparative method in education*. New York, NY: Rinehart and Winston.

Bishop, C. (2006). The social turn: Collaboration and its discontents. *Artforum International, 44*, 178–195.

Blumefeld-Jones, D. (2008). Dance, choreography and social science research. In A. L. Cole & J. G. Knowles (Eds.), *Handbook of the arts in qualitative research: Perspectives, methodologies, examples, and issues* (pp. 175–184). Thousand Oaks, CA: Sage.

Bourdieu, P. (1984). *Distinction: A social critique of the judgement of taste*. London: Routledge & Kegan Paul.

Bray, J. (2012). Concrete poetry and prose. In J. Bray, A. Gibbons, & B. McHale (Eds.), *Routledge companion to experimental literature* (pp. 298–309). New York, NY: Routledge.

Cahnmann-Taylor, M. (2008). Arts-based research: Histories and new directions. In M. Cahnmann-Taylor & R. Siegesmund (Eds.), *Arts-based research in education: Foundations for practice* (pp. 1–13). New York, NY: Routledge.

Creswell, J. (1998). *Qualitative inquiry and research design: Choosing among five traditions*. Thousand Oaks, CA: Sage.

Denzin, N. (2005). Emancipatory discourses and the ethics and politics of interpretation. In N. Denzin & Y. Lincoln (Eds.), *The Sage handbook of qualitative research* (3rd ed., pp. 933–958). Thousand Oaks, CA: Sage.

Dewey, J. (1958). *Art as experience.* New York, NY: Capricorn Books.

Eisner, E. (2006). Does arts-based research have a future? *Studies in Art Education, 48*(1), 9–18.

Eisner, E. (2008). Art and knowledge. In A. L. Cole & J. G. Knowles (Eds.), *Handbook of the arts in qualitative research: Perspectives, methodologies, examples, and issues* (pp. 3–25). Thousand Oaks, CA: Sage.

Finley, S. (2005). Arts-based inquiry: Performing revolutionary pedagogy. In N. Denzin & Y. Lincoln (Eds.), *The Sage handbook of qualitative research* (3rd ed., pp. 681–694). Thousand Oaks, CA: Sage.

Gaut, B. (2003). Art and knowledge. In J. Levinson (Ed.), *The Oxford handbook of aesthetics* (pp. 436–450). Oxford: Oxford University Press.

Greene, M. (2002). *Releasing the imagination: Essays on education, the arts, and social change.* San Francisco, CA: Jossey-Bass.

Guba, E. G., & Lincoln, Y. S. (1994). Competing paradigms in qualitative research. In N. K. Denzin & Y. S. Lincoln (Eds.), *Handbook of qualitative research.* Thousand Oaks, CA: Sage Publications.

Guyer, P. (2013). Monism and pluralism in the history of aesthetics. *The Journal of Aesthetics and Art Criticism, 71*(2), 133–143.

Halls, W. D. (1977). Comparative studies in education, 1964–1977: A personal view. *Comparative Education, 13*(2), 81–86.

Haseman, B. (2009). Performance as research in Australia: Legitimating epistemologies. In S. R. Riley & L. Hunter (Eds.), *Mapping landscapes for performance as research: Scholarly acts and creative cartographies* (pp. 51–61). New York, NY: Palgrave Macmillan.

Jenoure, T. (2008). Hearing Jesusa's laugh. In M. Cahnmann-Taylor & R. Siegesmund (Eds.), *Arts-based research in education: Foundations for practice* (pp. 153–181). New York, NY: Routledge.

Johnson, J. R., Onwuegbuzie, A. J., & Turner, L. A. (2007). Towards a definition of mixed methods research. *Journal of Mixed Methods Research, 1*(2), 112–133.

Kieran, M. (2011). Aesthetic knowledge. In S. Bernecker & D. Pritchard (Eds.), *The Routledge companion to epistemology* (pp. 369–379). New York, NY: Routledge.

Levinson, J. (2003). Philosophical aesthetics: An overview. In J. Levinson (Ed.), *The Oxford handbook of aesthetics* (pp. 3–24). Oxford: Oxford University Press.

Manzon, M. (2011). *Comparative education: The construction of a field.* London: Springer.

Marginson, S., & Mollis, M. (2008). "The door opens and the tiger leaps": Theories and reflexivities of comparative education for a global millennium. *Comparative Education Review, 45*(4), 581–615.

Mertens, D. M. (2007). Transformative paradigm: Mixed methods and social justice. *Journal of Mixed Methods Research, 1*(2), 212–225.

Mienczakowski, J. (2006). Ethnodrama: Performed research – Limitations and potential. In S. Hesse-Biber & P. Leavy (Eds.), *Emergent methods in social research* (pp. 235–252). Thousand Oaks, CA: Sage.

Mikkonen, J. (2015). On studying the cognitive value of literature. *The Journal of Aesthetics and Art Criticism, 73*(3), 273–282.

Miller, B., & Paola, S. (2005). *Tell it slant: Writing and shaping creative nonfiction.* New York, NY: McGraw-Hill.

Mitter, W. (1997). Challenges to comparative education: Between retrospect and expectation. *International Review of Education, 43*(5–6), 406–412.

Morris, M. (2012). The meaning of music. *The Monist, 95*(4), 556–586.

Neilsen, L. (2004). Aesthetics and knowing: Ephemeral principles for a groundless theory. In L. Neilsen, J. G. Knowles, & T. Luciani (Eds.), *Provoked by art: Theorizing arts-informed research* (pp. 44–49). Halifax, NS: Backalong Books.

Pariser, D. (2009). Arts-based research: Trojan horses and shibboleths. *Canadian Review of Art Education, 36*, 1–18.

Phillips, D. C. (1987). *Philosophy, science, and social inquiry: Contemporary methodological controversies in social science and related fields of research.* Oxford: Pergamon Press.

Radman, Z. (2012). Body, brain, and beauty: The place of aesthetics in the world of the mind. *Diogenes, 59*(1–2), 41–51.

Ruscoe, G. C., & Nelson, T. W. (1964). Prolegomena to a definition of comparative education. *International Review of Education, 10*(4), 385–392.

Teddlie, C., & Tashakkori, A. (2009). *Foundations of mixed methods research: Integrating quantitative and qualitative approaches in the social and behavioral sciences.* Thousand Oaks, CA: Sage.

Tikly, L., & Bond, T. (2013). Towards a postcolonial research ethics in comparative and international education. *Compare, 43*(4), 422–442.

Torres, C. (2013). Comparative education: The dialectics of globalization and its discontents. In R. Arnove, C. A. Torres, & S. Franz (Eds.), *Comparative education: The dialectic of the global and local* (4th ed., pp. 459–483). Lanham, MD: Rowman & Littlefield.

Vulliamy, G. (2004). The impact of globalization on qualitative research in comparative and international education. *Compare, 43*(4), 422–442.

Zha, Q., & Tu, D. (2016). Doing mixed methods research in comparative education: Some reflections on the fit and a survey of the literature. In A. W. Wiseman & E. Anderson (Eds.), *Annual review of comparative and international education 2015.* Bingley: Emerald Group Publishing.

CHAPTER 5

Interrogating Impact: Whose Knowledge Counts in Assessment of Comparative and International Education Interventions?

Karen Ross

Abstract

This chapter explores evaluation and impact assessment in the context of comparative and international education research. I begin by contextualizing evaluative research within the broader comparative and international education field, highlighting the disjuncture between approaches favoured by local organizational actors and the randomized control trials favoured by international funders and donor agencies mandating assessment. I then draw upon a decade of evaluative research I have conducted in partnership with Sadaka Reut, a Jewish-Palestinian educational organization in Israel, to illustrate the significance of long-term researcher-organization partnerships to create shifts in research emphases from outsider-driven areas of focus to questions raised by organization staff. I discuss this within the broader context of Sadaka Reut's approach to organizational learning and the systems it has developed to balance conflicts between its own internal needs and the demands placed upon it by outsiders.

Keywords

impact – evaluation – legitimate knowledge – insider knowledge – outsiders – experts – assessment

1   Introduction

The priorities of comparative and international education (CIE) research have shifted as the field has developed, moving from predominantly positivist approaches to a more inclusive umbrella of onto-epistemological frameworks that have brought a range of discourses into the field. However, both comparative and international education research broadly, and evaluative inquiry and assessment of impact within the CIE field more specifically, largely define legitimate knowledge from the perspective of outsiders. In the case of evaluative research, both the form and content of legitimate knowledge has been overwhelmingly defined by donors and funding agencies in the Global North (Bamberger, 2000), while the expertise of local actors who develop and implement educational programming is often marginalized (Chouinard, 2013; Delandshere, 2004; Williams, 2010).

In this chapter I focus on who gets to determine legitimate knowledge as it applies to defining the "success" or "impact" of educational interventions and the implications of this for enabling such interventions to meet local needs. I do so by exploring the post-positivist orientation towards impact assessment that is modelled by funders in the Global North. Then, drawing upon a nearly decade-old partnership with the Israeli organization Sadaka Reut, I contrast this orientation with possibilities for understanding impact that can occur in the context of organizational learning and reflection, as well as through long-term academic research partnerships. My discussion also addresses the implications of defining impact according to the priorities set by outsiders – that is, individuals or agencies not directly involved with educational programming – rather than emphasizing impact as it relates to local organizational actors in terms of the concepts most central to their programming goals and values.

2   Comparative Research, Educational Assessment, and Legitimate Forms of Knowledge

As a field, comparative education has long looked to explore similarities and differences across educational systems. Over the years, comparative and international educational research has shifted in both its substantive and methodological foci (Wiseman & Matherly, 2016). This is reflected in, among other things, the changing emphases of manuscripts published in *Comparative Education Review*: from editor George Bereday's focus on "empirical scientific" studies, to editor Harold Noah's emphasis on "establish[ing] generalizations that can apply across contexts" (Cossa, 2016, p. 135), to the greater range of epistemological and methodological frameworks in published manuscripts that can be seen today, including decolonial/postcolonial (e.g., Takayama, Sriprakash, & Connell, 2017) and participatory (e.g., Shah, 2015) approaches.

Even within this broader range, comparative and international education research is still largely characterized by two methodological approaches: cross-national comparison and case study research, each emphasizing different aspects of investigation into education around the world. Cross-national comparisons are useful for theory-building and for understanding "the multiple ways in which societal factors, educational policies, and practices may vary and interact in otherwise unpredictable and unimaginable ways" (Arnove, 1999, p. 4; see also Bray & Thomas, 1995; Manzon, 2007; Meyer, Ramirez, & Soysal, 1992). Cross-national comparisons also provide a methodological framework for advancing knowledge about education in a global context. For instance, literature on globalization in education that uses world systems and on world culture theories, is predicated on methodological approaches that can illustrate commonalities and differences between education systems in multiple countries.

Methodologically, cross-national comparison is not well suited to learning about the nuances of educational interventions and in particular how these interventions are experienced by multiple stakeholders, in part because comparison across nation-states obscures unique and distinguishing features of different regions, districts, schools, and pupils within those nations. However, while scholars have turned to comparisons that account for broad differences within countries, this comparative approach continues to privilege scholars who are more often than not outsiders to educational intervention settings in making choices about how to explore the similarities and differences across different contexts. Thus, this approach provides few opportunities for developing an understanding of educational interventions from the perspective of local policy makers, practitioners, educators, or students.

In contrast to this broad mode of comparison, case study approaches emphasize particularities, offering an opportunity for understanding micro-level processes in education (Crossley & Vulliamy, 1984) and acknowledging "the contingencies of particular sociocultural milieu and historical formations" (Ragin, 1987, p. 16, quoted in Arnove, 2001, p. 496). Bartlett and Vavrus (2017) have called for case studies of education that address vertical, horizontal, and transversal dimensions of comparison: multiple scales through which cases are explored (micro- to macro-level); comparison of similar units of analysis across distinct locations; and comparison that historically situates processes under examination. Importantly, their approach emphasizes the need to focus on power relations as well as attending to social relations, political processes, and networks that exist across multiple scales and times. Yet, whether in the form of the implicit comparisons that accompany single case studies or in research that engages comparison more explicitly, case study approaches generally also place outside researchers at the center of the decision-making process about both points of comparison and issues to compare. Thus, although the comparative education field has moved away from positivist, "scientific" or hypothesis- and variable-driven approaches, nuanced case study approaches retain an emphasis on the production of knowledge as it is determined by 'experts' particularly researchers located in the Global North.

3 Evaluation and Assessment in Comparative and International Education Research

Within the field of CIE research is a specific focus on assessment and impact evaluation of educational interventions, which Phillips and Schweisfurth (2007) describe as focused on "judging the merit, value, or worth of any given program or technique" (p. 85), in order to facilitate decision making – an endeavor that is comparative in nature, though not always explicitly so. Silova, Read and Mundy (2016) note the rise of assessment and evaluation in the field of comparative and international education as a political endeavor, pointing out that, "Rising demands on limited resources and a general culture of accountability have produced, at least in much of the industrialized world, a political climate emphasizing the need for 'evidence-based' policy and practice in all public service sectors", including within the field of education (p. 155). In other words, even as CIE as a field has moved away from a sole prioritization of positivist and post-positivist research, evaluative inquiry within the field has not.

Even more so than other elements of CIE research, impact evaluation is predicated on assumptions that reify the expertise of researchers/evaluators/decision-makers. Although non-governmental organizations (NGOs) are accountable both upwards to their donors/funding agencies and downwards to their beneficiaries, the "technical, expert, and standardized knowledge" that flows upward towards donors is privileged by many organizations over the contextually-bound, intimate, and much deeper forms of knowledge that emerge in the enactment of downward accountability (Williams, 2010, p. 34). In other words, evaluation does not privilege those forms of knowing that organizations perceive as most effective for understanding their own work and the needs of their beneficiaries, but rather what others – those with power to continue funding these organizations or not – perceive as legitimate forms of meaning making. As Busza (2004) notes, the implications of this power dynamic are that local organizations and programmatic staff are often caught in a fraught situation of trying to address the tension between their contextually-situated concerns and desire for participatory knowledge creation, and the need to meet demands of funders in order to continue project implementation. Moreover, in the context of educational initiatives occurring outside of the Global

North, the primary sponsors of evaluation are often international funding agencies (Bamberger, 2000). Thus, "donors' information priorities and evaluation methodologies continue to exert considerable influence on how evaluation is practiced and used" (Bamberger, 2000, p. 96): priorities that are often expressed in a preference for approaches perceived to be neutral and objective, and that gather evidence primarily about efficiency, cost-effectiveness, or program relevance (Chouinard, 2013). Moreover, it is political actors in the form of government officials or international agency staff, rather than local educators or program implementers, who determine the criteria by which decisions about the worth or value of different policy/program options will be made. And while these actors often have backgrounds in education relevant to their work, they do not have the nuanced understanding of local context or organizational needs held by the educators and program implementers whose work is evaluated.

4   Criteria for Success: Causal Relations and the Outside Expert

As Ginette Delandshere (2004) highlights in her discussion of federal (U.S.) education research, the criteria most commonly utilized to assess impact are "evidence-driven" models of success, in particular randomized control trials (considered the "gold standard" of assessment) and quasi-experimental designs. These models privilege a specific conception of causal inference: for instance, impact evaluations implemented at United States Agency for International Development (USAID) are based on "models of cause and effect [that] require a credible and rigorously defined counterfactual to control for factors other than the intervention that might account for the observed change" (USAID, 2016, p. 3). In privileging this conception, the "evidence-based" assessment trend limits what kind of knowledge is regarded as valuable by focusing on variables deemed by researchers *a priori* to examine; moreover,

> [This trend] is also quite disconcerting precisely because it imposes great homogeneity and particular values and interests on a world of differences without much concern for peoples' and communities' welfare and quality of life, that is their own values and interests. It positions scientific research exclusively in service of global economic interests – not in service of humanity – at a time when the idea of the common good is ignored or strictly equated with economic growth and technological progress. (Delandshere, 2004, p. 252)

In other words, these models of research ignore the values and interests of individuals and communities who are subjects of that research, and most crucially, "ignore[s] people's voice, their will and agency, and the interpretations they make of their own reality" (Delandshere, 2004, p. 253).

Delandshere's discussion illustrates that instead of deeply contextualized, bottom-up knowledge, what funding agencies value is the ability to illustrate causality within the framework of variable-oriented methodological approaches. This holds true even when lip service is paid to incorporating the voices of program beneficiaries and bringing in varied methodological approaches. For instance, a USAID evaluation of one youth-focused civil society project in Kenya, *Yes Youth Can!* (YYC), included data "collected through focus group discussions and key informant interviews in order to incorporate the views of program participants and other stakeholders in their own words, and provide further depth to the findings" (Linkow, Heidenrich, Cao, Haddaway, & Damon, 2014, p. 5). However, this data was included only as a supplement to the "rigorous statistical methods [used] to compare outcomes for YYC beneficiaries to a counterfactual, and provides evidence of causal impact of the program" (p. 1). And while this is but one example out of hundreds of evaluations USAID implements annually, it exemplifies an evaluation approach privileging a framework set in accordance with criteria determined by program funders, both substantively and methodologically, and including participant voices only as a way of "providing further depth" – that is, as a way of confirming or nuancing findings, rather than in shaping the focus of the evaluation's design or substantive focus. As such, this example as many others suggests that terms like "local ownership" are subject to broad interpretation and that local *voices* and *knowledges* remain undervalued at best.

5   Interrogating Impact Evaluation: Local Knowledges, Long-Term Partnerships

The preceding pages illustrate that in comparative education research and more specifically in the assessment of educational interventions within the comparative and international education field, significant challenges exist to prioritizing or even creating space for voices that push against dominant perspectives. However, possibilities do exist for interrogating dominant approaches to CIE research and assessment of educational initiatives. Moreover, when such possibilities are instantiated, they help us understand "impact" and what makes educational programs "work" (or not) with far more nuance than do traditional frameworks.

To illustrate this, in the remainder of the chapter I explore the work of one Israeli educational organization to illustrate both the possibilities and the challenges inherent in transgressing epistemological and methodological norms when assessing educational impact. Specifically, I discuss the work conducted by Sadaka Reut, a non-formal educational organization working with Jewish and Palestinian[1] youth in Israel. I focus on my own engagement with Sadaka Reut since 2009 as a way of highlighting how long-term relationships in the form of researcher-practitioner partnerships enable alternate approaches to impact assessment to be explored. My discussion of Sadaka Reut's work also exemplifies the depth of knowledge local organizational actors can hold and points to the importance of this knowledge in relation to external perspectives about "impact" and its measurement.

5.1   Sadaka Reut

Sadaka Reut is a veteran Israeli non-governmental organization. Founded in the early 1980s, for the past 30+ years Sadaka Reut has focused on bringing together Jewish and Palestinian youth in order to counter dominant societal narratives, foster partnership for social change, and empower participants to be active agents of that change. Since its founding, the organization has implemented two main programs: *Building a Culture of Peace* (BCP), a weekly, after-school initiative for junior and senior high school students; and *Community in Action* (CiA), a year-long, 3 day/week intensive program for recent high school graduates during which participants engage in facilitated discussions with Sadaka Reut staff, volunteer together in local community organizations, and engage in social justice work, including meeting with activists, traveling to sites of social justice activities, and implementing initiatives of their own. More recently, Sadaka Reut has expanded to institutions of higher education with the *Partners in Shaping Reality* program, which brings together students on university campuses around the country that focus on Jewish-Palestinian dialogue and activism.

In its early years, Sadaka Reut's primary emphasis was on inter-personal relationship building, given the near-total segregation experienced between Jewish and Palestinian citizens in most realms of Israeli society. However, over time, especially in the wake of the Al-Aqsa Intifada that began in 2000, its approach shifted to a more direct focus on systemic injustices in Israel. Since then, Sadaka Reut has placed greater emphasis on the importance of engaging in social change activities within Israeli society, and on the significance of Jewish-Palestinian binational partnership as a means to that end. In recent years, the organization has also placed a heavy emphasis on recruiting participants from marginalized Jewish and Palestinian communities within Israel, rather than young people who are being raised in the social identity groups most active in peace-building activities (Helman, 1999).

5.2 Shifting the Focus of Knowledge Production through Long-Term Research Partnerships

I have been involved with Sadaka Reut since 2009, when, as a doctoral student, I first approached the organization about working with them as part of my dissertation research. That summer, I spent 2 months in Israel, during which I met with Sadaka Reut staff/directors and board members in order to learn more about the organization, explain my research interests, and explore possibilities for working together. When I began my discussions with Sadaka Reut, a central goal of mine was to help think through what "impact" might look like over long periods of time, in the context of programs bringing together Jewish and Palestinian youth. Sadaka Reut staff with whom I spoke were very interested in this topic, and I received quite a bit of support from them in the lead-up to my dissertation fieldwork, including a letter of recommendation that was used to help me secure fieldwork funding, a point person to whom I could turn for recruiting potential participants to my study, and so forth. The conversations I held with staff also shaped my dissertation proposal significantly, as they helped me better understand the focus of the organization and its work, and what might be able to be addressed in terms of "impact".

Still, the questions at the focus of my work were based primarily on what *I,* rather than Sadaka Reut staff, perceived as important. When I defended my proposal prior to heading back to Israel for fieldwork, my research questions were the following:

– What are the experiences of individuals when they participate in these programs, and how do these experiences compare to the goals of organization personnel?;
– How does participation in educational encounter programs influence participants' identity claims, their ties with individuals from the other side of the conflict, and their desire to participate in additional coexistence activities?; and
– How do different factors following participation in coexistence education programs influence participants? Specifically,
    – How do personal connections and experiences following participation in coexistence education programs influence identity claims, networks, and continued participation in peace activities?; and
    – How do changes in Israel's political context following participation in coexistence education programs influence identity claims, networks, and continued participation in peace activities?

At the time, I wrote in my proposal:

> Through my answers to these questions, I hope to make a contribution at two levels. Practically, I hope to help these organizations understand what happens to their alumni after programming ends. At the theoretical realm, I hope to offer scholars of peace and peace education a new perspective for thinking about the impact of educational and peace-building interventions in conflict contexts.

While my proposal and questions had been shaped by conversations with Sadaka Reut, the emphasis on examining impact in terms of identity, social ties, and continued participation in what I referred to at the time as "coexistence activities"[2] was determined by me alone, without direct input from the organization. I quickly learned, however, that my conceptions of what might indicate impact were quite different from what program participants and certainly what organizational staff felt should be the emphasis of an exploration of transformation. For example, as my research questions suggested, one of my hopes was to map out social networks of Jewish and Palestinian participants: how ties across conflict lines were created and maintained over time. This aim was based on an emerging line of research exploring social networks in relation to conflict that has attracted significant attention (Nan, 2008), and an emphasis among both scholars of peace-building interventions and funders on encouraging a lessening of social distance as a focus of such programs (e.g., Maoz, 2003). However, after I arrived in Israel, one of the Sadaka Reut directors quickly disabused me of the notion of disseminating the networking survey I had diligently created: in addition to pointing out logistical reasons why doing a social network survey would be problematic, she noted that asking questions about inter-personal relationships would not be relevant for the organization's work. Rather than building relationships, the director suggested that a more relevant question to ask former participants might be, "What are you doing for the purposes of ending the conflict?", emphasizing that a primary goal of Sadaka Reut for participants was for them to begin to ask themselves critical questions about reality and how to change that reality.

It was easy enough for me to shift my questions, and indeed, over the course of my fieldwork and during analysis of my dissertation data, my areas of emphasis changed numerous times to better reflect issues that program participants and organization staff themselves had brought up during interviews. Moreover, as I spent time with and met with Sadaka Reut staff regularly, I learned more about what interested *them* in terms of assessing the impact of their programs. In return for their support with my dissertation, I worked with program coordinators to develop internal monitoring and evaluation surveys that could be used for assessment. During these discussions I noted that issues such as political knowledge, desire to be involved in one's own community, feelings of belonging to the organization, and ability to critique both one's own narrative and that of the other side, were of particular interest among staff. These questions overlapped in part with the ones I had assumed were important to emphasize, for instance with respect to desire for continued involvement. However, there were clearly significant differences between my questions addressing relationship-building and continued participation in joint Jewish-Palestinian "coexistence" activities, and the emphasis on critical socio-political awareness, knowledge, and engagement expressed by Sadaka Reut staff.

Sadaka Reut staff also expressed interest in using the outcomes of my research for their own purposes. As one example, during a meeting with one of the organization's co-directors about halfway through my fieldwork, she expressed interest in seeing preliminary results from my research that could be useful for the organization, in particular information about levels of activism among Sadaka Reut alumni during different time periods. She also told me that information about the degree to which alumni were "active" would be helpful for them to present to donors as evidence of success. Indeed, as I remained in touch with Sadaka Reut while writing up my dissertation, I was asked several times for data that the organization could use when reporting to donors and applying for additional funding. However, it was never clear from my conversations with staff whether this data would be helpful for the organization's own learning processes, or whether it was necessarily primarily as a way of appealing to donors based on funding agency priorities.

The flexibility of my own status as a doctoral student, and the initial approach I took to working with Sadaka Reut, allowed the assessment of "impact" in my dissertation to shift from prioritizing outsider understandings of what was significant, to emphasizing the knowledge and issues important to the organization itself. In the years since completing my dissertation, I have continued to work with Sadaka Reut. In these more recent projects, the emphasis placed on *their* ownership of the questions asked, and of the research process as a whole, has become far more explicit. For instance, we have established a relationship via which we determine research questions together, through conversations among myself and staff and board members of the organization. Thus, the inquiry in which I am engaged emerges from their internal organizational learning processes and is not imposed upon them, in contrast with much of the research on "impact". My more recent research with Sadaka Reut also explicitly addresses the questions to which they feel they need answers but do not have the capacity, mostly due to time constraints, to address on their own, and which do not align with the questions asked *of* them by the donors who fund their work.

5.3 *Internal Learning Processes*

Beyond my long-term relationship with Sadaka Reut, the organization's own learning process highlights possibilities for developing an understanding of impact as it emerges from deeply embedded knowledge about the context in which educational interventions are implemented. In particular, I argue that the culture of reflection and learning characterizing Sadaka Reut has created the flexibility required for the organization to succeed in its programmatic endeavors, as well as the expertise to understand and articulate the mechanisms leading to that success.

In my most recent set of conversations with Sadaka Reut staff and board members, a recurring theme was that the organization was a place where everything is open to critique: where, by virtue of the organizational culture, questions about process, pedagogy, staff interactions and so on are constantly examined, and those examinations acted upon, in order to facilitate Sadaka Reut's ability to move forward and continue to engage in effective work, within the ever-shifting socio-political context in Israel. Embedded into this organizational culture is an internal monitoring and evaluation approach that Sadaka Reut has developed over the years. Although this approach is attuned to the need to meet donor demands, internal evaluation of impact occurs through active, dialogic learning at the organizational level, balances methodological assessment and support for practitioners, and leaves decision-making in the hands of program staff. In other words, Sadaka Reut has developed an approach *internally* that is congruent with its commitment as an organization to its program work and its organizational culture as a whole. Among other things, what this means is that the organization utilizes a far more sustainable approach to monitoring and evaluation than any outsider-imposed framework could mandate.

Sadaka Reut's development of an approach to evaluation that is *part of* a holistic process of organizational learning, highlights a different way of thinking about understanding program impact as well as providing insight into the way that an emphasis on insider knowledge can enable intervention success. Development of this approach has been crucial in enabling Sadaka Reut to shift its programming focus as the context in Israel has changed to better meet the needs of the young people with whom the organization works. In a way, this has also created a virtuous cycle: due to its successful programming, Sadaka Reut is better placed to receive donor funding that helps the organization meet its current needs. Moreover, as I describe further below, my own relationship with Sadaka Reut affirms the potential of long-term research partnerships to help the organization better meet its own needs in terms of knowledge production and internal learning. The dissemination of findings from research conducted through this partnership has also provided opportunities to highlight to other organizations possibilities for achieving programming success as well as how development of internal organizational learning processes is significant in doing so.

However, it is important to remember that my work with Sadaka Reut has been in the form of a partnership between the organization and myself as a scholar accountable only to myself, that is, without a requirement to report my findings (or report them in specific ways) to funding agencies. In many ways my relationship with Sadaka Reut has been fortuitous for us both – my status as an academic scholar has allowed for significant flexibility in the ways that we have explored questions of impact. In the context of funder-initiated evaluations, there is a far greater need for Sadaka Reut to focus on external priorities rather than emphasizing the particular issues that are most relevant to its internal learning process.

Another way of putting this is that the meaning of "what works", or what is "successful" or "effective", according to program managers and staff at Sadaka Reut, can be quite different from the notions of success as articulated by external funders who ask for outcome and impact evaluations. However, it is precisely the organization's deep expertise and its constant internal interrogation of programmatic work, which make Sadaka Reut a successful and thus fundable organization; it is Sadaka Reut's internal process of reflection that has made the organization's programs successful and thus attractive to outside funders. Yet, the need to speak the language of donors, to use their cognitive frames and knowledge production tools, limits possibilities for articulating the organization's success and indeed takes resources from the very processes that enable it. As such, it seems as though there is something of a paradox to consider here.

6   Reconsidering Impact

So, what can we take from this? Ultimately, I believe we need to reconsider the concept of "impact" as something that should be locally known rather than globally or universally applied. Requests from funders for assessment will not diminish any time soon, given their need to be accountable and transparent to stakeholders (whether these be taxpayers, individual donors, or others).

However, a pertinent question to ask might be: if organizations have proved their work is sustainable, why is outsider criteria of impact/effectiveness necessary? And if it is, how might local ways of knowing be incorporated into those outsider criteria in a way that is meaningful and authentic?

At a broader level, it is worth noting that within the evaluation field, culturally-specific and participatory approaches to evaluation have gained traction in recent years: for instance, the American Evaluation Association now includes a Collaborative, Participatory and Empowerment Evaluation Topical Interest Group (TIG) as well as a TIG focused on International and Cross-Cultural Evaluation issues. However, what is needed is a way to bring these issues out of the periphery and into the mainstream – of the international development field and the comparative education field as well as the realm of evaluation. Also necessary is a way of aligning, or at minimum bringing into conversation, the insider knowledge that is used to increase the effectiveness of organizational programming, with outsider criteria required to demonstrate impact.

The intersection of comparative and international education research and the field of educational evaluation highlights a key question about *who* can know about the impact of educational initiatives as well as what knowledge counts in this realm. My experiences working with Sadaka Reut over nearly a decade highlight possibilities for engaging in research partnerships that bring the insider expertise of organizational staff to the fore in assessing impact, even as this expertise challenges dominant approaches to knowledge production. More importantly, Sadaka Reut's work, independent of research partnerships with myself or any other external actors, illustrates the organization's deep capacity to understand and assess its own initiatives, developed through years of ongoing reflection and a commitment to a flexible, changing model of program design. While there are challenges associated with developing this kind of internal buy-in to a reflective learning process, Sadaka Reut serves as an important example showing us not only what non-dominant research in CIE might look like, but also how local educational organizations can navigate the challenges of speaking up to donors.

Notes

1. My reference to "Palestinians" is to citizens of Israel who are of Palestinian descent or identify as Palestinian with respect to their ethno-national identity. I use this term (rather than Israeli Arab or Arab Israeli) because this is how the large majority of individuals with whom I have conducted research in the Israeli context describe themselves.

2   It was in fact due to my fieldwork and ongoing conversations with Palestinian citizens of Israel that I stopped using this term, given the perception among many Palestinians that "there can be no coexistence without existence" – in other words, that the basic needs of Palestinians and Palestinian citizens needed to be addressed before issues of "coexistence" could be prioritized.

References

Arnove, R. F. (1999). Introduction: Reframing comparative education. In R. F. Arnove & C. A. Torres (Eds.), *Comparative education: The dialectic of the global and the local*. Lanham, MD: Rowman & Littlefield Publishers, Inc.

Arnove, R. F. (2001). Comparative and International Education Society (CIES) facing the twenty-first century: Challenges and contributions. *Comparative Education Review, 45*(4), 477–503.

Bamberger, M. (2000). The evaluation of international development programs: A view from the front. *American Journal of Evaluation, 21*(1), 95–102.

Bartlett, L., & Vavrus, F. (2017). *Rethinking case study research: A comparative approach*. New York, NY: Routledge.

Bray, M., & Thomas, R. M. (1995). Levels of comparison in educational studies: Insights from different literatures and the value of multilevel analyses. *Harvard Education Review, 65*(3), 472–490.

Busza, J. (2004). Participatory research in constrained settings. *Action Research, 2*(2), 191–208.

Chouinard, J. (2013). The case for participatory evaluation in an era of accountability. *American Journal of Evaluation, 34*(2), 237–253.

Cossa, J. (2016). Shaping the intellectual landscape. In E. H. Epstein (Ed.), *Crafting a global field: Six decades of the comparative and international education society*. Hong Kong: University of Hong Kong, Comparative Education Research Centre (CERC); Dordrecht: Springer.

Crossley, M., & Vulliamy, G. (1984). Case-study research methods and comparative education. *Comparative Education, 20*(2), 193–207.

Delandshere, G. (2004). The moral, social and political responsibility of educational researchers: Resisting the current quest for certainty. *International Journal of Educational Research, 41*, 237–256.

Helman, S. (1999). From soldiering and motherhood to citizenship: A study of four Israeli peace movements. *Social Politics: International Studies in Gender, State & Society, 6*(3), 292–313.

Linkow, B., Heidenrich, T., Cao, Y., Haddaway, S., & Damon, M. (2014). *Yes Youth Can! Impact evaluation final report*. Chicago, IL: NORC.

Manzon, M. (2007). Comparing places. In M. Bray, B. Adamson, & M. Mason (Eds.), *Comparative education research: Approaches and methods*. Hong Kong: Comparative Education Research Centre.

Maoz, I. (2003). Peace-building with the hawks: Attitude change of Jewish-Israeli hawks and doves following dialogue encounters with Palestinians. *International Journal of Intercultural Relations, 27*, 701–714.

Meyer, J., Ramirez, F., & Soysal, Y. (1992). World expansion of mass education, 1870–1980. *Sociology of Education, 65*(2), 128–149.

Nan, S. A. (2008). Social capital in exclusive and inclusive networks: Satisfying human needs through conflict and conflict resolution. In M. Cox (Ed.), *Social capital and peace-building*. New York, NY: Routledge.

Phillips, D., & Schweisfurth, M. (2007). *Comparative and international education: An introduction to theory, method and practice*. London: Continuum Books.

Ragin, C. (1987). *The comparative method: Moving beyond qualitative an quantitative strategies*. Berkeley, CA: University of California Press.

Shah, P. (2015). Spaces to speak: Photovoice and the reimagination of girl's education in India. *Comparative Education Review, 59*(1), 50–74.

Silova, I., Read, R., & Mundy, K. (2016). The mobilization of knowledge. In E. H. Epstein (Ed.), *Crafting a global field: Six decades of the comparative and international education society*. Hong Kong: University of Hong Kong, Comparative Education Research Centre (CERC); Dordrecht: Springer.

Takayama, K., Sriprakash, A., & Connell, R. (2017). Toward a postcolonial comparative and international education. *Comparative Education Review, 61*(S1), S1–S24.

United States Agency for International Development. (2016). *USAID evaluation policy*. Washington, DC: USAID.

Williams, S. A. (2010). Intersections of accountability: Measuring the effectiveness of international development NGOs. *Berkeley Journal of Sociology, 54*, 27–58.

Wiseman, A. W., & Matherly, C. (2016). Professionalizing the field. In E. H. Epstein (Ed.), *Crafting a global field: Six decades of the comparative and international education society*. Hong Kong: University of Hong Kong, Comparative Education Research Centre (CERC); Dordrecht: Springer.

PART 2

Decolonizing Methodology by Invoking Local Voices

CHAPTER 6

Decolonializing Voice and Localizing Method in Comparative Education

Gerardo L. Blanco

Abstract

The author expertly ties together the three other chapters in this part by pushing a bit on the notions of giving/finding voice. This introductory chapter discusses how the contributions in this part demonstrate ways in which research and methods are pushing boundaries instead of treating local methods and knowledge as fragile. The write-up concludes by sharing that these chapters allude to ways in which research can be done differently and that researchers/practitioners can/should consider abandoning familiarity, making space for "difference".

Keywords

voice – local – decolonizing – differences – boundaries

1   Introduction

This chapter frames a series of contributions that originated from a plenary session at the 2017 Fall Symposium of the Comparative and International Education Society convened at George Mason University. Titled *Decolonizing Methodology by Invoking Local Voices*, the session engaged with knowledge production and the processes of legitimation in Comparative and International Education (CIE). While the focus of both the panel and the subsequent chapters is on methodology, the discussions are grounded on research experiences, and ethically important moments (Guilleming & Gillam, 2004) that triggered reflection, reflexivity and interrogation of assumptions and taken-for-granted practices.

The deeply evocative title "Can the subaltern speak?" of Gayatri Spivak's (1988) essay reminds us that colonization, gender and identity are often intertwined with voice metaphors. Too often the purpose of research is articulated in terms of *giving voice* to those who cannot speak for themselves, or more precisely, to those who speak but remain ignored. The abovementioned plenary panel explored the role of CIE scholars in these entanglements of voice and identity, with a focus on postcolonial contexts.

2   Finding Voice on the Margins

The plenary panelists, including me, traverse multiple boundaries on a regular basis and are acquainted with oppressed and privileged identities. I will speak personally, although I experienced a strong affinity among my colleagues on the plenary. Even though I am a member of several minoritized communities, made evident by my name, accent and phenotypical characteristics, when it comes to scholarship, research and international engagement, I am associated with a research university in the Global North. I am, as Spivak (1993) would phrase it, the margin in the center, or the South within the North. It is this borderland identity (Anzaldúa, 2009) that sets apart the upcoming contributions; the following chapters explore the many contradictions inherent to any attempt to make claims about educational systems from a comparative perspective, and the complexity involved in connecting research and practice.

Given that the plenary contributions that inspired the chapters in this part have a regional focus on South Asia, it seems appropriate to illustrate my argument with some of my own experiences conducting research and collaborating with colleagues in the region (Blanco Ramírez & Haque, 2016). I contend that my Bangladeshi colleagues understand much better than I do, much more intuitively, the performativity of research methodology. They seem to be more closely in tune with the realization that all our knowledge is a claim to power. This is indeed a reason for hope, especially if the goal is decolonizing knowledge and learning from Southern theory (Connell, 2007). However sometimes we fall in the trap of treating Southern knowledge as fragile, as a sort of endangered species. Nevertheless, as the upcoming chapters illustrate, South Asia presents a myriad of examples where the limits of CIE research are being pushed, its assumptions about methods are questioned, and its processes of legitimation and knowledge creation are being thought anew.

3   Contributions in This Part

This part is comprised of three chapters. Radhika Iyengar and Matthew Witenstein analyze technical and vocational education for women in India and, in doing so, explore their aspirations, values and gender-based stereotypes to draw policy lessons for an inclusive vocational education program for India. Huma Kidwai complicates the notion of global knowledge and discusses what is lost when we privilege certain voices and positionalities in knowledge construction within our field. Erik Byker focuses on the tension between research and practice and the hierarchal relationship that quickly emerges whenever these concepts are presented next to each other.

3.1 Women's Voices in Technical and Vocational Education

Iyengar and Witenstein's chapter presents a detailed account of technical and vocational education for women in India. Most importantly, the chapter aggregates perspectives of women ranging from 15 to 56 years old. This is an unusually rich dataset, given the transformations that India and South Asia have experienced during the lifetime of the study participants. The multigenerational nature of the sample presents an interesting thread throughout the chapter.

The relative influence of women's voices in society seems to be closely connected with their influence in the economic sphere. Therefore, gaining a deeper and more sophisticated understanding of the existing mechanisms to increase women's participation in the economy can indeed result in their empowerment in other spheres.

3.2 Voices, Language, and Educational Institutions

What counts as an educational institution? This poignant question is at the core of Kidwai's chapter. By focusing on madrassas in South Asia, this chapter invites us to reflect on how our choices as scholars can exacerbate or reduce the existing hierarchies among different types of educational institutions. Moreover, this question emphasizes the power of quantification and the ways in which traditional research methods can render invisible, inaudible perhaps – to fit the theme of this part, the experiences of vast segments of the population.

This chapter encourages reflection about what topics we choose to investigate, the settings we consider acceptable for research and the implications of these choices. Kidwai reminds us that these choices take place not in a vacuum, but in a growing regime of citation metrics and within an English-dominant publication system.

3.3 Transforming Knowledge by Understanding Knowledge Workers

In order to counterbalance the often-abstract nature of discussions related to research methodology, Byker takes a close look at the producers of research. Specifically, he analyzes the work of volunteers who collect data for the Annual

Status of Education Report (ASER) in India. The chapter includes snapshots of the experiences of these volunteers, and presents a perspective in which knowledge creation is an embodied process. The values and experiences of these volunteers come through the chapter. This contribution stands as an invitation to further explore the role of knowledge workers in CIE research.

This chapter makes space for the voices and experiences of volunteers whose names are not listed as authors and yet whose contribution is central to knowledge production. The chapter presents an opportunity to reflect about the existing hierarchies within our own knowledge factories and the need to humanize our work.

4 Conclusion

Each of the contributions in this part advances knowledge in our field in at least two dimensions. Firstly, the chapters present important advances in different aspects of education in the South Asian subcontinent. Secondly, they provide examples of how CIE research can be done differently, in different settings and with different participants. This difference/alterity presents an invitation to recapture something that has been at the core of our field: abandoning our familiar settings. Let us, then, depart from our comfort zones. As this collection of chapters shows, the results are very promising. Maybe what I am advocating for is making space for difference/alterity. The disappearance of singularities as globalization takes hold (Baudrillard, 2001) has long been a concern among scholars in our field. It seems to me that singularities are still abundant across the Global South, and particularly in South Asia as the following chapters demonstrate. Therefore, we need to be careful about re-colonizing these settings with our methods and assumptions. What this means for me personally is embracing the necessary evil of being fetishized-exotified as a Northern expert, as an American (yet Mexican) academic, if that grants me the opportunity to engage with researchers and research participants in their own terms.

References

Anzaldúa, G. (2009). *The Gloria Anzaldúa reader*. Durham, NC: Duke University Press.
Baudrillard, J. (2001). *Impossible exchange*. London: Verso.
Blanco Ramírez, G., & Haque, M. J. (2016). Addressing quality challenges in the private university sector in Bangladesh: from policy formulation to institutional implementation. *Quality in Higher Education, 22*(2), 139–151.

Guillemin, M., & Gillam, L. (2004). Ethics, reflexivity, and "ethically important moments" in research. *Qualitative Inquiry, 10*, 261–280.

Spivak, G. C. (1988). Can the subaltern speak? In R. Morris (Ed.), *Can the subaltern speak? Reflections on the history of an idea* (pp. 21–78). New York, NY: Columbia University Press.

Spivak, G. C. (1993). *Outside in the teaching machine.* New York, NY: Routledge.

CHAPTER 7

Amplifying Indian Women's Voices and Experiences to Advance Their Access to Technical and Vocational Education Training

Radhika Iyengar and Matthew A. Witenstein

Abstract

This chapter questions gender biases that are entrenched in culture and traditions. It shows the gap between education policy and practice. The practice here is women's participation in non-formal and Vocational Education and Training programs. The chapter urges policy makers to bring reforms in the vocational track of the education system, by incorporating the reality that many women face. Through Participatory Action Research method, Iyengar and Witenstein try to illicit the cultural, religious, intergenerational practices that tend to thwart basic human rights for women in India.

Keywords

TVET – India – voices – gender – non-formal – skilling

1 Introduction

India is moving towards a "knowledge economy" (Misra, 2016) and therefore it is very important to supply its workforce with 21st century skills. However, the reality is that about 130 million young people in developing countries (15–24 years) are classified as 'illiterate' with women comprising 59% of that number (UNESCO, 2008). To ensure youth attain literacy and gain employable skills, India has instituted policies on Technical and Vocational Education Training, otherwise known as TVET. Diwakar & Ahamad (2015) highlighted that the 11th five-year plan (2007–2012) declared the importance of skill development for women in the workforce. The plan stated that both in the formal and informal workforce, skilled personnel comprise only two-percent of the total workforce.

Venn (1964) explained the meaning of the term 'vocational' (which derives from the industrial revolution) as a sort of 'calling', and Diwakar (2015) interpreted Venn's (1964) notion of vocational as education that enables one to get a "stable job". There are several challenges with vocational education and training in India including, quality and financing of the system; an ineffective funding model; strong mismatch between demand and supply side factors; and lack of match between labor market needs and vocational courses (Agrawal, 2013). Moreover, Agrawal (2013) suggested that major reforms in the abovementioned domains are required before expanding the TVET system and making it more responsive to labor market needs. Along with the strong skills mismatch with the requirements of the labor market, policies are largely neglectful toward creating conducive environments for women to access them. This chapter argues that to provide life-long learning opportunities and to meet United Nations' (UN) Sustainable Development Goal four (SDG4 – which aims to provide lifelong learning opportunities that are equitable and of high quality), women need much more than labor market skills alone. Additionally, we argue they need opportunities to reflect and be critical about gender stereotypes, to question patriarchal practices, and become active, participating Indian citizens.

1.1   *Mahashakti Seva Kendra*

In order to learn more about the intersections of TVET/labor-upskilling in concert with women's reflections regarding gender (as mentioned above), we worked with women at a non-formal skilling program in Bhopal, India via participatory action research (PAR) approaches. The participating women toil in skill development, making handicrafts at Mahashakti Seva Kendra (MSK). Mahashakti has been in existence for more than 25 years and originated to provide skill development opportunities to the 1984 Bhopal Gas disaster victims. The organization is funded by the National Textile Ministry and under the *Jan Shikshan Sansthan* scheme of the Government, which is a skill development program run by the Government of India. Though MSK's work is not part of TVET, it provides the target clientele for TVET. Since the women at MSK did not access TVET concurrently, it served as an appropriate group to ask about the potential of accessing TVET institutions locally.

1.2   *Purpose and Research Questions*

On the supply side, this study explored options women have outside of school education and on the demand side, it explored factors, stated through the voices of Indian women, about why they are unable to take advantage of educational opportunities. The purposes of this study were to: a) develop a space to unpack, explore and discuss gender stereotypes that could impede successfully attaining SDG4; and b) begin understanding how the values systems at home and at the workshed[1] (as expressed by women's voices in India) position them to meaningfully access TVET to be lifelong learners. The research questions guiding this study were: What are the challenges in meeting SDG4 for young women in India? What are some of the practices and mental models that become hurdles and opportunities to availing women at the workshed of life-long learning opportunities? How might a participatory approach foster meaningful foundational knowledge about the ways in which Indian women desire to access and engage with TVET programs to support theirs and the country's aspirations regarding skilled training?

2 TVET Historical and Policy Review

This section explores the historical context of TVET in India, a program providing a viable option toward enhancing citizens' skills for the labor market. To begin with, policies and approaches to technical and vocational education and training underwent major re-adjustment in the 1970s and 1980s. Diwakar & Ahamad (2015) noted that the importance of skill development, especially for the female workforce, was highlighted in India's 11th five-year plan (2007–2012). The plan stated that both in the formal and informal workforce, skilled personnel comprise only two-percent of the total workforce population, with the objective of increasing it to 50% by 2022. The plan also mentioned that women form a significant portion of the total workforce but are mainly concentrated in the informal sector, where they face the challenges of low earning wages, have low productivity, and work in poor working conditions without any social protection.

Vocational training includes institution-based training programs which fall outside the formal schooling cycle, mainly provided through public Industrial Training Institutes (ITIs), private Industrial Training Centers (ITCs) and polytechnics (both public and private) (Agrawal, 2013). The Department of Women and Child Development runs Support to Training and Employment Programs (STEP), a Norwegian Agency for Development Cooperation (NORAD)-assisted program on employment cum income-generation. The scheme offers women condensed courses of education and vocational training programs.

Under the Prime Minister's National Skill Development Mission launched in 2008, the focus was on skill development aligned to the demands of the employers with "aspirations of Indian citizens for sustainable livelihoods". The government's other initiative, the Beti Bachao, Beti Padhao initiative was announced in June 2014 with the Ministry of Women and Child Development as the nodal agency in collaboration with the Ministry of Health and Family Welfare and the Ministry of Human Resource Development. The Ministry of Women and Child Development, through STEP, offered support for skill upgradation of women in informal employment in eight selected sectors – initially agriculture, small animal husbandry, dairying, fisheries, handlooms, handicrafts, khadi and village industries, and sericulture. Later, two more sectors, social forestry and waste land development, were added (Sudarshan, 2012).

In 2011, the Aajeevika Skill Development Programme (ASDP) was initiated by the Ministry of Rural Development (MoRD) as a sub-mission under National Rural Livelihood Mission (NRLM). The ASDP provided young people from poor communities an opportunity to gain work skills, thence joining the skilled workforce in growing economy sectors. The program aimed to provide employment-linked, market-oriented training to those 18–35 from families below the poverty line across India. The aim of this program was to equip this group with necessary skills and ensure their employment (five million youth) in the formal sector by 2017 (Das, 2015). The top 12 trades preferred by trainees, training providers and the national program management unit for imparting training under ASDP were: retail sales, hospitality, security guard, IT-enabled services, welding, Process Outsourcing and Call Centre, industrial sewing machine operator, electrical, ITES-data entry, tally and bookkeeping, and tailoring and cutting (Das, 2015).

The vocational training programs at the higher secondary stage are aimed to develop competencies, knowledge, skills and attitudes required by respective occupations (Goel, 2011). The programs provided for administrative structure, area vocational surveys, preparation of curriculum, text books, work book curriculum guides, training manuals, teacher training programs, strengthening technical support system for research and development, training and evaluation etc. (Sudarshan 2012). Vocational education is provided in 9,619 schools with 21,000 sections, reaching approximately 1 million students. The Government proposed to expand vocational education to 20,000 schools and student intake capacity of 2.5 million by 2011–2012 (Sudarshan 2012). About 150 job-oriented courses at +2 level[2] are provided in the areas of Agriculture, Business and Commerce, Engineering and Technology, Home Science, Health and Paramedical, Social Sciences, Humanities, etc. (Sudarshan, 2012).

Students could opt for Polytechnic Education which is a diploma program after class 10. It is typically a three-year program, and students become employable by age 19. These institutions also provide one to two years of specialization. Typical courses are Electronics, Computer Science, Medical Lab technology, Hospital Engineering, Architectural Assistantship etc. In 2011–2012, the student intake numbers were: degree (653,000) and diploma-level

(354,000) technical institutions. Nevertheless, some challenges remained, including, non-availability of new courses that meet the market demand; inadequate infrastructure; obsolete equipment; lack of technically-trained staff; antiquated curriculum, etc. (Sudarshan 2012).

National Skill Development Corporation (NSDC) identified the main TVET challenges as the following: the large number of women who need to be trained since currently most are in the informal, non-skilled sector; inadequacies in the quality and relevance of TVET; inadequate infrastructure, acute shortage of trained women workers; poor quality of training; lack of mechanisms to judge and certify quality; inequity in access to TVET for women; low level of education of potential women trainees that limits training of women in the formal sector; lack of recognition of prior learning of potential women trainees; and relatively high opportunity cost of learning involved for training women (Diwakar & Ahamad, 2015).

According to Biavaschi et al. (2012), the main problems for the labor market prospects of the Indian youth are, low levels of general education; weak foundations to build employable skills; low enrollment in vocational training and poor match with demands in industrial sector; and low quality of informal vocational training and apprenticeships. Agrawal (2013) added an ineffective funding model as a further challenge to youth employment. The authors suggested that major reforms in different areas are required before expanding the TVET system and making the system more responsive to the labor market's needs.

3   Conceptual Framework

People tend to create and re-create identities based on their context. This concept could be applied to the definition of how Mahashakti women are defining their identity. Easthope (1998) and Witenstein and Saito (2015) explained Bhabha's concept of "third space" which is how people create their own identities given their contexts. The authors explained that "fixed identifications" become flexible and open up to "cultural hybridity" which does not conform with any existing hierarchy. Even though traditions, culture and patriarchal legacy still consume their reality, this notion of cultural hybridity has seeped into their conscience. The dichotomy in which they are caught includes the one at their homes where they play a very traditional life as mother, wife and daughter-in-law and following many traditional practices which are not all socially just, yet are gendered norms that "need" to be followed. This contrasts with the workshed where they are re-discovering themselves through their creativity, confidence and collaboration among peers. At the workshed, they discuss political opinions, taboos as well as current affairs. Not all views at their work place are in conformity with their lived experience at home. However, they are trying to negotiate their identity in the "third space" which is a hybrid of what people expect them to be with what they may aspire to be. This transition and in-between space cannot be explained solely by the colonial past or patriarchy; nevertheless, they are a part. Therefore, in this globalized world, they are crafting identities of their own on the border of multiple identities and expectations.

Witenstein and Saito (2015) engaged research by Moje et al. (2004) where the third space is defined as an amalgamation of the first space, which is the family and community, with the second, institution-based space. Moje et al. (2004) suggested that the third space is an appropriate lens to use when individuals are trying to define their identity through their schooling experiences, which can be quite different from their home culture. In the case of Mahashakti, the third space is at the intersections of their home and workspace. The women struggle internally while they listen to more bold ideas by co-workers and colleagues. Each day at the workshed their limits of what is the acceptable norm may get pushed slightly further. While doing so, they may be in constant tension, yet find the courage to enter into the in-between, third space, which is pushing and pulling them and constantly evolving.

In many ways Witenstein and Saito's (2015) discussion about third spaces is similar to Appadurai's notion of "scapes" (Appadurai, 1996). Oonk (2000) discussed Appadurai's idea of "scapes", beginning his discussion by stating "we all live in a global village" (p.157) and that the "world is shrinking" (p. 157) so there is nothing new to say about globalization. However, when traditions and cultural practices clash with contextual reasoning and "modern thought", identity crises may ensue. Appadurai (1996) explained "scape" with these amalgamation-appropriate prefixes *ethno-, media-, techno-, finance-, and ideo-*. Central to Appadurai's (1996) theory is that the new global cultural economy "cannot longer be understood in terms of existing center-periphery models" (Oonk, 2000, p. 158). Oonk (2000) suggested that the idea of "scapes" is that there is constant motion and that it is not linked to one landscape. These "scapes" are the building blocks of contemporary imagined worlds. Therefore, the lives Mahashakti women lead at home and at the work institution are not separate. They are flowing into one another since culture and one's own identity are not defined by any one physical space. Oonk's (2000) observation about Appadurai's work is that "scapes" can potentially help explain the cultural changes within the sphere of globalization. Therefore, the idea that modernity is fluid and not linked to a physical space could also explain how globalization is affecting the identity of women in India.

4 Methodology

4.1 Research Design

This is a qualitative Participatory Action Research (PAR) study. Since this study was deeply rooted in social contexts, and because both action and research were needed to support the study's purposes, PAR was deemed the best method (Setty & Witenstein, 2017). PAR derived from work in marginalized and oppressed communities. In fact, historically, PAR has meaningful roots in Indian contexts, leading all the way back to Kaluram and the Bhoomi Sena when scheduled tribes engaged in community meetings to safeguard their rights due to land loss (Setty & Witenstein, 2017).

As Hall (1981) and Fals-Borda and Rahman (1991) noted, PAR offers the opportunity to concurrently engage in learning, research, and action in a space where all participants (including the researchers) contribute, acquire knowledge, and experience transformation. Since discussing gender biases can induce heightened sensitivity in this context, activity-based approaches were used to conduct the data collection sessions. Hence, the study provided a "brave space" (Araro & Clemens, 2013) where women learned to challenge their ingrained biases and assumptions, particularly those serving to repress them.

Qualitative data was collected via group activities that were video-recorded. The raw footage formed the data for the study and was analyzed to develop themes. Discussions included biases in education, jobs, daily responsibilities, household decision-making and other dimensions. The activities were adapted from the Life-Skills and Leadership Manuals of Peace Corps and customized to the Indian setting with local examples. Rather than overtly discussing gender roles, assessing mental models using values and realizing how communities impact individual practices was deemed a productive exercise.

4.2 Sample

There were forty participants between ages 15–56. Many MSK women suffer from health-related ailments due to the gas tragedy. Others come from families with health ailments. The majority have not reached beyond grade eight. A few others lack basic literacy skills and have never attended school. The participants come from the same community where the workshed is located.

4.3 Procedures

The procedures to get the participants engaged in a conversation required activities that the participants could relate to. These activities included realizing the characteristics about self-confidence. In this activity the participants were asked to create at least 3 affirmations about themselves and "put-down" what people may think about them and "turn-them" around into affirmations. Since women in similar settings have often witnessed disappointment, distrust, and lack of confidence, this activity was meant to turn these negative insights into positives by starting to believe in themselves. The second activity was concerned with the formation of cultural values, and their importance to each participant individually. The participants were to identify a value they treasure and explain its importance in their lives. This activity was helpful in identifying and understanding participants mental models. This self-awareness could help translate into positive behaviors. Activity three carried the same theme of self-awareness about their mental models but was done through showing photos. The photos included non-traditional selections such as two pilots who were women, two girls playing hockey, a woman taxi driver and others.

Activities and ice-breakers were carefully planned to make the exercise inclusive. The main take-away for all the stakeholders was to collectively discuss and question practices and attitudes starting from the workplace, leading to homes. The intention of this discussion-driven, activity-based MSK workshop was not to challenge nor judge existing belief systems and opinions of MSK women. Rather, it allowed women to recognize that they are often powerfully affected and impacted by their surroundings. Essentially, the goal was to build awareness of where beliefs, values and perspectives come from. In doing so, it can give value to considering varying perspectives, recognizing that our own perspectives, decisions and lives are affected by external factors – and that we are all capable of change and growth. It is to present the reality that people have the capacity to change and empower themselves, build self-confidence and choose positive values, regardless of where they live.

Discussions on gender roles and stereotypes are sensitive on many accounts. This topic is laden with layers of customs, traditions and culture. Therefore, it became extremely important to carefully broach this topic. The participants were to share their opinions and be receptive to hearing others. The participants shared their lived experiences in the activities planned. As a part of the methodology, the researcher showed pictures and initiated discussions without presenting opinions. Since the researcher's[3] background was very different from the participants, this could have caused the participants to give socially desirable answers. Therefore, the role of the researcher was to ask the "why" questions and challenge the assumptions rather than to present opinions. Activities were sequenced from having generic discussions to more targeted discussions on gender roles. The NGO's program coordinator was a part of the exercise to ensure that the participants viewed the activity as part of their daily work. However, these activities were voluntary and were organized based in consent by the MSK participants.[4]

5 Findings

Detailed analysis of video footage revealed five noteworthy strands. Each one is shared in the subsections below.

5.1 Household Work Defined by Gender

First, roles are divided based on gender. Housework and looking after children were primarily women's jobs. The participants complained all their housework goes unnoticed by their husbands. If the women performed work typically not done by them (e.g., repairing the roof to prevent rain coming in, work possibly requiring more manual labor), it was considered heroic. They took pride in performing these tasks; however, it increased their ever-expanding chore list. The women agreed the workshed provided some respite where they get to enjoy work, be creative and engage their colleagues to talk about their lives.

A few younger participants spoke about sharing the household work with their husbands. They remarked that workload must be shared. However, one respondent mentioned this is subject to the income the person earns. Unpaid "home" work did not equate to working for an income even though the workload with household chores was higher. There was a unanimous voice that girls have dreams and can have careers too. Therefore, parents need to support them to achieve their career goals. They also agreed that marriage should not be the only goal for girls. While older participants said women can work outside the home, she would still be the primary person to look after the household and family once married. Some others justified that men are the primary breadwinners and need to derive income to run the family. Whereas some believed women can also perform unconventional roles like taxi driver, others believed men and women are different and cannot perform all tasks expected of the other.

5.2 Younger Women Question More

The younger women questioned the unfairness in terms of gender roles and are negotiating their practices at home with their husbands and extended families. Whereas the older women, despite understanding the gender dynamics, were more likely to continue with the status-quo. For instance, in the photo exercise, a younger woman mentioned it is acceptable for girls to wear pants or shorts (as shown in the photo). She believed times were changing; hence, everyone must accept the reality. However, an older woman found it highly inappropriate for a girl to wear shorts or pants because it is not societally acceptable. She believed girls would be judged in the neighborhood for wearing unconventional clothes. Some others suggested it depends on one's immediate community if it is acceptable to wear certain types of clothes and the community decides what is appropriate. One person noted if the girl is wearing short dresses or pants, she is inviting trouble from neighborhood men.

5.3 *Patriarchy Still Exists*

Patriarchy still exists and men in the family make the decisions. There is a sense of dependency that women have on their male counterparts. One participant noted if men are around, she feels more confident. She further noted this is true because men are "stronger" (not sure if she only meant physically stronger). Another participant mentioned that women are unsafe alone and need male support to do their work. However, another participant mentioned women can be strong on their own if they learn "judo karate" and can protect themselves. One of the participants explained that to be able to join the workshed, her father had to visit, and only after his approval was the place considered decent enough for her to join. Another participant noted that she needed to get approvals from her husband to come in the morning hours. Whereas, men in the family do not have to get approvals from adult household females. But, the norm was accepted by the women and none of the participants seemed to mind it.

5.4 *Visible Intergenerational Differences*

Intergenerational differences in terms of men in the family taking more progressive decisions holds true. The patriarchal grip is easing for the younger generation. For instance, an older woman shared that her mother was not allowed to continue her education post-marriage. Her father-in-law's opinion was that since the daughters of the house were not allowed to study after the primary grades, the same rule was applicable to the 15 year-old daughter-in-law. The interviews illuminated nuanced contrasts of decisions made previously versus those in contemporary times. In the younger generation, in one case the father was against the 18-year old daughter working; however, when he escorted her to the workshed and found it was only for ladies, he allowed her to work. Clearly, issues of safety are more of a concern among the fathers. This could be related to increased rape case numbers in the State at present as compared to the recent past. The women who did not finish schooling said that financial issues forced them to drop out. However, it was not clear whether their brothers were allowed to study. Therefore, for the older generations, the restrictions imposed by their fathers were often more work-prohibitive than those imposed by younger participants' fathers.

5.5 *Community Forms Norms*

Family and community environment were still huge challenges to achieving gender equity in education and skill development. The TVETs are still not easily accessible due to their fees, timings and majority male student composition. One participant added that sometimes the girl does not get everyone's permission to work outside, but later, if she persists, the parents will realize their daughter is capable of working outside. She continued that in this case, the daughter needs to take the first step and then everyone else may agree after she shows they can trust her.

6 Discussion and Conclusion

The results of the study need to be considered in the following light. Even with participatory approaches, it was difficult to be certain if responses were socially desirable or true reflections. Some participants presented an overly optimistic and positive picture. However, there were others who expressed, with examples, their long lists of daily chores and responsibilities that they experienced as limiting their opportunities to pursue further education and employment. There may have been a generational bias where the young women were not as expressive as older participants since there is a strong sense of respect toward the elderly. Younger participants may also not like to oppose older participants' views. In these cases, the NGO's program coordinator played a more active role in asking everyone's opinion if she perceived a certain group of women did not participate equally. Since she has a personal connection with everyone, she helped to explain the activity as well as prompt some of them to speak up. All participants came from the same neighborhood. This may cause a bias in two ways, firstly, participants did not reveal their thoughts since they did not want to deviate from their common understandings or assumptions. Since opinions can be viewed as a societal reflection, they may have wanted to show congeniality. Unsurprisingly, it may also be the case that they did not want their thoughts to somehow reach their parents or in-laws. The researcher attempted to circumvent this issue by noting that no one will be pointed out or ridiculed based on their reflections and everyone's individual opinions need to be respected. The researcher conveyed there are no right or wrong answers.

With the changing times and with more exposure due to globalization, media and other influences, the women seemed to struggle and challenge themselves and each other in the third-space. They listened to each other patiently, opening their worlds to dimensions they did not previously explore. The ongoing internal reflections and struggles created and re-created their third-spaces and they continued to define and redefine the way they understand and employ their roles in their home and work spaces. Their workspace, homes and their community are the "scapes" that define their identity in its changing narrative.

Discussions centered on what is acceptable in "our culture" and per "our traditions". The photos shown as part of the activity required participants to reflect on the culture and traditions. The activities were created in a way to question the status-quo or current thinking, without explicitly asking to do so. One of the activities was aimed at realizing that values are formed by the social environment. Therefore, questioning those values and reasoning may help them break away from gender stereotypes.

The mismatch between demand and supply regarding the TVET system cannot be resolved with only policy changes in the TVET system. The demand-driven factors, the psycho-social aspect biased against women, need to change as well. Women are not allowed to work outside, enhance their skills due to safety concerns, or the males in the families do not give permission. From the data it was clear that women themselves tend to feel safe(r) with men and rely on their decisions. In many cases if the women needed to go outside, they might be the first ones in their families to venture out, which requires courage. Male dominance and female dependency may not provide a conducive environment to access and avail of skill development opportunities through TVETS.

Given the strong gender issues that have emerged from this study, TVETs that are only for women, at flexible hours, yet linked to local jobs, may stand a chance. Counselling the males in families is highly important for female participation and ensuring the utility of the courses in their daily lives. Therefore, revamping the existing courses which include retail sales, hospitality, security guard, welding, etc., to match skills with local employers' needs might be a good strategy resulting in more job opportunities for women. The courses could include computer basics, typing, cyber security, wellbeing, gender studies, public health, etc.

The UN is aiming for the world to meet SDG4 by 2030. Life-long learning opportunities are being expanded to ensure access, inclusiveness and quality skills. This study adds value to the current education discourse by highlighting the voices of Indian women. Many of these women have never been asked to provide any opinion on their lives. They inherit and are born into a patriarchal society/structures heavily laden with norms and expectations concerning the virtues that "good Indian women" must have. This study included insight from the rich discussions about gender, patriarchal rules and education that will help to understand the challenges in meeting the SDG for Education.

Unpacking the contextualized components of gender equality by constant dialogue and discussions is much needed. SDG5 on Gender Equality and Women's Empowerment needs to be integrated into SDG4 to make any impact on girls' education. Education should not be limited to schools but should be made inclusive to provide meaningful education to all ages. Research is needed to understand the ways in which TVETs can be made more inclusive to the needs of women through participatory approaches. This research also needs to inform TVET policy from the bottom up to not only be more inclusive of women generally, but to involve them by including their input into how programs reflect women's interests. Future research strands should focus on the gender empowerment work done by various NGOs and taking some of the key lessons to integrate them within all avenues of learning for all ages.

Notes

1. Workshed is the working place for the NGO. The workshed is given to the NGO by the Government of India. It is a temporary arrangement with no concrete roof. It is where the women attend all the workshops and get trained on various handicraft making skills.
2. In the Indian education system grade 10 plus 2 years is the completion of the schooling till grade 12.
3. Radhika Iyengar conducted the data collection with the MSK participants. She belongs to the same hometown as the participants. She also shares many cultural and religious aspects of the participants. However, there are many differences in terms of education levels and economic background that needed to be kept in mind for this study.
4. The research study protocol is registered under IRB at Columbia University. Formal consent were obtained by the participants to collect any data.

References

Agrawal, T. (2013). Vocational Education and Training programs (VET): An Asian perspective. *Asia-Pacific Journal of Cooperative Education, 14*(1), 15–26.

Appadurai, A. (1996). *Modernity at large: Cultural dimensions of globalization.* Minneapolis, MN: University of Minnesota Press.

Arao, B., & Clemens, K. (2013). From safe spaces to brave spaces: A new way to frame dialogue around diversity and social justice. In L. Landreman (Ed.), *The art of effective facilitation: Reflections from social justice educators* (pp. 135–150). Sterling, VA: Stylus.

Biavaschi, C., Eichhorst, W., Giulietti, C., Kendzia, M. J., Muravyev, A., Pieters, J., Rodríguez-Planas, N., Schmidl, R., & Zimmermann, K. F. (2012, October). *Youth unemployment and vocational training* (IZA DP No. 6890). IZA. Discussion Paper Series.

Das, A. K. (2015). Skill development for SMEs: Mapping of key initiatives in India. *Institutions and Economies, 7*(2), 120–143.

Diwakar, N., & Ahamad, T. (2015). Skills development of women through vocational training. *International Message of Applied Research, 1*, 79–83.

Easthope, A. (1998). Bhabha, hybridity and identity. *Textual Practice, 12*(2), 341–348.

Fals-Borda, O., & Rahman, M. A. (Eds.). (1991). *Action and knowledge: Breaking the monopoly with participatory action research.* New York, NY: Apex Press.

Goel, V. (2011). *Technical and Vocational Education and Training (TVET) system in India for sustainable development.* Ministry of Human Resources, Department of Higher Education, Government of India.

Hall, B. L. (1981). Participatory research, popular knowledge and power: A personal reflection. *Convergence, 14*(3), 6.

Hartl, M. (2009). *Technical and Vocational Education and Training (TVET) and skills development for poverty reduction – Do rural women benefit?* Policy Paper for Pathways out of Poverty, Gender and Rural Employment.

Misra, S. K. (2015). Skill development: A way to leverage the demographic dividend in India. *GSTF Journal on Business Review, 4*(2), 28–36.

Nitika Diwakar, N., & Ahamad, T. (2015). Skill development of women through vocational training. *International Journal of Applied Research, 1*(6), 79–83.

Oonk, G. (2000). Review of modernity at large: Cultural dimensions of globalization. *Journal of World History, 11*(1), 157–159.

Setty, R., & Witenstein, M. A. (2017). Defining PAR to refine PAR: Theorizing participatory action research in South Asian educational contexts. In *Participatory action research and educational development* (pp. 13–47). Cham: Palgrave Macmillan.

Sudarshan, R. (2012) *National skills development strategies and the urban informal sector: The case of India.* (Background paper prepared for the Education for All Global Monitoring Report 2012. Youth and skills: Putting education to work). UNESCO.

Witenstein, M. A., & Saito, L. E. (2015). Exploring the educational implications of the third space framework for transnational Asian Adoptees. *Berkeley Review of Education, 5*(2), 117–136.

CHAPTER 8

Contemporary Traditions of State-Madrassa Relationships in India

Huma Kidwai

Abstract

The author forces the readers to question the beliefs around formal schooling. She narrates the resistance of the madrassa teachers and leaders against the State at the same time highlighting the inherent biases of the State against the madrassas. Many interesting findings are narrated in the chapter, including the power of the official language used in Government documents. These documents are written in a language that is alien to the madrassa leaders and thus create a direct disconnect between the Government, its mandates, and the madrassa. Kidwai also does an interesting hierarchical analysis of the Government officials at various ranks and confirms that the ranks do make a difference in the belief structures. Beliefs around the madrassa are also influenced by the religious affiliation of the Government officials. The Muslims seems much more flexible and empathetic about the madrassa than the Hindu officials. The chapter presents insightful findings on how culture and religion gets entangled with politics and bureaucracy to shape education policy.

Keywords

madrassa – India – non-formal education – religious schools

1   Introduction

In this chapter I present the case of State-madrassa relationship in Uttar Pradesh (UP) province of India under the context of presently employed policies for "madrassa modernization". I attempted to map out the various social, political, and economic factors that influence policy while it is conceived, implemented, and re-imagined, from central to local levels.[1] These levels are: national capital (located in Delhi), state capital (Lucknow city) and four districts (across the state of UP). The study was carried out using a mixed-methods vertical case study research design (Vavrus & Bartlett, 2006).

The role of bureaucracy forms an important aspect of present State-madrassa relationship in India, particularly in understanding policy processes – policy conception and implementation by bureaucrats, and reception and local interpretation by madrassas. Most modern research and thinking about bureaucracy has been strongly influenced by Max Weber's model of bureaucratic organizational structure from the 1900s. According to Weber (1968), there is a general, historical tendency for administration to move towards the bureaucratic type. The bureaucratic structure is characterized with full-time, salaried, career administrators appointed on merit, technically qualified, arranged in a hierarchy and subject to rules and discipline (Weber, 1964). Bureaucracy possesses several advantages including efficiency, certainty, reliability and the "stringency of its discipline" (Weber, 1964, p. 337). Organizational size and communication technologies further promote bureaucratic structure development, Weber argues. For this research, I utilized literature on post-Weberian conceptualization and critique of bureaucracy to understand the incongruity between the colonial design for administrative structure and postcolonial realities of the Indian context. I employed this critique of bureaucracy structures to understand transformations and resistances of madrassas as they are exposed to the cooptation strategies of the State.

2   Conflicting Beliefs and Ideologies

This study's findings demonstrate the significance of the concept of bureaucratic norms: unwritten and unofficial, yet widely observed rules within the State that shape the behavior of public officials and structure their interaction patterns with actors outside the State, in this case the institution of madrassas. According to Akshay Mangla (2014), in his analysis of bureaucracy and public provision of education in India, "bureaucratic norms guide public officials on how to enact their roles and responsibilities in carrying out the tasks associated with policy implementation" (p. 3). In addition to the formal design of institutions, informal practices that shape social expectations and behavior of bureaucrats are pertinent. These informal practices are greatly influenced by the respective backgrounds and belief systems of government officials, and the culture of bureaucracy that encapsulates all policy processes in India.

A majority of interviews with administrators of education and minority welfare programs in the State revealed a severe gap in the perceived relevance of madrassas and their idea of educational development. While these officers are implementing policies intended for the development and support of madrassas, there is an obvious lack of conviction in these programs. At the same time, there is little faith in the institutional capacity of the State to bring about long-term change. The following is an excerpt from a transcript of an in-depth interview with a low-ranking bureaucrat in Bareilly district. It reveals his perception of the role he plays as a government representative, and his views on the relevance of madrassas in the world today. His viewpoint is far from exceptional among this category of study respondents.

Interviewer (I): In what ways is madrassa education important [relevant] in your district?

Respondent (R): In today's time, madrassa education is not important. Can a child going to a madrassa compete with children of "normal" schools and become a doctor or an engineer? He can just become a mulla [priest].

I: Then why do you think the government wants to support madrassas?

R: It's all politics to make the minority community happy. To be honest, there is no point in continuing support to madrassas. Nowadays, there are government schools in every neighborhood. If the government is providing free education to all then why should parents send their children to madrassas? I will never send my child there, will you?

I: Have you ever conveyed your views to the state level officials?

R: It is not our job to do that, madam. Who will listen to our views? The minority community will think I am discriminating against them because I am Hindu. The higher ups will transfer me or suspend me. I am here to just quietly carry out the instructions I am given. After 20 years of service with the government I have learnt that nothing much changes in the system, no matter how much you try. (District level Hindu bureaucrat, Interview, Bareilly)

There are several layers to understanding bureaucratic norms governing this response. First, there is a problem of *relatability*. Lack of belief in the relevance of madrassa education is a common sentiment among most Hindu government officials interviewed for the study. They regard this educational choice as a deviation from what they consider "normal" schooling. Implementers of the program find it difficult to relate with madrassas as credible systems of education.[2] They consider the curricula outdated and irrelevant to the needs of what they consider modern society. This is reflective of the officials' backgrounds in terms of religious and educational ideology they identify or empathize with, the nature of education they received, and the nature of progress and development they believe is an outcome of "normal" education.

After conducting interviews with two officials in Barabanki, I realized the need to include certain background information about officials I had not initially considered necessary. It turned out that, without exception, all government officials working at the district level in the four study districts were educated in schools and colleges offering standardized curricula regulated by either state or National Boards. Not a single employee had graduated from a madrassa. This indicates the complete absence of representation in the administrative staff that deals with madrassa managers and staff daily. According to a madrassa teacher,

> ... they [government officials] do not know much about our curricula and teaching practices. How can they understand us when they cannot even read Urdu? Instead, they want us to understand them and learn the language they are comfortable in. (Teacher, private madrassa, Interview, Azamgarh)

Even those officials and policymakers who have the "best intentions" for the Muslim community's development, a national level Islamic scholar posits, may not completely understand the needs of madrassa education reform. He explained the best solution to the community's social and economic upliftment, according to these "education and policy experts", is to mainstream madrassas and convert them into schools with standardized curriculum they regard as "modern and secular". He further remarked,

> ... you see, these policymakers are products of Western education. It is difficult for them to understand that some people may have different value systems and that to some people it is not as important to become doctors and lawyers as it is to understand and follow their faith. They [policymakers] have a different paimaana (system of assessment) for measuring development and they are so confident about it. (Teacher, private madrassa, Interview, Azamgarh)

According to three scholars of Islamic Studies and Sociology of Education interviewed for this study, the *burden to reform* carried by most well-intended participants of educational policy-making is reminiscent of colonial rule and its early imperialistic justifications. Madrassa representatives, as evident in their perception of the government's motive to mainstream their education, take phrases like "modernization of madrassas" and "upliftment of the community" as metaphors for their "condescending" attitude toward "underdeveloped" community culture and traditions. On probing answers to *what has changed in your relationship with the Sarkar (State/government) after the end of the British rule*, one category of responses is "did we ever decolonize?" The country inherited its bureaucracy and systems of education from the British. The educational ideology of independent India, which denies integration of religion with science, has been "exactly the same" as it was during colonial rule. Policymakers and implementers are, hence, "no different from the Western colonizers with regards to their beliefs about the purpose of education" (Madrassa manager, private madrassa, Interview, Azamgarh).

However, there are respondents who see this conflict somewhat differently. A senior teacher from a renowned female Muslim girls' madrassa in Lucknow asserted this situation is not as much a "clash of cultures" as it is a "clash of conveniences". According to this respondent, government officials and policymakers are too quick coming to conclusions about what form of education is relevant and what is not. She argues,

> It is inconvenient to understand the other. It takes time and effort. Government officials do not have so much time. Even if they have time, they lack the will to extend themselves to understanding the complexity and purpose of the [madrassa education] system. (Senior teacher, girls' madrassa , Interview, Lucknow)

Hence, officials impose the norms of administration most opportune for themselves, often creating conflicts of "culture" and "conveniences". Language policy for government administration in UP, as illustrated in the following section, is one example of the political and cultural conflict between State norms and madrassas.

2.1   The Power of Official Language

Official notices and paperwork are all issued in Hindi language that, according to several madrassas as well as low-level government officials, is becoming more and more *sanskritized*[3] with time.

> We are not that well versed in Hindi language, particularly the difficult Hindi they [government offices] use in their official documents. We

recently hired a clerk who can read and write official Hindi but even he finds it difficult. The language is getting more difficult to understand day by day. It is nothing like the Hindi you and I speak. (Manager, partially funded madrassa, interview, Barabanki)

The increasing complexity of the official Hindi vocabulary has reportedly been a form of alienation that creates communication gaps between madrassas and state administration in UP. While Hindi is the most dominant and widely used state language, there seems to be a wide rift between written and spoken forms. This gap widens for Urdu speaking communities. This had not been the case historically, since the vernacular forms of Urdu and Hindi are similar. Despite official statements to not associate language with religion, it cannot be denied there are and always have been more Muslim than Hindu speakers of Urdu. Hence, Muslims and their institutions are at the greatest disadvantage with the increasing sanskritization of Hindi in official spaces. Some Muslim participants regard this *difficult to understand* Hindi as a form of cultural attack and imposition. The situation is reflective of how language policies in governance can help to create, sustain, or reduce political conflicts among various linguistic groups, and how State authorities can manipulate access to language rights for political and cultural governance (Vaugier-Chatterjee, 2005).

Consistent exclusion of Urdu from official spaces and school curricula has been considered a major cause for economic depression among Muslims post-independence (Husain, 1965; Sachar Committee Report, 2006). Participating scholars of Islamic studies and History of Islam in India argue that the domination of Hindi and exclusion of Urdu from schools and official spheres was a form of neocolonialism put into practice by the majoritarian policies of the government. Bureaucrats, respective of their regional or religious identity, have no choice but to follow instructions from higher-ups, thereby institutionalizing non-secular practices with seemingly secular intentions.

Regardless of the influence official language policies have had on alienating madrassas, the policy reflects the hierarchy of written and oral materials that reinforce bureaucrats' self-consciousness of their superiority. This domination of one linguistic tradition over another through a bureaucratic structure is reminiscent of British colonial policies of imposing English as the administrative language, which created social divisions and a favored class of Anglicized Indians (Evans, 2002). Official documentation produced by the State is invested with "magical powers", as Gupta (2012) notes in his observations of "subaltern and illiterate people" and their care and regard for the official papers (pp. 20–21). These papers are difficult to procure and even more difficult to comprehend. Those who master the art of bureaucratic language have immense power over others. Of course, this power is not always put to good use:

> We wanted to apply for the maanyata (certification of recognition). We went to the office and asked for an application form. The clerk asked us to come later. After several visits we finally got the form ... we could not make any sense of it. We went back to the clerk to help us fill the form. He asked us to pay Rs.1000. We brought it down to Rs.600. Finally, we submitted the form and received an acknowledgment receipt. We have not even started working with the government and we have already killed our conscience and participated in corruption. (Madrassa manager, Interview)

2.2 *Identity of the Bureaucrat*

Religion inevitably emerges as a seemingly significant predicting factor in understanding behavioral aspects of State bureaucracy. In all four district level offices of the Minority Welfare Department and the Education Department, the staff had very few Muslims and Muslim employees were predominantly lower in rank. On segregating officials' responses on the subject of "contemporary relevance of madrassa education" by their religious identity,[4] a pattern of findings was discovered. Muslim officials, though of the view that madrassa education at large has limited relevance given the demands of a modern job market, pointed towards the *religious and cultural needs of the community* as the primary reason parents choose madrassas over public schools. In comparison, for most Hindu officials, the primary factor determining this choice was *poverty* followed by *illiteracy* or *poor educational background*. Table 8.1 outlines some of the most commonly occurring responses to the question: *Why do you think parents choose madrassas over free public schools in their neighborhood?* Responses are listed in the decreasing order of their frequency, segregated by the apparent religious identity of the government officials.

While most Hindu officials consider selection of madrassas over government schools a result of financial helplessness and educational "backwardness", Muslim officials regard it as a conscious decision to fulfill and preserve the community's religious and cultural needs. Another striking feature is that in comparison with Muslim officials, fewer Hindu officials felt parents reject government schools due to their poor "quality standards". Several Muslim officials pointed out the absence of clean toilets and separate toilet areas for female students kept many Muslim parents from sending children, particularly daughters to schools. Additionally, more Muslim officials listed greater teacher and student absenteeism in government schools as impacting parents'

TABLE 8.1　Government officials' perceived reasons for parents choosing madrassas (based on 29 semi-structured interviews conducted first-hand by the author)

Muslim officials	Hindu officials
Religious needs of the community: read Quran, learn about Islam and Islamic history, "become a good Muslim"	*Poverty*: Many madrassas offer free housing and boarding
Similar cultural practices: dress codes, language, Islamic calendar and holiday schedule, etc. At girls' madrassa, they wear hijab and are taught by female staff. Not so in public schools.	*Illiteracy/lack of education*: "they are illiterate, and do not know what is best for their child"
Poverty: Many madrassas offer free housing and boarding	*Religious needs of the community*: To preserve sectarian beliefs (e.g., Sunni, Shia, Barelvi, Deobandi, etc.)
Lack of trust in the quality of government schools: teacher absenteeism, poor student attendance, poor hygiene and cleanliness standards, no separate toilet for girls, "children are not disciplined", poor learning outcomes, no guarantee of employment or higher education after schooling	*Similar cultural practices*: dress codes, language, Islamic calendar and holiday schedule, etc.
Hindu and anti-Muslim nature of curricular content in government schools	Quality concerns at government schools:teacher absenteeism"government school children misbehave"poor learning outcomes

perceptions about institutional quality, pointing out madrassas seemingly have stricter practices to ensure behavioral discipline and compliance among students and teachers. Similarly, while no Muslim official pointed out illiteracy or lack of education as a factor for selecting madrassas over public schools, no Hindu official mentioned the possibility of perceived anti-Muslim, Hindu-dominant curricular content in government schools.

Perhaps a more structured set of surveys with quantitative analysis might reveal a more scientific comparison. However, based on qualitative analysis of my data from semi-structured interviews, it seems Muslim officials have more detailed and possibly more empathetic understanding of parent choices. Most Muslim officials regard parents as active selectors of faith-based education they regard as essential. They consider parental choice a conscious selection of madrassas over "poor quality" and "culturally inappropriate" government schools. Moreover, many, if not all, Hindu officials consider these parents passive and uneducated decision-makers. They do not stress the inadequacies of public schools as much as their Muslim colleagues do as a factor determining parent choices. [5]

With the absence of Urdu in public schools in UP and a complete shift to Hindi as a medium of instruction, employability of teachers from madrassas in government schools and employment of madrassas graduates in the public sector has dropped significantly. This shift in language policy, as discussed earlier, has had serious ramifications in segregating work and cultural spaces for communities from different linguistic backgrounds. It is thus not surprising to hear bureaucrats refer to Muslims and their culture as "those people", "their traditions", "their education", "their children", etc. Several Hindu officials feel Muslims are to blame for their economic and social "backwardness", as they place more than necessary emphasis on preserving and transmitting, from one generation to the next, the tradition of what is regarded as Islamic learning and a sense of Muslim identity. This sentiment is common among upper and upper-middle class Muslims and their writings about education and development of Muslims.

Educated and elite Muslims of the country, according to a scholar of Islamic history in India, feel pressure to assimilate with the dominant culture at the cost of their traditions and identity. Some of their Hindu friends and colleagues begin to see them as enlightened and educated Muslims, whereas those who pray five times a day, fast during Ramadan, and abstain from alcohol as traditional and "fundamentalist". "Fundamentalist", which as a word has adopted connotations of being "extremist" and "separatist", is regarded in popular media and writings as a highly detrimental trait to the national interest of the country.

Many scholars and madrassa teachers have expressed concern over policies and political media promoting sentiments of nationalism by imposing an order of identity. This pattern is commonly found in textbooks and media campaigns such as "we are first and foremost Indians". This sentiment forms the basis for an ideological critique of madrassa education systems and their purpose. Bureaucrats and policymakers, who privilege a certain notion of Indian national identity as being of overriding importance, find any kind of "excessive" stress placed on separate communitarian identity based on religion to be greatly troubling. This could be madrassas in the case of Muslims, and schools run by right-wing Hindutva groups in the case of Hindus. Bureaucrats and policymakers consider these institutions to be a significant hurdle in the process of developing a common national identity. According to Sikand (2005), while there is merit in this argument, there are perils of the same kind in the whole ideology of nationalism, which at the global level is as divisive and problematic as communalism based on religion. The following quote illustrates the nationalistic concerns of government officials against faith-based schooling in general.

> We need to promote feelings of unity and nationalism. We need to teach our children about the greatness of our country and how they should be proud to be Indians. Religious schools like madrassas and [Hindu] paathshaalas divide the society. A divided society cannot make India the most powerful country of this world. This is why our neighboring countries [primarily Pakistan and China] take us so lightly. (Hindu official, Interview)

Indian bureaucracy and policymaking, as argued by scholars participating in this study, is socially conditioned to support State decisions and actions to prove nationalistic vigor. Madrassa teachers expressed great concern over the Hindu nationalism rise in India and increasing displays of majoritarian culture as national culture on television, cinema, fashion, books, etc. In one focus group discussion, a group of madrassa managers and teachers discussed how the government's ideology of nationalism clashes with the sentiment of *ummah* (a collective community of Islamic people). The following two quotes illustrate this conflict:

> We believe we are first Muslims and then Indians. We feel we have ties with Muslims all over the world. The world is talking about global citizenship. But the Indian government wants us to prove that we are first Indians and then Muslims. (Madrassa management committee member, Focus group, Azamgarh)

> We feel the plight of Palestinians. They are fellow Muslims. 'Til some 20 years ago the Indian government too supported Palestine. But now they are friends with Israel. Government's international policy is a mirror of its in-country relations. If our government truly cared for our sentiments,

they would not have joined hands with Israel. (Madrassa management committee member, Focus group, Azamgarh)

When probing responses about national integration concepts and how schools and madrassas can play an important role in encouraging or discouraging it, focus group participants' discussions were highly critical of government school textbooks, particularly history textbooks, and for teaching skewed versions of history favoring a Hindu narrative about contributions to Indian society.

3 The Dichotomy of Politics and Government Administration

Interviewer (I): I have been visiting different kinds of madrassas; some work with the hukumat and some do not. In what different ways do madrassas relate with the hukumat of India?
Respondent (R): Madam, what exactly do you mean by hukumat?
I: The usual meaning ... I mean the government of India.
R: I know that, but you see Madam, we live in "jamhuriat" (democracy). The government means two things – the administration, and the political party. Which of the two are you talking about? (Manager of an applicant madrassa, Interview, Barabanki)

Three months into my data collection I began noticing how multifaceted the idea of a government was. Even though participants may have used the term indiscriminately with reference to any organization or a body of individuals receiving salary from the national treasury, a closer analysis of data and follow-up interviews with select participants revealed variations in the implied meaning. While some aspects of government (like the ruling political party) change too often, others(bureaucrats) stay longer than desired. Political instability is an important concern related to successful administration of policies.

The volatility of this structure leads to a practice of politics that is rife with corruption and exploits of public sentiments based on caste and religion. Amidst this political chaos, most public welfare programs that lack an instantly visible outcome often get sidelined. Alternatively, programs are designed to have an immediate impact on public opinion. Public welfare programs are often announced close to election dates to garner positive public opinion, so these programs are often rushed and half-baked with little planning for long-term sustainability or regular monitoring and evaluation. Often, these projects dry up mid-way and are either suspended temporarily or reworked into seemingly different packages.

The administrative section of the government is regulated by an ongoing system of official staff appointments. Once tenured, there are limited and highly complex procedures for terminating employment. The stability of a government job is one of its biggest attractions, as well as one of the most exploited and misused features. Higher-level bureaucrats tend to have shorter postings in one location than lower level bureaucrats. This, according to many government officials interviewed for the study, prevents team building.

At the district level, what brings madrassas together with the government is not mere policy programs but individuals working in the two organizations. According to a state level bureaucrat in UP, district and block level variation in the uptake of government policies for madrassas and the minority community is evidence of the role local staff can play in mobilizing community awareness and support for a program. He said, "Forming relations of trust with representatives of the community is key to the success of the madrassa modernization program" (Senior bureaucrat, Interview, Lucknow). However, this trust is easily compromised by frequent transfers of officials. In the words of a senior teacher at a private madrassa, "... one should not trust these government officials to fulfill their promises. They themselves have no idea when they will be transferred" (Teacher, private madrassa, Interview, Saharanpur).

The distinction between policymakers and policy executors becomes relevant here. Policies for madrassas are pushed by political parties and designed by high level bureaucrats – both of whom have a short lifespan in any one location of policy implementation. It is the low level bureaucrats, with their limited authority and role in policy planning and decision making, who mostly stay on in one location until the end of their tenure. Even though politicians are under high pressure to deliver results and be accountable to their respective constituencies, their goals and emphasis lack sustainability and long-term planning. Given their short terms and the desperate need to show results, especially close to the end of the political term, there is a tendency to place populist projects ahead of more fundamental economic and social overhauls.

High level bureaucrats, by contrast, are unaccountable to the wider public and are appointed with a high degree of job security. Despite their job security they have very little time to control the implementation and outcomes of policies at hand. Besides, their relatively higher status in the organizational hierarchy makes it extremely difficult for common citizens to approach these high level bureaucrats with their issues. At the end of the day, it is low level bureaucrats, including sub-district level officers, clerks, and peons, who interact directly and more consistently with the recipients of any policy.

4 Politicization of Bureaucracy

Several participants, both madrassa representatives and government officials, expressed concern over the corrupting and politicizing influence of political party individuals and organizations on administrative affairs. Corruption related to distribution and uptake of government programs for madrassas is a common occurrence. References to politicization of bureaucracy were higher among government officials' responses at the district level than at the state or national levels. However, this may not be an accurate reflection of how the state and district level administrations compare with each other. Participants at the district level invariably seemed more candid in their conversations about the government and its policies than higher-level officials at the state and central levels. Nevertheless, their narrative of the State-madrassa relationship reveals several ways politics guide administrative interactions with madrassas in the four districts.

Bureaucracy is ideally supposed to be operated by officially appointed and politically neutral individuals. However, that is rarely the case in practice. Here I would like to make a distinction between two kinds of politicizations of bureaucracy I observed in the responses of government officials. The first kind of politicization has to do with the infiltration of political party representatives within the organizational structure of various departments. With every electoral change in the political party causing significant reshuffling of officials across departments and locations, party *loyalists* are rewarded with more prestigious and influential positions. The previously mentioned process of transfers is a particularly effective strategy that allows political control over administrative matters.

Loyal officials support politicians in a number of ways. A few examples that came up during interviews with madrassa representatives and a few low level government officials included: (a) a case where the local district collector altered the plans for road reconstruction to benefit specific villages recommended by a powerful local political leader, (b) a case where a district level high-ranking officer issued recognition certificates to unqualified madrassas belonging to the relatives of a state level minister, (c) a case where the local administrative head delayed the release of funds for the construction of new classrooms in targeted schools in order to time the sanction with election dates so this development could be used, as in the campaign, for re-election of the existing minister, and (d) numerous cases of illegal bidding of tenders for public works to construction companies that sponsor local politicians.

The purpose of citing these examples is to make a point that there is incongruity between the rhetoric of political neutrality of State bureaucracy and the reality of its politicized nature and role. This assertion has been made repeatedly in literature claiming that politicization of bureaucracy in developing countries, particularly those in South Asia and Africa, is a feature of colonialism. The continuities in structural, normative, and behavioral formations across the colonial-postcolonial divide are undoubtedly more than just rhetorical flourish.

The second kind of politicization, a form most gravely feared by madrassa representatives, is to do with the possibilities of the influence that a political party's religious ideology may have on the behavioral conditioning of bureaucrats. Religion is a big factor in any state or national level elections in India. Religious divisions affect both party organization and voting habits in the country. There is a history of cases where political parties have exploited religious tensions to grab power.

Communalization of bureaucracy under the influence of, or irrespective of, the political influence has been a widely recognized reality in the country. A number of civil society organizations as well as the central government of India acknowledge the harsh reality that civil and police functionaries of the government have not played a fair role while performing their duty to protect vulnerable communities during outbursts of ethnic violence. It has been argued widely in media that these functionaries have either been negligent during inter-community conflict situations and, in worse cases, have actively shown bias.

On a more regular basis, madrassa teachers and managers believe that Muslim officials are treated unfairly by their Hindu superiors, Muslim students are discriminated against by their Hindu teachers at school, and police are a constant threat to the safety of Muslims. "These days it is so easy for police to charge Muslims with false cases of terrorist or extremist activities and ruin their lives", pointed out a madrassa teacher during a focus group discussion.

Given the deep entrenchment of politics with religion, it seems, the liberal theory of political anonymity has no reality in the Indian context. As discussed earlier, India, like most other postcolonial contexts, has inherited its administrative framework from the West. However, patterns of local culture remain significantly different. It is clear that ethnic and religious heterogeneity has important implications for public policies – both official and unofficial. Hence, there is often disparity between formal bureaucratic rules and codes of conduct representing the Western/colonial model and the actual behavior of officials based on societal norms and in-group expectations (Haque, 1997). This is yet another example of how vestiges of colonial influence on the existing bureaucracy of the State continue to maintain gaps between official policies and unofficial practices. Similar observations have been made by senior madrassa teachers in Bareilly.

> ... democracy will always mean the rule of the majority community over the fate of minorities. Democracy cannot be fair to the minorities in India. ... this majoritarian rule was what the supporters of [India-Pakistan] partition had the foresight to see. But then, power is such an addiction that even they [Pakistan] created a majority and minority within the same religion. They are in no better state, maybe even worse.
> (Private madrassa teacher, Interview, Bareilly)

Fear of this behavioral adaptation of bureaucracy to ideological expectations of the ruling political party is both an experience and a deep-rooted perception of Muslims living in the state. It obviously translates into hostility of madrassas and the Muslim community towards the government and its efforts for collaboration. On the other side, simultaneously, a relationship of indifference has been created, which often leads to further misinterpretation and misunderstanding of social problems. As a result of this increasing misunderstanding between the two groups, unrealistic or impractical public policies and programs are created based on imitative models of modernization (Rondinelli, 1982).

5 Subalterns in the Bureaucracy

The Urdu word for government is *hukumat,* which roughly translates as "the rule of *Hakim*" or the "rule of the one who can give orders and judgements". A more officially used word for government in Hindi speaking states is *Sarkar,* which translates as "master" or "overlord". Even though the local administration of states and provinces has changed dramatically in political nature from the monarchy of the Mughals, through feudalization under the British, to the rule of bureaucracy in democratic India, the linguistic semantics for "administrator" as denoting an authority figure have remained unchanged. The nature of these words, *hukumat* and *Sarkar*, that are commonly and officially used for the government of India, is characterized by features such as elitism, despotism, hierarchical rigidity, secrecy and distrust, and urban bias. Continuation of this linguistic culture is not far from the reality of day-to-day bureaucratic practices in UP. It is evident that, despite postcolonial rehabilitation and reforms in the administrative superstructure, the most dominant features of State bureaucracy are its inherited colonial and pre-colonial feudal legacy.

An obvious use (and misuse) of authority, no matter at what rung of the organizational ladder, is what defines the work environment of a government office in India. As discussed earlier, lower level bureaucrats, though most knowledgeable about local needs and developments, exercise little control over policy making processes. Although there are formal reporting structures in place to allow for communication of village and block level developments to district and state level officials, the rigidity of hierarchy and frequent changes in administrative leadership at the district level obstructs an effective upward flow of information. Fear of authority often keeps low ranking officials from honest reporting. This group of order-takers is what Akhil Gupta (2012) refers to as the subalterns in bureaucracy. This group is perhaps the most powerful in terms of information and inter-community relations with the recipients of any government policy, but least commanding of the project distribution and decisions. Furthermore, it was observed personally, as well as pointed out by study participants, that a low ranking official's dignity is compromised on a daily basis. The unofficial code of conduct empowers higher ranking officers to often mistreat and humiliate lower ranking officials. According to a group of madrassa representatives who participated in a focus group, unless one works as a high-ranking officer there is no self-respect working within – or even with – the government. A participant shared the following example to illustrate why he cannot encourage madrassas to be involved with the government:

> I am friends with the office clerk in the Minority Welfare Department. He is a very good man. Everybody in my village respects and consults him on important decisions. But it breaks my heart when I see him taking orders, standing and bent, from his officer who is half his age. This is why I don't want my fellow teachers to work with the government. In no time we will end up becoming their [high officials'] slaves. (Madrassa manager, private madrassa, Azamgarh)

The fear of losing autonomy, which is the most commonly given line of argument presented by madrassas resisting government interference, has a more practical than ideological implication. This fear comes from their observations of how low ranking staff members are treated in offices and how little respect government teachers have within the system. It is crucial for low-level staff to present themselves as servile, with no apparent pride or defiance, when engaging with higher authorities. This form of self-subjugation is reminiscent of the subaltern attitudes discussed widely in literature based on postcolonial theory (Spivak, 1988, Morris, 2010).

Another common narrative, in discussions with high-ranking officials and policymakers at government offices, revolves around the inefficiency and incompetency of low ranking officials. Failures of policies to yield expected results commonly generate, in the words of Gupta (2012), "a colonial complaint of the incompetence of the natives and a class bias toward subalterns in the bureaucracy" (p. 25). Within this narrative, following is one of the typical concerns of education officers and policymakers:

> Nothing is wrong with the curriculum. Look at our National Curriculum Framework. It is such a high class document. We even give training to teachers to teach that curriculum. But what do we do if we do not have intelligent and hardworking teachers anymore? Nothing will change in the education system 'til the teachers start doing their job. (Education officer, Interview, Lucknow)

Ascribing inefficiency to teachers for the poor quality of education in the country is one of the ways we can see subalterns in the bureaucracy being blamed for the failures of development programs.

6 Resisting Bureaucratization of Madrassas

Bureaucracy is a culture of its own. According to Ralph Hummel (2008), in his most famous work on the subject of public administration, *The Bureaucratic Experience,* he contends that bureaucracy is "dehumanizing". Its structures "force bureaucrats into behaviors that alter the psyche's processes by which knowledge is acquired and by which emotions are felt" (p. 96). This dehumanizing effect of bureaucracy is argued by most of the madrassa representatives and Islamic scholars interviewed for the study to be one of the most important factor perceived to shape the Muslim community's resistance against State-madrassa collaboration for the education of Muslims in India.

A number of respondents posit that it is crucial to maintain distance between madrassas and the government in order to protect the *zameer* (the conscience) of the institution. According to Hummel (2008), bureaucrats are asked to become people without judgment about right and wrong, as that is to be left to the discretion of the supervisor or to the organization as a whole. The following excerpt illustrates one of many ways the study participants believe that bureaucratization negatively impacts the decision-making ability and capacity of an individual:

> There is nothing like a good or a bad government employee. They just need to follow orders. Orders from the authority are their rules. Now [if I am a government employee] I will have to follow my superior's orders in order to be a good employee. Those police officers who were firing shots at innocent Muslims in Gujarat were just following orders .... I might have

to do the same if I was in their position. This is why ... I cannot join an organization that is likely to be ruled by the likes of Narendra Modi. (Participant identity not be disclosed)

Teachers, along with the janitorial staff, are, in practice, the lowest ranking members of the bureaucratic hierarchy. Office clerks and peons, though lower in social standing, tend to have certain degree of procedural control over teachers. Nevertheless, while I point out the abjectness of the low ranking workforce, including public school and State-funded madrassa teachers, I want to underline the importance of not looking at these individuals as passive or docile victims. Collective agency and socio-political networking are another common feature of Indian bureaucracy that allows low ranking officials to stand up for their rights, and often to turn the tables. While an individual teacher may not have much authority in the organizational structure of bureaucracy, as a collective they are a power to be reckoned with. This reactionary form of revolutionary attitude among teachers becomes a major concern for madrassa managers and their traditional values regarding intra-staff relationships. For example:

It is the character of government teachers to leave classrooms to go for strikes and protests. At madrassas our first priority should be teaching. There have been times when, due to lack of funds, we could not pay our teachers for months or paid them a quarter of their salaries – but we are one community and understand each other's problems and look for solutions together. But in a government school environment, teachers have no care for the problems of the government, the government is corrupt and stealing away from teachers ... is that a kind of environment we want to educate our children in? We do not want our teachers to become government employees because we do not want to engage in union-baazi [roughly translates as union-ism]. (Teacher, private madrassa, Interview, Saharanpur)

Little is written about the effects of the special constitutional privilege granted to teachers in India, namely their guaranteed representation in the Upper House of the state legislatures. It is argued that the existence of separate teacher constituencies for electing members to the Upper House encourages teachers' participation in politics. Teacher unions are used by teacher leaders to launch and buttress their own political careers, in particular to become members of the Legislative Council or the Legislative Assembly. Several Chief Ministers and cabinet ministers have been teachers.

The political influence of teachers in UP comes not only from their representation in the state legislature but also from the strength of their unions. The pressure of the teachers' lobby often leads the government to accept teacher demands to avoid public resentment caused by prolonged disruption of the schooling system. Those who resist government policies for aiding madrassa teachers use the example of the political context in which government teachers find themselves, as a basis for their opposition. They fear that the inclusion of madrassa teachers in these unions and campaigns will politicize teacher interests and distract them from their teaching activities.

7 A Bureaucrat's Dilemma: Are Madrassas That Irrelevant?

While conducting interviews with a wide range of bureaucrats in UP, I noticed a common contradiction in their evaluation of madrassas. While most did not strongly feel that they can trust madrassas to lead children towards a "modern" and "developed" life, they admire madrassa teachers and managers for their conviction and work ethic. According to a few respondents, if a formal evaluation of literacy skills is conducted to compare madrassa students of primary grades with the corresponding age group in public schools, controlling for language differences, madrassa students will undoubtedly perform better. However, they feel this literacy advantage of madrassa students over public school students will take them only so far, since Urdu and Arabic are rarely used in public domains. Nevertheless, there is high regard for the institutional structure and practices of madrassas, particularly the bigger and private institutions.

I: How do you compare students from madrassas with those from public and private schools?
R: There is a lot of difference, especially if you are looking at average madrassas.
I: Then let's talk about an average madrassa, an average public school and an average private school.
R: You see, madrassa students are really good with languages and [have] very well-mannered students. They can read and write Urdu quite well and also learn some Arabic and Persian. But that is not education. That is just literacy. Now if you look at a private school child. My children go to private schools. You went to private schools, right? From pre-primary they learn ABCD, 1234, etc. They are getting both education and literacy. On the other hand, our poor public school children get only a little bit of both.
I: How do you differentiate literacy (saaksharta) and education (shiksha)?
R: Literacy is about learning to read and write. Education is about what to read and write. Both are important. (State level bureaucrat, Interview, Lucknow)

Nevertheless, most government participants feel that public schools are still more relevant in two ways. One is that they expose students to a variety of "modern" subjects that help students mainstream themselves with future employment opportunities and higher education. The other is the greater legitimacy of graduation certificates that students receive from public schools compared to their madrassa counterparts. Even though the government has begun to issue graduation certificates for graduates of madrassas affiliated with the government, they do not reflect the same acceptance rate with college admissions or prospective employers.

8 Conclusion and Ideas for Future Research

In this chapter, I explored the micro realities of State-madrassa relationships in UP by looking at the everyday interactions between State bureaucrats and madrassa representatives. I employed a postcolonial critique to deconstruct policy processes at the district level.

Development policies and bureaucracy in India, I argue, continue to be structurally and ideologically governed by the imperialistic culture of the British colonizers and present day seemingly imperialist pressures from the dominant West. The educational purpose, organizational structure, and networking policies of madrassas in the region, I observe, have not yet overcome their historic response to colonization. Present activism against State intervention is rooted in Muslim fear of external control and forced cultural assimilation. From the madrassa point of view in India, the government's vision of "modernization", "upliftment of the backward communities" and "educational reform" is a policy for political control and identity conversion. The fact that Muslims constitute a minority in a Hindu majority country with a history of interreligious tensions further reinforces these role perceptions. Hence, colonial patterns continue in terms of perceptions and expectations that entrench relationships of mistrust and aloofness, and an inevitable gap exists between official policy, unofficial interpretations, and resulting practices of madrassa education reform in India.

The colonial conditioning of bureaucracy, as described both theoretically and empirically in the discussion of findings, presents us with a question of whether the behavior of bureaucrats is determined by their particular history and environment or whether they feel and act out of personal choice and agency. It is a philosophical dilemma and I personally find it difficult to discern between the *lack of choice* and the *lack of will*. The same applies to madrassa representatives and their decisions on working or not working with the government, which has been explored further in the study (Kidwai, 2014).

Research suggestions in this section are not limited to contexts where Muslims constitute a minority, nor are they regionally confined to the Indian subcontinent. Given the history of Islamic scholarship in India and increasing movements of ideas and scholars between India and other parts of the world, a better understanding of the madrassa system of education in India is likely to have valid implications for similar investigations in other parts of the world. I have outlined the following ideas for future research keeping in view the need and relevance of comparative studies about madrassas in contemporary times.

First and foremost is the need to analyze and translate into English some of the prominent curricular documents and prescribed textbooks at madrassas. Without this work, it is difficult to make evidence-based arguments about the efficacy of madrassa education, or the lack thereof. Second, there is an urgent need to develop an effective educational management and information system that includes data on madrassas in India. Availability of data on certain key education and household level indicators can open doors for a whole new area of research to support policy goals and claims. Third, it would be important to devise a study that compares student performance in madrassas with student performance in government and other secular private schools. This research should entail a detailed format of performance indicators that fairly represent student outcomes in common areas of learning. Fourth, an area of important work would be to study the transformative agency of madrassa education in the contemporary context of rural India. Fifth, an ethnographic study could follow the life of students after they graduate from different levels of madrassa and explore their experiences as they move to cities and interact with society and culture they were previously not a part of. Some of the interesting locations for such a study would be universities and colleges that admit madrassa graduates and private and government offices that hire them.

Finally, this research reasserts the need to acknowledge the postcolonial realities of development policies and practices. A postcolonial critique of the State's policy for the institutions and culture of the marginalized, I argue on the basis of this study, is likely to reveal the hegemonic tendencies of the majoritarian perspectives on change and progress. To understand the present mode of reactions and resistances of the marginalized towards the dominant view of education is crucial to make sense of local needs and perspectives on development.

Notes

1 This chapter is drawn from my dissertation: "Postcolonial challenges to madrassa education reform in India: Bureaucracy, politics, resistance, and cooptation"

submitted at Teachers College-Columbia University in May 2015. It is based on an extensive qualitative study of state-madrassa relationship for educational reform in India. Data about policy processes were collected at the national level in New Delhi, at the provincial level in Uttar Pradesh, and at the district level in Barabanki, Azamgarh, Bareilly, and Saharanpur. Twenty-eight madrassas were sampled to capture a classification of madrassas based on their relationship with government funding as well as their sectarian ideology for religion and education. In the process, a total of 148 interviews, 25 focus groups, and 32 sessions of non-participatory observations were conducted. Data was gathered over a course of 1.5 years ending in April 2014.

2   However, it will be discussed later in detail how most of these respondents, who do not believe in the relevance of madrassas as a system of education, openly praise certain institutional practices of madrassas, particularly in comparison with public schools.

3   Sanskritization is a theory of social change in India proposed by M. N. Srinivas (1952), a celebrated sociologist in India. With regards to language, sanskritization refers to the adoption of spoken Hindi words from Sanskrit, the ancient language of upper caste Hindus.

4   Participants were not asked about their religion. Their identity was deciphered by their names.

5   This interaction and variation in perceptions between a community insider (Muslim officials) and a community outsider (Hindu officials) could be further elaborated through the lens of postcolonial theory that describes the subaltern as a person rendered without agency, as someone incapable of complex thinking (Young, 2003).

References

De, A., Khera, R., Samson, M., & Kumar, S. (2011). *PROBE revisited: A report on elementary education in India.* New Delhi: Oxford University Press.

Evans, S. (2002). Macaulay's minute revisited: Colonial language policy in nineteenth-century India. *Journal of Multilingual and Multicultural Development, 23*(4), 260–281.

Gupta, A. (2012). *Red tape: Bureaucracy, structural violence, and poverty in India.* Durham, NC/London: Duke University Press.

Haque, M. S. (1997). Incongruity between bureaucracy and society in developing nations: A critique. *Peace and Change, 22*(4), 432–462.

Hummel, R. P. (2008). *The bureaucratic experience. The post-modern challenge* (5th ed.). New York, NY: M. E. Sharpe Inc.

Husain, A. (1965). *The destiny of Indian Muslims.* Bombay: Asia Publishing House.

Iyer, L., & Mani, A. (2012). The transfer raj. *Ideas for India.* Retrieved from http://www.ideasforindia.in/article.aspx?article_id=25

Kidwai, H. (2014). *Postcolonial challenges to madrassa education reform in India: Bureaucracy, politics, resistance, and cooptation* (Doctoral dissertation). Teachers College, Columbia University, New York, NY.

Mangla, A. (2014). *Bureaucratic norms and state capacity: Implementing primary education in India's Himalayan region* (Harvard Business School Working Paper, No. 14-099). Retrieved from http://www.hbs.edu/faculty/Publication%20Files/14-099_31b21487-2a82-4200-83ec-6e5efa89388c.pdf

Morris, R. C. (2010). *Can the subaltern speak? Reflections on the history of an idea.* New York, NY: Columbia University Press.

Rondinelli, D. A. (1982). The dilemma of development administration: Complexity and uncertainty in control-oriented bureaucracies. *World Politics, 35*, 43–72.

Sachar Committee Report. (2006). *Prime Minister's high level committee on social, economic and educational status of the Muslim community in India.* Retrieved from http://minorityaffairs.gov.in/newsite/sachar/sachar.asp

Sikand, Y. (2005). *Bastions of the believers: Madrasas and Islamic education in India.* New Delhi: Penguin Books.

Spivak, G. C. (1988). Can the subaltern speak? In C. Nelson & L. Grossberg (Eds.), *Marxism and the interpretation of culture* (pp. 271–313). Urbana, IL: University of Illinois.

Vaugier-Chatterjee, A. (2005). Plural society and schooling: Urdu medium schools in Delhi. In R. Chopra & P. Jeffery (Eds.), *Educational regimes in contemporary India* (pp. 99–118). New Delhi: Sage.

Vavrus, F., & Bartlett, L. (2006). Comparatively knowing: Making a case for the vertical case study. *Current Issues in Comparative Education, 8*(2), 95–103.

Weber, M. (1964). *The theory of social and economic organization.* New York, NY: The Free Press.

Weber, M. (1968). *Economy and society: An outline of interpretive sociology.* New York, NY: Bedminster Press.

CHAPTER 9

'I Walk Each Village': Transforming Knowledge through Citizen-Led Assessments

Erik Jon Byker

Abstract

The chapter attempts to address two research questions pertinent to this book. How can the CIE field destabilize and transform knowledge hierarchies through research and practice? What are research practices that promote and enact a socially just and transformative ethos anchored by an ethics of engagement between the researcher(s) and the researched? The chapter takes us to Punjab, India, with motivated volunteers who use data to energize common citizens. It helps us to understand the motivation of these foot-soldiers, the volunteers, who walk village after village to build awareness on learning levels of the students. The author interviews and follows the volunteers to be a part of the action in the villages.

Keywords

volunteers – village – India – ASER – NGO

1 Introduction

It was 10 in the morning. Two young men led a small company of volunteers into a *pind* or village outside of Hoshiarpur, Punjab, India. The group began their journey on a paved road, which they shared with bullock carts piled high with long, white radishes ready for market. Soon, though, they turned on to a dirt trail, which meandered around a field of carrots and past a *gobar* (dry cow dung) storage area. The volunteers, who followed behind the two young men, were being trained to collect field-based research data about the schooling and basic learning levels of India's children. Most volunteers carried backpacks that hold their notebooks, pens, pencils, and their water bottles. Their first stop was to meet the *sarpanch* or village elder and explain the purpose of their visit. One of the young men leading the group knocked on the door of the elder's home. A young girl answered the door and invited the entire group to enter a small courtyard where an elderly lady sat. The young men introduced themselves and shared the purpose of the visit, which was to collect data for Annual Status of Education Report (ASER) in India. They explained how the data collection included a visit to the village's government-run primary school as well as door-to-door interviews with some of the parents and children in the pind. The young men asked for the matriarch's permission to collect these data. The matriarch agreed and invited everyone to drink a cup of *chai* tea before starting their field work.

This vignette captures how ASER's citizen-led assessment process commences at the ground level. Since 2005, many *lakh* (hundred thousand) of India's young adults – mostly college undergraduates – have volunteered to collect ASER data (Banerjee & Mutum, 2014). Similar to a door-to-door census, the Indian young people who volunteer for ASER walk from village to village to collect data on Indian children's ability to read and complete basic math figures (Bhattacharjea & Byker, 2017; Byker, 2014a, 2017; Byker & Banerjee, 2016). The ASER volunteers contribute to a program known as the "citizen-led basic learning assessments" (ASER, 2014a, p. 2). ASER's citizen-led assessment initiative was designed by Pratham – one of the largest non-governmental organizations (NGOs) in South Asia. Pratham's mission is to improve the learning levels of India's children. Pratham links assessment with improvement. They created the initial assessment tool for conducting household surveys. The tool was known as the Pratham Assessment Survey, but was renamed the Annual Status of Education Report or ASER for short (Banerjee & Mutum, 2014). The survey is now supervised and implemented by the ASER Centre, an autonomous organization in New Delhi. The ASER Centre's mission is to assess and measure children's basic learning levels in South Asia. The ASER Centre conducts the "the largest household survey of children in India by citizens' groups, which is carried out by more than 25,000 volunteers and covering over 700,000 children in 15,000 villages" (Vagh, 2009, p. 2).

The chapter has two purposes connected to the larger inquiries which this book examines related to the field of Comparative and International Education (CIE). The first inquiry is: How can the CIE field destabilize and transform knowledge hierarchies through research and practice? The second is: What are research practices that promote and enact a socially just and transformative ethos anchored by an ethics of engagement between the researcher(s) and the researched? The chapter's first purpose, then, is to investigate a case study of how ASER volunteers are engaged in participatory research in order to transform knowledge hierarchies. The second purpose is to argue that the participatory research engagement of the ASER volunteers reflects a transformative ethos anchored in social justice and the conceptions of what it means to be a citizen.

I have organized the rest of this chapter into five sections. First, I provide background information about the process of ASER data collection. Second, I examine how the ASER data collection is informed by a conceptual framework of evidence-based action (Byker, 2016). Third, I explain the case research design, which shapes the study's methodology. Fourth, I report on the findings from a case study of ASER volunteers. Last, I discuss how the case study reflects the implementation of participatory forms of research for enacting social justice. I then connect this discussion with the notion of being a citizen assessor.

2 ASER Background

The ASER data collection starts with the recruitment of volunteers to collect the survey data. Across India's rural districts, volunteers are recruited from local colleges and universities, NGOs, and District Institutions of Education and Training (DIET). A DIET is a school that prepares teacher candidates to teach in India's government-run public schools. After recruitment, the ASER volunteers are trained. The training includes a written test about the ASER philosophy and methodology. It also includes a field component, which was described in the opening vignette. The training finishes with a graduation where the ASER volunteers pledge that they have decided as a citizen of India to volunteer for the Annual Status of Education Report.

They also acknowledge in the pledge that participation in the ASER process is a way to ensure quality education for the children of India. They finish the pledge with a commitment to record accurate information in their survey notebook and pledge to do so with complete honesty as they have been entrusted with this volunteer role in order to help build a better India. The pledge is the verbal start to how ASER volunteers translate a type of participatory action research (PAR) into a large-scale data assessment (Byker & Banerjee, 2016; French & Kingdom, 2010; Hickey & Mohan, 2004). The ASER data collection connects everyday citizens with their localities and regions. The ASER data collection has a tremendous scope in terms of the assessment scale as almost one million children in India are assessed. The duration and efficiency of the assessment is as impressive as the scope. Almost all the assessment data gets collected within a four month time period; it is an expeditious process of data collection.

The quick turn-around of the ASER survey helps to ensure the "availability of results in the same school year, which is a tremendous feat for such a large survey because it enhances its potential as a tool to inform educational practice and policy" (Vagh, 2009, p. 1). Thus, the short time window for data collection means that the actual data collection process is highly participatory and comprehensive. Most of the ASER volunteers conduct their surveys over an intense two day time period in almost all of India's rural districts. The ASER volunteers are given surveying notebooks for data collection. The notebooks include three sections: (1) the village information sheet; (2) the school information sheet; and (3) the household survey sheet.

The first day of data collection is usually on a Saturday, which is still a school day in most regions of India. The second day of data collection is on Sunday, which is typically a day off. ASER divides the volunteers into pairs and assigns each pair to a village to conduct the survey. The first day's mission is to obtain the village leader's permission to conduct the survey, as well as to gather information about the village. The volunteers also visit the village's government-run schools. They record the school information in their surveying notebooks. The notebooks include places to record the student and the teacher attendance for that day, the computer technology hardware, and whether the school facilities are operable – like working toilets for both girls and boys. The ASER volunteers finish their first day of data collection by walking the perimeter of the village and drawing a map in their notebook of the village's geography. The mapping activity allows them to divide the village into four quadrants; which ensures that households are sampled from each quadrant of the village during the second day of data collection.

Volunteers start early on the second day to conduct the household surveys. Five houses are selected from each quadrant and are surveyed for a total of 20 households per village. They fill out the household survey sheets in their notebook to record the basic household information data. These data include: (1) the material the home is built from, (2) the parents' highest education levels, (3) the reading materials available in the house, and (4) if there is electricity in the home. The volunteers also record data about the ages and number of children living in the home. They finish the survey with an assessment of the children's basic reading, math, and English skills. The objective of this part of the assessment is to record what the children "can do comfortably in terms of their basic reading in the first language, mathematics, and communication in English" (ASER Centre, 2014b, p. 12).

3 Conceptual Frame

At the ground level where the ASER volunteers are in the field collecting data, they are engaged in executing one of ASER's core principles: evidence informs action. This core principle can be summed up in the phrase "evidence-based action" (Byker & Banerjee, 2016, p. 6). Evidence-based action is the notion that social action should be informed by data. Situated in a participatory framework, evidence-based action is grounded in the understanding that effective assessment requires accessibility of data that is both instructive and empowering. For example, ASER empowers everyday citizens to engage with their communities by participating in the assessment and measurement of the children in the community. Indeed, the ASER data collection "balances on the shoulders of citizen volunteers spread across the huge geographic area of India … to engage more people, communities, and parents" (Banerjee & Mutum, 2014, p. 24). Measuring the education levels of India provides a pathway toward improving the education of India's children. For the participants in this chapter's case study, for instance, the educational improvement of India's children was a highly motivating reason to volunteer for ASER.

Evidence-based action is part of ASER's vision. This vision equips citizens with data collection tools for assessment. The vision also emphasizes how data collection is a catalyst for taking action to change education levels for the betterment of a child's future. Evidence-based action comes with the promise of more citizen-oriented engagement within the community. It can be summed up in the following way: "When ordinary people are empowered with knowledge, they can bring about extraordinary change" (Banerjee & Mutum, 2014, p. 6). Evidence for action nurtures citizenship and is a conceptual frame built on agency and a data-driven lexicon for citizens to communicate and take action steps for improving their communities.

In this case study, I investigated the ASER volunteers and their notions of what it means to be a citizen and data collector. The study is guided by the following research questions:
– Who volunteers for the ASER assessment?
– Are there common dispositions that orient the ASER volunteers? If so, what are those dispositions?
– How, if in any way, are those dispositions connected to citizenship and a transformative ethos?

4   Method

I examined the aforementioned research question using a case study research design. Yin (2008) argued that case study research design allows for the mixing of qualitative and quantitative data in order to investigate the complex nuances of a context or phenomenon under study. The inclusion of a mixed methods approach to data collection is one reason I chose the case study design. Another reason is because case study research design afforded a way to "thickly describe" (Geertz, 1973) the ASER process of data through a first person account (Creswell, 2014). A final reason for the selection of the case study research design was connected with Yin's (2008) assertion that the strength of case study research design allows the researcher to examine how and why questions. A how question is useful for identifying the processes of the ASER data collection; whereas, the why question is important for understanding the reasoning and purposes behind the ASER data collection as it relates to citizenship development.

4.1 Data Collection

I utilized a mixed-methods approach to the case study's data collection. The quantitative data source was the ASER Volunteer Survey (see Appendix A), which is a questionnaire that includes demographic related questions and Likert Scale questions. Following Fink's (2003) advice about the validity of survey research, the questionnaire was adapted from two already established surveys. Most of the survey items were broad enough to be used in an Indian setting, but some questions had to be contextualized. For example, when participants were asked to identify where they grew up, I included the words village and pind with the rural setting choice selection. Specifically, I derived and combined the International Association for the Evaluation of Educational Achievement's (2010) International Civic and Citizenship Education Study (ICCS) and Flanagan, Syvertsen, and Stout's (2007) Civic Measurement Model to develop the ASER Volunteer Questionnaire Survey. All the case study participants (n = 458) completed the survey.

The case study's qualitative data source included field notes from participant observation. I was a participant observer in the ASER volunteer trainings and data collection in three locations: Haryana, Punjab, and New Delhi. The sites were selected because they were neighboring states in which the ASER data were being collected at the time of the study. The field note observations were recorded using time stamp notations and the note-taking was guided by an observation protocol. The protocol included collecting field observations and notes about the following aspects: (1) the ASER data collection process; (2) the data collection schedule; and (3) any discussion among the volunteers about the data collection.

4.2 Data Analysis

The quantitative analysis of the ASER Volunteer Questionnaire Survey is at a descriptive level. These descriptive statistics are intended to provide "snapshots" of the participants' perceptions and interpretations for involvement in the ASER data collection. The quantitative analysis reports on the participants' demographics. I analyzed the case study's qualitative data – the field notes from the participant observation – using Miles and Huberman's (1994) interpretive approach. Their approach includes the following three steps: (1) reduction of data; (2) displaying data; and (3) drawing conclusions from the data. Using this interpretive approach, I identified frequencies in the data to establish patterns. I then displayed the data in visual ways to analyze the findings. I drew conclusions and developed themes based on the study's research questions. I employed the constant comparative method as part of this interpretive process in order to compare and organize larger themes from the data.

5 Findings

I organize the case study's findings by revisiting and answering the research questions. The findings are based on the study's three research questions. First, I describe the demographics of who volunteers for the ASER assessment and how they identify as citizens (i.e., global citizens, citizens of India, etc.). Second, I examine the common dispositions and values that orient the ASER volunteers. Third, I analyze whether the common dispositions are connected to citizenship and a transformative ethos.

5.1 *Volunteers' Demographics*

The demographic data from the ASER Volunteer Survey revealed that most of the volunteers are young adults, with the ages ranging from 18 to 25 years of age. Almost 62 percent of the volunteers are male and 38 percent are female. More than one quarter (28%) of the volunteers participated two or more times in the ASER data collection. Almost 85 percent indicated that they would volunteer again to collect ASER data. One participant explained, "If my 10 days of volunteering can help my nation; then I will do it again".

Another participant wrote, "Yes, I would participate again as I found volunteering to be a genuine effort to help mankind standup again for the good. Moreover, if volunteering can help my country, then why not stand for such a good cause?" In response to the question about whether their parents were educators or school teachers, only 14 percent responded yes. Related to the location where the volunteers were born and raised, 39 percent indicated it was a rural area of India, 35 percent indicated it was in one of India's suburban area, and 26 percent indicated it was in an urban area of India (see Table 9.1).

TABLE 9.1   In what area did you grow up?

Area location	Percentage
Rural area	39
Suburban area	35
Urban area	26

All of the ASER volunteers are educated. On the survey question about their highest level of education, all of the participants indicated that they had received their Secondary School Leaving Certificate (SSLC). All of the survey participants also indicated that they were currently enrolled in either a college program or part of a District Institution of Education and Training. Among the surveyed ASER volunteers, almost 28 percent indicated they were studying in an engineering related field, 23 percent indicated they were studying in an information and communication technology (ICT) related field, and about 21 percent were studying business administration, and 16 percent were in the field of education and preparing to become teachers. The remaining 12 percent were comprised of several different areas of study (i.e., arts, psychology, etc.) Volunteers also responded to a question about citizenship and identity. The question inquired: As a citizen, how do you identify yourself most often? See Table 2.2 for a percentage breakdown of the volunteers' responses.

TABLE 9.2   Citizenship and identity

Citizenship identifier A citizen of my ...	Percentage
Town, village, or pind	15
State or region	10
Nation (e.g., India)	26
World (e.g., Global)	20
Other: please comment	2

As Table 2.2 shows, more than half – 53 percent – of the volunteers most often identified as a citizen of India. Next, 20 percent most often identified as a global citizen. Whereas, 15 percent of the volunteers identified as local citizen, and 10 percent most often identified as citizen of their state or region. Only 2 percent of the volunteers selected the other category. One participant who checked this category explained the selection, "In my opinion, all the above categories are based on our willingness and location. But as a human being, the entire world is our home and we are the citizen of it". Most of the other volunteers who selected the Other category in the survey commented that they were undecided.

5.2   Common Dispositions

The second research question inquired about whether there are common dispositions that orient the ASER volunteers. By dispositions, I mean the "attitudes and habits of mind" (Center for Civic Education, 1991, p. 11) that unify a person's logical thoughts with their moral beliefs (Dewey, 1933; Kumar, 2004). In reporting on the dispositions among the volunteers, I examined the most often repeated words related to their notions of citizenship and to why they chose to become an ASER volunteer. There were two words that stood out: responsibility and openness. In response to the open-ended survey question about why they decided to volunteer for ASER, most participants wrote in something related to the responsibility of social service. One volunteer, for instance, explained that, "I have been a NSS (National Service Scheme) volunteer for the last 3 years. I feel happy when I do the type of work to help my country. It is a responsibility which I do not ignore". The National Service Scheme (NSS) is an important part of this story and I have more to say about the NSS in the discussion section. The volunteers connected responsibility with the future and with understanding the education levels of children in the rural areas of India. They also expressed a strong belief about how responsibility is tethered to education. For example, in their response to the statement: Being concerned about education and schooling is an important responsibility of all India's citizens; there was no dissent among the volunteers, 72 percent strongly agreed and 27 percent agreed with this statement.

Openness was the other disposition that was often repeated. The ASER volunteers connected openness with two aspects: communication and respect. Related to communication, the participants indicated that openness starts with language. One volunteer put it this way, "It is important that we [ASER volunteers] are good communicators of local language in order to interact with people". The idea here is that openness starts with an understanding of a person's mother tongue. Being able to communicate in a local language is also a sign of respect. The participants indicated that openness is connected with respect for the people and children they were surveying as part of the ASER data collection. By respect, the ASER volunteers meant a combination of being courteous and open-minded. I witnessed this first-hand in the field as the team of ASER volunteers that I followed would greet the people they encountered with the phrase, "May I have five minutes of your precious time?" Showing respect was a key part of gaining entry into a family's home in order to conduct the ASER survey.

5.3 Citizenship Connections

The study's third research question asked about whether the dispositions of responsibility and openness are connected to citizenship. In addressing this question, I recognize the question's limitation. It draws too much on suggesting inferences from the data rather than citing data as evidence. With that caveat, the data suggest: Almost 86 percent of the ASER volunteers either agree or strongly agree that they are better citizens of India because of their ASER volunteer experience. Likewise, more than 84 percent of the ASER volunteers either agree or strongly agree that they are more invested in India's future because of their ASER volunteer experience. Almost 95 percent indicated that they know more about schooling in their community because of their ASER volunteer experience. In addition, 92 percent of the participants indicated that they better understand the challenges of teaching because of their ASER volunteer experience. The disposition of developing a deeper understanding of India's educational context and the disposition of developing a stronger commitment to the future of India's educational system are two dispositions connected with the ASER volunteer experience. These dispositions – along with the dispositions of responsibility and openness – are connected to the ASER volunteers' notions of citizenship. Additionally, the dispositions help to anchor the ASER volunteers' commitment as citizens to the future of India's education system.

6 Discussion

The disposition and citizenship connection might be best summed up in the statement of one volunteer who wrote, "I walk each village knowing that the progress of the children is also the progress of India". To this participant, at the very least, the ASER experience compelled her or him to action – to walk each village – for the progress of India. Yet, this chapter is more than just the perception of one individual. It a snapshot of the perceptions (n = 458) of almost 25,000 people who annually volunteer to conduct the ASER data collection. At first glance, it seems like a fool's errand to equate a large scale assessment with a transformative movement to disrupt notions of education, schooling, teaching, and learning. However, in this discussion section, I argue that the volunteers who conduct the ASER data collection are citizens propelled by a transformative ethos for the communities where they are situated.

But, what is meant by a transformative ethos? In unpacking the term, I followed Paulo Freire's understanding of transformation as emancipation, which includes the development of conscientization or critical consciousness (Freire, 1970). A transformative ethos is emancipatory. It requires a reading and re-writing the world and becoming critically cosmopolitan (Byker, 2013, 2016, 2017; Freire, 1970). Being cosmopolitan should not be equated with something urbane, but rather cosmopolitan is connected to a concern for larger humanity. The Greek etymological root – which is *kosmopolitês* – means citizen of the world. Appiah (2010) asserts that cosmopolitan means that one has a shared "value in human lives and humanity" (p. xv). Related to a transformative ethos, being cosmopolitan is connected with the ethic that a person understands and acts upon their shared humanity towards the production of knowledge and improvement of practice (Bhattacharjea & Byker, 2017; Byker & Banerjee, 2016; Byker & Thomas, 2018; Kumar, 2004; McTaggart, 1991).

Citizenship dispositions – like responsibility and openness – foster a transformative ethos as citizens take action and participate in knowledge building about a community. It is as UNESCO (2015) explains that active citizenship "aims to be transformative, building the knowledge, skills, values and attitudes that learners need to be able to contribute to a more inclusive, just and peaceful world" (p. 15). Evidence-based action, which is the conceptual frame for this chapter, supports the work of citizenship towards a transformative ethos. Indeed, a transformative ethos is reflected in ASER's commitment to evidence-based action, which is captured in the ASER mission statement: "Measure to understand, understand to communicate, and communicate to change" (Banerjee & Mutum, 2014, p. 6). Through the embrace of evidence-based action, the ASER volunteers have helped to improve and transform education processes, especially in India's rural areas (Banerji, 2014). Yet, for evidence-based action to be transformative it needs to be rigorous and comprehensive in data collection, but also accessible to the very communities where the evidence is collected. Accessibility – in regard to ASER – includes transparency of the data results, reports written in the multiple languages that encompass the Indian subcontinent, and findings that direct enough to move policymakers, educators, and everyday citizens to action. Fostering agency among everyday citizens is one of the hallmarks of the ASER data collection. Such agency is furthered supported by ASER's institutional partners – like India's colleges and DIETS – who often help promote the volunteer opportunities with ASER. The citizens and institutional partners have a strategic role in carrying out the ASER measurement as well as communicating the findings from their survey and assessment work.

7 Conclusion: CIE Connections

Moving to the chapter's conclusion, I revisit the two larger inquiries that frame this entire book: (1) How can the CIE field destabilize and transform knowledge hierarchies through research and practice? and (2) What research practices promote and enact a socially just and transformative ethos anchored by an ethics of engagement between the researcher(s) and the researched? In sharing the case study of the ASER volunteers, a reader could interrogate the case study with a cross-examination of the case study's sample size, the age of its participants (i.e., relatively young and, perhaps, idealistic), as well as self-report issues that go along with survey research. All of these are limitations of the case study.

As in all studies, context matters greatly. It needs to be noted that India has a policy related to volunteerism and service. One of the participants mentioned this policy – called the National Service Scheme (NSS) – in response to the question about the reason for choosing to volunteer with ASER. The NSS is a policy inspired by Mahatma Gandhi and has been an official policy in a policy in India since the late 1960s (Banerjee & Mutum, 2014). It is a scheme that is primarily for India's undergraduate students. The program's purpose is to encourage volunteering and social service in order to obtain some work experience and get a sense of the scope of India's national development. The NSS encourages undergraduates not to overly indulge during their time at college or university study, but to also see that time as citizenship development through a dedication of service for the common good. The NSS vision of service echoes in what one volunteer wrote about being a citizen: "A citizen is a responsible person who not only thinks about his own family, society, country, but considers this whole world as his family and do everything in order to serve or for the betterment of this world". The NSS policy makes the ASER recruitment of tens of thousands of volunteers more manageable.

There are implications from the ASER case study for the field of CIE in terms of destabilizing and transforming knowledge. One implication is the value of what could be termed grassroots participation, but what I call "door-to-door citizenship". Being invited into someone's home for data collection offers a window into how they live and how policies get worked out on a familial level. ASER supports this familial notion as it engages volunteer citizens in participatory field research that eventually converts into a large data assessment; yet, the assessment starts with a door knock. This participatory nature of ASER volunteering can help to destabilize stereotypes about villages where the data are collected.

In terms of transforming knowledge, much of this transformation of knowledge seems to be dependent on the mission (i.e., evidence-for-action) and the volunteers who are collecting the data. Overall, in this case study, the volunteers could be characterized as young, educated, and altruism – which is the care and selfless concern for other people. It goes beyond the scope of this current case study, but a future research agenda would include an investigation into a possible correlation regarding whether the ASER volunteers are naturally altruistic, or whether the volunteers gain altruistic competencies because of their service. Future research would also examine the any relationship between altruistic competencies and the transformation of knowledge hierarchies.

This book poses a vital question about how research practices promote and enact social justice through the engagement with the researcher and researched. As a form of participatory researcher, the ASER volunteer experience is expanding through the CIE field. Citizen-led assessments have been replicated now in several countries around the globe. As examples, Pakistan, Kenya, Uganda, Tanzania, Mali, Senegal, and Nigeria have utilized ASER's citizen assessment methodology in collecting data about the primary education levels of their children. The adoption and contextualization of the ASER methodology in the aforementioned countries speaks to the methodology's flexibility and appeal. Part of the appeal seems to be the engagement that everyday citizens have in tackling the challenges of providing equitable access to schooling.

Another reflection of the research engagement is how the ASER survey tool was renamed to connect with culture and citizenship values of the country where it was adopted. In Mali, for instance, ASER is called *beekungo*, which means "we are in it together. In Kenya, ASER is named *uwezo*, which means "capability" and in Senegal, ASER goes by the name *jangandoo*, which means "learn together". Citizen-led, large-scale assessments have now reached over one million children in South Asia and Sub-Saharan Africa (Banerjee & Mutum, 2014). The scope of use for the ASER survey is a testament to how the methodology provides elementary school assessment date through community engagement and the mobilization of a citizenry. Contextualizing educational improvements into the research engagement and the practices of localized school settings is a hallmark of social justice (Byker, 2014a; Iyengar, Witenstein, & Byker, 2014; Kumar, 2004). Banerji (2015) asserted that "Citizens-led assessments have a very strong potential to lead to citizen-led action for improving learning" (para. 12). Indeed, stronger engagement and socially just practices on behalf children and schools reflects the raison d'etre for citizen-led assessments. As the case study illustrates, the ASER volunteer experiences is a model that has linkages to greater awareness and service to a community and nation. The case study also demonstrates how everyday citizens – guided by a transformative ethos – become highly invested into the future of their country's education system because of their volunteer service through research.

References

Appiah, K. A. (2010). *Cosmopolitanism: Ethics in a world of strangers.* New York, NY: WW Norton & Company.

ASER Centre. (2014). *Annual status of education report 2013.* New Delhi: Pratham Resource Center.

ASER Centre. (2014). *History of ASER – 1996–2005: Foundations.* Retrieved from http://www.asercentre.org/p/158.html

Banerjee, A., & Mutum, A. (2014). *The ASER assessment and survey framework.* New Delhi: Pratham Resource Center.

Banerji, R. (2014). An intervention improves student reading. *Phi Beta Kappan, 95*(6), 74–75.

Bhattacharjea, S., & Byker, E. J. (2017). The ASER "translating policy into practice" toolkit: From participatory action research to evidence-based action. In H. Kidwai, R. Iyengar, M. Witenstein, E. J. Byker, & R. Setty's (Eds.), *Participatory action research and educational development: South Asian perspectives* (pp. 75–96). New York, NY: Springer International Publishing.

Byker, E. J. (2013). Critical cosmopolitanism: Engaging students in global citizenship competencies. *English in Texas Journal, 43*(2), 18–22.

Byker, E. J. (2014a). ICT oriented toward nyaya: Community computing in India's slums. *International Journal of Education and Development Using ICT, 10*(2), 19–28.

Byker, E. J. (2014b). ICT in India's elementary schools: The vision and realities. *International Education Journal, 13*(2), 27–40.

Byker, E. J. (2015). Teaching for 'global telephony': A case study of a community school for India's 21st century. *Policy Futures in Education, 13*(2), 234–246.

Byker, E. J. (2016). Developing global citizenship consciousness: Case studies of critical cosmopolitan theory. *Journal of Research in Curriculum & Instruction, 20*(3), 264–275.

Byker, E. J. (2017). Reading and rewriting South Asia. In H. Kidwai, R. Iyengar, M. Witenstein, E. J. Byker, & R. Setty's (Eds.), *Participatory action research and* educational development: South Asian perspectives (pp. 271–279). New York, NY: Springer International Publishing.

Byker, E. J., & Banerjee, A. (2016). Evidence for action: Translating field research into a large scale assessment. *Journal of Current Issues in Comparative Education, 18*(1), 1–13.

Byker, E. J., & Thomas, V. (2018). Culturally responsive webquests: Connecting technology with inquiry-based learning. *Journal of Teaching Social Studies, 18*(2), 19–25.

Center for Civic Education. (1991). *Civitas*. Calabasas, CA: Center for Civic Education.

Creswell, J. W. (2014). *Research design: Qualitative, quantitative, and mixed methods approaches* (4th ed.). Thousand Oaks, CA: Sage.

Dewey, J. (1933). *How we think*. Lexington, MA: D.C. Heath and Company.

Fink, A. (2003). *The survey handbook*. Thousand Oaks, CA: Sage.

Freire, P. (1970). *Pedagogy of the oppressed*. New York, NY: Continuum.

French, R., & Kingdon, G. (2010). *The relative effectiveness of private and government schools in rural India: Evidence from ASER data*. London: Institute of Education.

Geertz, C. (1973). *The interpretation of cultures: Selected essays*. New York, NY: Basic Books.

Hickey, S., & Mohan, G. (2004). Towards participation as transformation: Critical themes and challenges. In S. Hickey & G. Mohan (Eds.), *Participation: From tyranny to transformation? Exploring new approaches to participation in development* (pp. 3–24). New York, NY: Zed Books.

Iyengar, R., Witenstein, M. A., & Byker, E. J. (2014). Comparative perspectives on teacher education in South Asia. In A. W. Wiseman & E. Anderson (Ed.), *Annual review of comparative and international education 2014* (pp. 99–106). doi:10.1108/S1479-3679_2014_0000025010

Kumar, K. (2004). Perspectives on learning in elementary schools. Plenary address. *National Conference on Leadership in India's Elementary Schools*. Retrieved from http://www.azimpremjifoundation.org/downloads/Plenary%20Address.pdf

McTaggart, R. (1991). Principles for participatory action research. *Adult Education Quarterly, 41*(3), 168–187.

Miles, M. B., & Huberman, A. M. (1994). *Qualitative data analysis* (2nd ed.). Thousand Oaks, CA: Sage.

UNESCO (United Nations Educational, Scientific and Cultural Organization). (2015). *Global citizenship: topics and learning objectives*. Retrieved from http://unesdoc.unesco.org/images/0023/002329/232993e.pdf

Vagh, S. B. (2009). *Validating the ASER testing tools: Comparisons with reading fluency and the Read India measures*. New Delhi: Pratham Resource Center.

Yin, R. (2008). *Case study research: Design and methods* (4th ed.). Thousand Oaks, CA: Sage.

Appendix A: Survey Questions

1. What is your gender? _____Male _____Female

2. What is your age? A. 18–21 B. 22–25 C. 26–30 D. 31–39 E. 40 or above

3. What State are you from in India?

4. Open response: When you think about your experience volunteering for ASER, what words or phrases come to mind? (Please list 2 or 3)

5. Open response: How do you define the word "citizen" and explain what it means to be a citizen?

6. As a citizen, how do you identify yourself most often?
    a) As a citizen of my town or village
    b) As a citizen of my state or region (i.e., a Goan)
    c) As a citizen of my nation, "Indian"
    d) As a global citizen
    e) Other (please specify in the comment box)

7. Before volunteering for the Annual Status of Education Report (ASER) in India, were you interested in a teaching career? _____Yes _____No

8. After volunteering for the Annual Status of Education Report (ASER) in India, are you now interested in a teaching career? _____Yes _____No

9. If you answered "Yes" to question 5, at what level would you like to teach?
    a) Elementary   b) Secondary   c) Higher education

10. Open response: Why did you decide to volunteer for ASER?

11. Would you volunteer for the Annual Status of Education Report (ASER) in India again? _____Yes _____No

    Comment box: Briefly explain why or why not:

12. I better understand the challenges of teaching because of my ASER volunteer experience.
    Strongly agree   Agree   Undecided   Disagree   Strongly disagree

13. I know more about schooling in my community because of my ASER volunteer experience.
    Strongly agree   Agree   Undecided   Disagree   Strongly disagree

14. Open response: What do you believe will be the 3 biggest problems or challenges in the future of India's education system?

15. I am a better citizen of India because of my ASER volunteer experience.
    Strongly agree   Agree   Undecided   Disagree   Strongly disagree

16. Open Response: The two most important skills for being an ASER volunteer are: _____

17. I believe that I can make a difference in my community.
    Strongly agree   Agree   Undecided   Disagree   Strongly disagree

23. How many times (including this year) have you volunteered for ASER?

24. Yes or No: Is either your father or mother a teacher, headmaster, or professor? *If yes, please identify who does what.*

25. Where did you grow up?
    a) Rural area (pind)   b) Suburban (town or small city)   c) Urban (big city)

26. What kind of computer technology do you own? (check all that apply)
    a) Cell/mobile phone   b) Tablet or iPad   c) Laptop
    d) Desktop computer   e) All

PART 3

Destabilizing Power and Authority: Taking Intersectionality Seriously

CHAPTER 10

Destabilizing Power and Authority: Taking Intersectionality Seriously

Payal P. Shah and Emily Anderson

Abstract

In this chapter we provide an overview of the third part of the book, Destabilizing Power and Authority: Taking intersectionality seriously. We focus on epistemological issues of what can be known and how, challenging dominant and hegemonic discourses and presenting alternative perspectives/knowledge. We do this by detailing the epistemological underpinnings of the third symposium and presenting the knowledge produced during this symposium using participatory visual methodologies – namely word collages. The chapter closes with an overview of the three chapters comprising this part. These chapters seek to interrogate, from an intersectional perspective, the legitimization of knowledge in scholarship, funding and evidence-based practices in comparative and international education. Two questions guide this part's focus: (1) How can CIE investigate power and authority dynamics and their implications for gender and education research and practice? (2) In what ways can research and practice destabilize and transform knowledge hierarchies?

Keywords

intersectionality – arts-informed research – participatory research – challenging authority – legitimate knowledge

1 Introduction

Picking up on some of the epistemological issues and questions raised in the first section of this volume, and first plenary section of the symposium, our focus for this section of the volume is on epistemological issues of what can be known and how, challenging dominant and hegemonic discourses and presenting alternative perspectives/knowledge. The three chapters in this part seek to interrogate, from an intersectional perspective, the legitimization of knowledge in scholarship, funding and evidence-based practices in comparative and international education. Two questions guide this part's focus: (1) How can CIE investigate power and authority dynamics and their implications for gender and education research and practice? (2) In what ways can research and practice destabilize and transform knowledge hierarchies? We hope this part can engage in an interactive discussion to (re)consider how scientific knowledge is constructed and disseminated in the field.

2 The Symposium

As we reflected on the questions structuring this part of the volume, we designed a plenary section that sought to challenge the very ways that knowledge was produced and disseminated within a conference/symposium structure. In this spirit, we designed a plenary format that encouraged engagement and reflection. In order to prepare our panellists and participants for this session, we asked the panellists to consider and prepare formal comments on how we might conceptualize and account for intersectionality in research, policy and practice; how existing power and authority dynamics shape CIE research and practice; and how the field of CIE can confront internal and external power and authority dynamics. These comments were shared with all conference members ahead of the plenary sessions so all participants had access to the panellists' considerations as a common platform for discussion and dialogue during the plenary session.

We began this, the third plenary session of the symposium, with commentaries from our four distinguished panellists: Emily Bent, Barbara Dennis, Oren Pizmony-Levy and Patricia Parker. Each panellist was asked, drawing from their experience and expertise, to reflect on the ways that they approach intersectionality in and through their work. Specifically, they were asked to address the question: how does (or does not) intersectionality enable the creation or stability of colonized spaces? After offering up their experiences and thoughts, we moved into the primary arena of the session: an interactive collage activity. For this activity facilitators transitioned participants and panellists to roundtables for an interactive conversation/work session. Panellists were randomly assigned to roundtables by numbered cards located under their seats. Each roundtable had a one-page guidance document to support discussion of the essential question, "How do we create and sustain decolonized spaces within comparative and international education?" We encouraged participants to think broadly about the institutional and individual levels spanning research and practice. Participants were then asked to create a word collage to document their process and to identify one action item to share with the group during the activity debrief. The last portion of the panel session included each table reporting out to the larger group by sharing their word collage and action item. The comments shared by each table spurred a larger discussion highlighting connections across the different tables and initial plenary comments, and generated a list of potential action items moving forward.

3   Word Collages and Participatory Visual Methodologies

As a means of supporting social research that seeks to be democratic and participatory, we designed our symposium session in a way that might "help us access those elusive hard-to-put-into-words aspects of knowledge that might otherwise remain hidden or ignored" (Weber, 2008, p. 44). We see visual and arts-informed research as a means of engaging in collaborative meaning making as itself a mode of inquiry, of representation, of dissemination, and of potential transformation (Mitchell et al., 2011). We turned to visual and arts-informed research to engage our participants to participate in the knowledge production process that goes beyond the primary format of conferences and symposiums: discussion. We also sought to decenter the traditional hierarchy of "expert" panellists and audience by having all panel members collectively engage. We consider this to be a "performative research methodology that is structured on the notion of possibility, the what might be ..." (Finley, 2011, p. 562), enabling us to move beyond discussion and towards action. Finally, we believed that using participant created drawings provided us an accessible, low tech and low cost method to capture the ineffable and act as a platform for deeper collaborative meaning-making during our plenary session.

Once the symposium was complete, we saved and photographed each word collage as artistic products that themselves are both images to be read and images to be interpreted by their producers and audiences. Committed to the tenets of collaborative meaning making, we, as researchers, do not seek to interpret the image on our own, but seek to connect the content of the images with the larger formal and informal discussions at the symposium. Using photographs of the original word art created at each roundtable, we created a frequency matrix to list and count all the words included in the collages created by participants. The matrix was then uploaded to an online platform (http://mywordart.com) to generate a frequency table and an initial meta-collage visualization.

Once we created this visualization, we created construct codes by frequency of word use across word collages created by participants. Constructs were refined through iterative review of the codebook created through the first round of data coding word with the matrix and visual created by the online platform. Constructs were then refined by frequency of words and co-occurrence (Miles, Huberman & Saldaña, 2014) across the word collages generated through participants' roundtable work.

Finally, we reviewed constructs using the codebook created through second-round coding procedures to refine thematic categories and to correct errors in data organization and analysis. We updated the matrix and visualization with each revision, and then reviewed to ensure data integrity. We reviewed the codebook, matrix, and visualization to check for errors and to confirm the decision rules used in data organization, analysis and visualization. Figure 10.1 visualizes the constructs sourced from the refined corpus.

FIGURE 10.1   Meta collage

The image in Figure 10.1 thus represents a *meta collage* encapsulating the primary 76 constructs that appeared across the individual word collages created during the symposium. The figure illustrates, by size of the words, which constructs appear with the most frequency, and thus can be considered salient themes emerging from the symposium session. For the rest of the chapter, we will focus on the three themes that appear with most frequency in this meta collage: disruption, sustainability, and tension. While each of these themes appeared with a frequency of 17, we acknowledge that many other themes also emerged and formed the basis of discussion, and thus we take them as serious and salient as well. In discussing the three major themes, we will create a dialogue of meaning making between the comments by our plenary speakers that illustrate the themes identified by the participants' word collages, instead of interpreting what *we* believe each of these themes mean.

4 Symposium Themes

4.1 *Disruption*

The theme of disruption appeared prominently across all of our plenary speakers' formal comments. Disruption is a concept core to many critical and poststructuralist theories, be they feminist, postcolonial, or decolonial. These perspectives seek to disrupt, or challenge, more traditional onto-epistemological assumptions about what constitutes knowledge, where knowledge can be found, and where meaning can be found. Applied in a more practical or concrete manner, these perspectives seek to disrupt systems of knowledge that work to reify the marginalization of the Other.

Barbara Dennis addresses this concept of disruption in her commentary by imploring those within the field of CIE to move the issues of White supremacy and racial injustice/racial oppression from the margins and to the middle of our work. She outlines how in assuming universally shared experiences, white women perpetuate the frame of White supremacy inside and outside academia. In this way, Dennis calls for a disruption of the dominant perspective of White supremacy where white, feminist, activist-scholars sideline race by prioritizing gender, in order to truly work against oppression.

Emily Bent similarly uses her positionality as a girlhood scholar to challenge normative patterns of research inquiry, design, and implementation. She states that "indeed to investigate girls and girlhood(s) requires the inherent disruption of knowledge under traditional hierarchies of power" (Bent, 2017). Central to her work is the assumption that girls themselves are legitimate, if marginalized, subjects with voice and knowledge. This onto-epistemological assumption recognizes the complexity of girls as subjects as being both regulated by and resistant to the discursive and material conditions of their lives. It is here "at the crossroads of voice, discourse, and materiality that I suggest transformative research and practice is possible" (Bent, 2017).

Oren Pizmony-Levy's comments take us from the micro to the macro level where he interrogates the assumptions underpinning international large-scale assessments (ILAS). Pizmony-Levy points out some of the limitations of such approaches by highlighting how gender has been encapsulated as an individual-level variable in simple binary terms, thereby ignoring how social-norms around gender affect students. He proposes that this line of research needs to recognize the complexities around "doing gender" and therefore expand general understandings of how gender dynamics can be captured. He urges us to recognize the fact that researchers themselves play prominent roles in perpetuating the current knowledge hierarchy.

Patricia Parker focuses extensively on the issue of the knowledge hierarchy in academia and begins her comments with an understanding "of the university as a colonizing space that is simultaneously (and historically) a site for revolutionary transformation" (Parker, 2017). She contends that the very structure of the academy continues to perpetuate a colonized academic knowledge production process that excludes the legitimization of knowledge from people in the Global South, people of color, women, and others. She contends that the potential for disruption – decolonizing the academy – lies at the level of teaching, scholarship and writing, and offers The Graduate Certificate in Participatory Research at the University of North Carolina at Chapel Hill as "one attempt to interrogate the legitimization of knowledge in scholarship, funding, and evidenced-based practice" (Parker, 2017). She asserts that disruptions to the colonial practices of knowledge production must occur from within the academy itself.

4.2 *Sustainability*

During the panel session, and across the symposium in general, one of the primary arenas of concern had to do with the issue of sustainability. Our analysis of the themes and constructs present in and across the word clouds produced by symposium participants highlights the interaction between *collaboration*, *ownership*, and *capacity-building* to create and sustain decolonizing research processes and relationships. Questions such as, once disruptions are made, how can we ensure that the disruptions are sustainable? And, how can we support these disruptions such that they lead to sustaining social transformation, were evidenced not only through each roundtable's work process and product, but also observed across the paper presentations, and plenary sessions at the CIES Symposium.

In this plenary session, the concept of sustainability was integrated into the comments of our speakers. Sustainability was discussed as both a process and an outcome of change in research practices. Parker, for example, pointed out that the development of the Certificate was the product of a participatory process that took a number of years before coming to fruition. She describes the three critical practices that she says have been vital in their path towards institutionalizing the affirmation and support of decolonizing research and decolonizing the academy: (a) disrupting gatekeeping mechanisms that maintain hierarchies of exclusion; (b) creating avenues for privileging a greater range of voices in knowledge production; and (c) providing training for research traditions that engage participants as co-producers of knowledge (Parker, 2017).

Emily Bent's symposium contributions remind that destabilizing the researcher-participant hierarchy creates spaces to challenge gender, power, and empowerment discourses through intergenerational collaboration. As offered by Bent and suggested across the symposium papers and plenaries, altering the roles of researcher and participants in the research process requires a commitment to relationship and capacity-building to sustain change in practice. In her plenary statement and remarks, Bent reflected on girls' nuanced sense-making with intersectional feminism as a catalyst to their engagement with the *United Nations' Working Group on Girls* and their roles as co-researchers, sharing that these collaborations "transform(s) the research relationship to promote a socially just ethics of engagement" (Bent, 2017, p. 2).

Committing to change, and then embedding changed practices into research processes, can build capacity to sustain new ways of conceptualizing and activating research. Barbara Dennis' written statement and plenary remarks brings the personal into public view by interrogating Whiteness in her identity as a scholar. She reflected, "I can write and speak and talk all day long about my oppressive experiences with gender and never have to admit my white privilege. And I was doing this while believing it was a legitimate form of knowledge" (Dennis, 2017, p. 1). Dennis demonstrates the importance of personal and critical reflection as a means to sustain change in research practices. As noted here, she remarks that appreciation and citation of women of color's contributions to the literature and acknowledgment of White supremacy is simply not enough. Dismantling systems of racial and gender oppression in and outside of the academy require White women to interrogate their own social locations to destabilize power and knowledge hierarchies within the academy that silence women of color across the gender identity and sexuality spectrums. As Dennis models through her contributions at the symposium, sustaining change in research practice requires that the personal become public in order to alter the systems that continue to marginalize the contributions of women of color in CIE and across education within the sciences and humanities, more broadly.

Oren Pizmony-Levy's written statement and remarks continue Dennis' and others discussions of personal reflection as a catalyst to create and sustain change. His written remarks position his work and engagement with the symposium within the contexts of identity, history and place. He begins by sharing that his early work in the non-governmental organization sector serving LGBTQAI+ youth in Israel informed his decision to ultimately pursue a doctoral degree in sociology and education (2017, p. 1). By first grounding his research interests and expertise within the contexts of his experience and identity, Pizmony-Levy highlights the interconnectedness of who we are with what we study. For example, from his foundational work with LGBTQAI+ youth-serving organizations, to his current scholarship, Pizmony-Levy shows the importance of positionality as a mechanism to destabilize knowledge hierarchies. This interconnectedness can sustain change in how research is conceptualized and activated across the research-to-practice continuum.

4.3   *Tension*

As reflected in the meta-collage presented earlier in this chapter, tension emerged as a salient theme across the plenary's activities. Roundtable participants included words ranging from *clash* to *contradiction* to describe the process of destabilizing knowledge hierarchies and to sustain change in research practices. As scholar-practitioners engaged in participatory and collaborative gender-focused research in CIE, we now turn to interrogate our position/s in this work so as to highlight the tensions we experienced in facilitating the third plenary session.

Our process in creating the plenary's activity involved extensive collaboration as well as consultation with our other colleagues on the symposium convening committee. One of the symposium's goals – and, one of our primary objectives in planning the third plenary session – was to reimagine the traditional conference space through participatory and visual arts-based approaches. This required that we engage in what we came to understand as *purposeful* tension as a means to interrogate our own expectations for the symposium and our dual roles as facilitators and participants. As part of our engagement with purposeful tension, we routinely questioned how we would balance giving clear instructions and setting objectives for the roundtable activity with participants' creative expression and interpretation of the activity's prompts. Our aim was to guide, but not dictate, how each table approached the activity. Some tables were more engaged compared to others, thus requiring us to restrain our instincts as educators to keep groups 'time on task' or to give directives on process.

At the time of the symposium's planning, we served together as Co-Chairs of the Gender and Education Standing Committee of the Comparative and International Education Society (CIES). In reflection of our service to the GEC, we sought to embed opportunities to confront gender within our contributions to the symposium. We approached this work with the understanding that the teaching space is a gendered space. Electing to 'teach' through facilitation of a participatory activity became a source of purposeful tension for us and (hopefully) for our participants to reflect on the ways in which gender shapes our interaction with others in knowledge production sites, and collaborative tasks, more broadly.

We engaged purposeful tension as a process of learning from and listening to each other to identify scholars within and outside of CIE to center gender within our activities, but to do so in a way that challenged gender binaries in knowledge production. As discussed at the Symposium by Bent, Dennis, Pizmony-Levy, and Parker (as well as in the latter's chapter in this part), transforming knowledge hierarchies requires a commitment to change and to accept the potential for making mistakes. Session participants also cited risk and the potential for mistakes as tensions in their roundtable activities and work products. This mirroring of purposeful tension in our experiences as facilitators with session participants' engagement illustrate how participatory knowledge-making can catalyze and sustain change in research practices.

5 Intersectionality and CIE

This part of our volume begins with a chapter by Patricia Parker who follows up on the themes of disruption, sustainability and tension raised during the third plenary session of the symposium. In her chapter, she sets the scene for how we can productively engage in conversations about the ideas, problematics, and opportunities for creating academic and community spaces that challenge existing power-knowledge dynamics in research. In particular, Parker offers her conceptualization of decolonizing the academy, and the role that she sees positionality playing as she engages in doing research with people in communities. She asserts that we need to have more conversations that "begin with people in the privileged spaces of the academy calling into question our complicity in advancing the colonial legacy of research practices that, among other things, establish knowledge hierarchies that objectify people and their life experiences" (Parker, Chapter 11, this volume). The primary claims that she addresses through detailing the development of a certificate in participatory research at the University of North Carolina – Chapel Hill include: (a) intersectionality is a necessary framework for enabling the creation and sustainability of decolonized spaces; (b) The university is a colonizing space that is simultaneously (and historically) a site for progressive transformation; (c) Decolonizing research involving academics and people in vulnerable communities that destabilizes and transforms knowledge hierarchies is possible, but requires commitments to decolonial participatory principles.

The next chapter in the part is provided by Kelly Grace and Sothy Eng who provide an alternative way of engaging in research to challenge existing power-knowledge dynamics. In particular, they seek to problematize hierarchies within the knowledge production process, focusing on the role of interpreters in CIE. By providing a reflective treatise on the development of a collaborative method to include the worldviews of the Cambodian interviewers, Grace and Eng offer a concrete way to broaden the knowledge production process and decolonize the research process using interviews and focus groups themselves. They argue that such transformation of knowledge hierarches requires a collaborative relationship between researcher and interpreter. In their chapter, they draw from their own research projects in Cambodia where they illustrate how traditional interpreter-researcher relationships reify existing power-knowledge dynamics, and provide an alternative method of how to include interpreters in the co-construction of human experience conveyed through interviews and focus groups.

The last chapter in this part, by Alisha Braun, uses PhotoVoice methodology as a way to bring the voices of people with disabilities more centrally into CIE research. After an overview of what the presence of disability in CIE development policy agendas and CIE research currently looks like, Braun argues that greater representation of the voices of people with disabilities is necessary. Her chapter details her use of PhotoVoice in a recent study on access to higher education for students with mobility disability in Ghana. Braun's chapter provides an excellent illustration of how broadening the breadth of intersectional research in CIE can be productive in transforming knowledge hierarchies as well as investigating power and authority dynamics related to whose experiences are excluded from mainstream CIE policy and research.

This part hopes to provide concrete examples of how shifts in onto-epistemological assumptions can support research and practice that can destabilize and transform knowledge hierarchies.

References

Bent, E. (2017). Symposium statement. In *Proceedings of the 2nd Comparative and International Education Symposium: Interrogating and Innovating CIE Research*. Arlington, VA: George Mason University. Retrieved from https://cehd.gmu.edu/2017symposium/speaker-statements

Crossley, M. W., & Tikly, L. P. (2004). Postcolonial perspectives and comparative and international research in education: A critical introduction. *Comparative Education, 40*(2), 147–156.

Dennis, B. (2017). Remarks. In *Proceedings of the 2nd Comparative and International Education Symposium: Interrogating and Innovating CIE Research*. Arlington, VA: George Mason University.

Dennis, B. (2017). Symposium statement. In *Proceedings of the 2nd Comparative and International Education Symposium: Interrogating and Innovating CIE Research*. Arlington, VA: George Mason University. Retrieved from https://cehd.gmu.edu/2017symposium/speaker-statements

Hickling-Hudson, A. (2006). Cultural complexity, post-colonialism and educational change: Challenges for comparative educators. *International Review of Education, 52*(1–2), 201–218.

Miles, M. B., Huberman, A. M., & Saldaña, J. (2014). *Qualitative data analysis: A methods sourcebook.* Thousand Oaks, CA: Sage.

Mitchell C., Theron L., Stuart J., Smith A., & Campbell, Z. (2011). Drawings as Research Method. In L. Theron, C. Mitchell, A. Smith, & J. Stuart (Eds.), *Picturing research.* Rotterdam, The Netherlands: Sense Publishers.

Parker, P. (2017). Remarks. In *Proceedings of the 2nd Comparative and International Education Symposium: Interrogating and Innovating CIE Research.* Arlington, VA: George Mason University.

Parker, P. (2017). Symposium statement. In *Proceedings of the 2nd Comparative and International Education Symposium: Interrogating and Innovating CIE Research.* Arlington, VA: George Mason University. Retrieved from https://cehd.gmu.edu/2017symposium/speaker-statements

Pizmony-Levy, O. (2017). Bent, E. (2017). Symposium statement. In *Proceedings of the 2nd Comparative and International Education Symposium: Interrogating and Innovating CIE Research.* Arlington, VA: George Mason University. Retrieved from https://cehd.gmu.edu/2017symposium/speaker-statements

Tikly, L., & Bond, T. (2013). Towards a postcolonial research ethics in comparative and international education. *Compare, 43*(4), 422–442.

Weber, S. (2008). Visual images in research. In J. G. Knowles & A. L. Cole (Eds.), *Handbook of the arts in qualitative research: Perspectives, methodologies, examples, and issues* (pp. 41–54). London: Sage.

CHAPTER 11

Notes on Intersectionality and Decolonizing Knowledge Production

Patricia S. Parker

Abstract

Participants at the Fall 2017 CIES Symposium engaged in provocative conversations about the ideas, problematics, and opportunities for creating academic and community spaces that challenge existing power-knowledge dynamics in research. This chapter summarizes my contributions to some of those conversations, drawn from prepared and extemporaneous remarks during the *Plenary on Intersectionality and Research*, as well as excerpts from a pre-symposium interview I did with Freshedx host, Will Brehm. Three key claims are developed in the chapter: (a) intersectionality is a necessary framework for enabling the creation and sustainability of decolonized spaces; (b) the university is a colonizing space that is simultaneously (and historically) a site for progressive transformation; and (c) decolonizing research involving academics and people in vulnerable communities that destabilizes and transforms knowledge hierarchies is possible, but requires commitments to decolonial participatory principles. The chapter concludes with a discussion of the Graduate Certificate in Participatory Research at the University of North Carolina at Chapel Hill as one example of what is possible in pursuing intersectionality in the co-creation of knowledge and decolonizing research as well as the academy itself.

Keywords

intersectionality – co-creation in knowledge production – decolonizing research – participatory research

1 Introduction

Holding true to its theme, the Fall 2017 CIES Symposium proved to be a productive space for "Interrogating Innovating CIE Research". As a participant in one of the plenary sessions and throughout the two-day Symposium, I engaged in provocative conversations about the ideas, problematics, and opportunities for creating academic and community spaces that challenge existing power-knowledge dynamics in research. This chapter summarizes my contributions to some of those conversations, drawn from prepared and extemporaneous remarks during the Plenary on Intersectionality and Research, as well as excerpts from a pre-symposium interview I did with Freshedx host, Will Brehm. The key claims are these: (a) intersectionality is a necessary framework for enabling the creation and sustainability of decolonized spaces; (b) The university is a colonizing space that is simultaneously (and historically) a site for progressive transformation; (c) Decolonizing research involving academics and people in vulnerable communities that destabilizes and transforms knowledge hierarchies is possible, but requires commitments to decolonial participatory principles.

2 Notes on Intersectionality: Enabling the Creation and Sustainability of Decolonize Knowledge Production

Panellists participating in the *Plenary on Intersectionality and Research* were asked to address the question, "What ways can research and practice destabilize and transform knowledge hierarchies?" My remarks focused on the importance of intersectionality for decolonizing knowledge production via research and other academic endeavours. To claim that the academy can be "decolonized", I argued, presumes an intersectional analysis, for it points to a process of making legible and calling into question the dominant colonial and class-based legacies of academic knowledge production and dissemination. Historically, the ontological and epistemological assumptions embedded in those legacies have contributed to the erasure or de-legitimation of certain sources and kinds of knowledge, while advancing and protecting others. Intersectionality (Crenshaw, 1989) is, in my view, a necessary framework for decolonizing research because it supports power analyses that make different *positionalities* legible for the purposes of *co-creating processes* that lead to more equitable and just social arrangements. Positionalities in this case can be distinguished from positions or interests. Rather positionalities are best understood as standpoints that are achieved through political struggle (See Collins, 1990). Because research is not, in any case, a neutral activity, researcher positionality must be understood as part of the decolonizing research process.

Co-creation also must be explained within the context of decolonizing knowledge production. In my view, processes of co-creation can enable research, activism, education, and policymaking. It can also be understood as a process that enables healing from the trauma of centuries of state supported violence and extreme capitalist practices. In the latter instance, a co-creative process that centers on the healing from trauma – or even acknowledging that trauma exists – becomes a form of knowledge production that informs research, activism, education, and policy. Marie Campbell (2016) made this point excellently. Drawing on Dorothy Smith's institutional ethnography approach as crucial for intersectional analyses, Campbell argued that researchers should generate knowledge through explication that is faithful to *social actualities*, recognizing that those actualities emerge via different discourses of power circulating through people's lives (Campbell, 2016; Smith 1987). That is, inquiry should stay "focused on explicating the problematics arising in people's everyday experiences" (Campbell, 2016, p. 250). This kind of intersectional co-creation in knowledge production, in my view, is a necessary condition for enabling and sustaining decolonized spaces in the academy and in communities.

What are the intersectional co-creation processes that produce explications faithful to social actualities? As I shared during the *Plenary on Intersectionality and Research,* Ella Baker's philosophy of group-centered community-led organizing for social justice provides one model. Born in 1903, Ella Baker was a civil rights and human rights activist whose activism spanned 50 years, leaving a legacy that has inspired grassroots social movements and work toward participative democracy around the world (see Ransby, 2003). Baker was a carrier of a tradition of anti-racist resistance that was connected to traditions of indigenous resistance globally but had roots in Black women's resistance to slavery and sexual violence in the United States. Her philosophy begins with a structural analysis of oppressive power structures (such as extreme capitalism, patriarchy, and White supremacy) as revealed in concert with, and through the lives of, people living under the heels of oppressive power regimes. It rejects notions of hierarchy in decision-making, except for the principle of tilting decision-making power toward the least powerful when it is their lives at stake. Her philosophy advances through practices grounded in a steadfast belief in the power of people living through oppressive power regimes to name their social actualities as it relates to power and to lead change (Ransby, 2003; Parker, forthcoming).

For the past 10 years, in my teaching, research, and service, I have attempted to understand and advance the philosophy and practice of what I've termed *Ella Baker's catalytic leadership approach* (Parker, forthcoming). That journey began with my participatory research with African American teen girls in public housing communities leading social change projects (see Parker, Sanchez,

Oceguera, 2011). More recently, Ella Baker's catalytic leadership approach has also inspired and informed my university service, including in my role as one of the founding board members and current director of the Graduate Certificate in Participatory Research at the University of North Carolina at Chapel Hill (see Parker et al., 2017: Parker, Dennison, & Smith, 2017). The Certificate is one example of what is possible for decolonizing research as well as the academy itself. I conclude the chapter with notes on those topics.

3   Notes on Universities as Colonizing Spaces: A Graduate Certificate in Participatory Research as a Decolonizing Mechanism

In the weeks leading up to the Fall 2017 CIES Symposium, the organizers arranged for FreshEd host, Will Brehm to conduct a series of interviews with plenary speakers and I was one of the interviewees. Questions for my interview were inspired by an article I published with colleagues at the University of North Carolina at Chapel Hill, about the Graduate Certificate in Participatory Research and its potential for decolonizing the academy (Parker, Holland, Smith, Dennison, & Jackson, 2017). In the excerpts from that interview that follow, I share my thoughts on universities as colonizing spaces and participatory research as a decolonizing mechanism. Some parts of the interview have been revised to adapt to the written (versus aural) context. However, the main ideas are consistent with the original interview.

Excerpts from the FreshEd Interview:

Brehm: What is the Graduate Certificate in Participatory Research at the University of North Carolina?
Parker: The Certificate is intended for graduate students who are seeking training in participatory research methods. A collective of faculty, students and administrators created the Certificate in 2013 in response to a particular need. The need was to create … a learning community for graduate students who want to pursue particular kinds of participatory methodologies where research is produced in partnership with communities, ideally from its inception of what the research is about, to the development of the research questions, to the implementation of the research and the dissemination of the research products (see Wallerstein and Duran, 2006). The Certificate was intended especially for those graduate students who might be questioning whether such methodologies are consistent with

[their particular] discipline's standards or perspectives. We wanted to provide a space where students could ask questions about doing research in equitable partnership with people in communities. Often times, in the academy, there are different ways of thinking about how knowledge is produced and what counts as knowledge. The Certificate allows questions, such as, "Who counts as experts in terms of producing knowledge?"

Brehm: So, why did all of these students and faculty think the academy is a colonizing space?

Parker: Well, we were not the first to think that. I mean there is a long tradition in the history of universities that, in the words of Carole Boyce Davies (2003) who has written quite a bit about this, that [the academy] might be considered one of the most colonized spaces. By that, it is meant that the university is a site for the production and reproduction of particular discourses that keep colonial structures in place. Those colonial structures are meant to maintain what has been referred to as Euro-American hegemonies at the level of thinking, and also in the larger world. This kind of thinking translates into the very idea of who belongs in the academy and who has access to particular ways of shaping thought .... Faculty of color, for example, coming from backgrounds in the US context as African American, Latinx, and Native American bring different histories and approaches to knowledge that often have been marginalized in the academy. The indigenous scholar, Linda Tuhiwahi-Smith (2013) has written about this in her book, *Decolonizing Methodologies*. Often for people who come into the academy from indigenous backgrounds and histories of colonial violence, they are thinking through complex questions about identity, research, and accountability to our communities.

Brehm: And this Certificate program allows you and other students to kind of wade through that history and complexity that you're talking about but having this unknown future because you don't know what will be produced through that process?

Parker: Yes, that's exactly right. Providing that opportunity to ask the questions that are emerging from their experiences and from their histories. And not being told that they're not legitimate questions. Not being told that these are questions that don't belong in the academy. That's what the Certificate does. It creates a space that legitimizes the experiences of people who are coming from traditions that are steeped in those histories.

Brehm: So, if I were a student today, what would this program look like? What would I be doing? What classes would I be taking? What would the experience be like?

Parker: The program is designed to provide students with tools for pursuing decolonizing research. Two required courses provide a practical and theoretical foundation – and introductory survey course on issues in participatory research and a core course called "Decolonizing Methodologies". The main intent of the decolonizing methodologies course is to get students thinking about destabilizing discourses that have maintained a particular structure within the academy in terms of how knowledge is produced and which knowledges are deemed legitimate. They also get hands-on experience "work-shopping" problems that come up in participatory research with people, such as, "How are community experts shaping the project?" "What if the research products bring more risk to an already vulnerable community?" There are also elective courses that the students are required to take, which provide additional exposure to participatory methods across multiple disciplines. A final requirement is for students to complete a practicum and a supervised, hands-on experience with participatory research. This is something that can be done with their current advisor. Oftentimes it is not. I think that's one of the needs that we were addressing is that while there may be departments that support participatory research methodologies and working in equitable partnership with communities, there may not be people with that expertise in that particular department at that time. We work with students to find research supervisors to work with them.

Brehm: I would imagine that with the bureaucracies inside the university it's very hard embracing the unknown.

Parker: The University has to be retrofitted for the kinds of initiatives that support the ways we're teaching the [decolonizing methodologies] course and administrating the Certificate. For example, as Director of the Certificate, much of my time is spent fundraising to support seed grants for students who want to start developing relationships with people in the communities where they will do their work. Most Certificates don't require funding, so it is sometimes a challenge translating that need to administrators. At the department level, [the interdisciplinarity of the Certificate] becomes tricky because one of the things that we are advancing is that our core course, Decolonizing

Methodologies, doesn't belong to any one department. It's a course that can be taught in almost any department with two instructors from different disciplines. There's no structure on campus that helps us to make that easy. But we've made it work for the past three years by building interdepartmental support with backing from department chairs and supportive deans.

4 Conclusion

The conversations I participated in at the CIES 2017 symposium and the pre-symposium interview advanced my thinking about my current research projects. They also reinforced my belief in the possibilities for decolonizing the academy through initiatives such as the Graduate Certificate in Participatory research. As an African-American woman-scholar-activist at a Research 1 university committed to doing research *with* people in communities, I welcomed the conversations with other scholars doing similar research from their own positionalities as indigenous, white women, and queer. I think such conversations are needed for the urgent decolonizing work toward ensuring indigenous futurity globally (Tuck & Yang, 2012) and reclaiming all humanity from the ruins of extreme capitalism, patriarchy, racism, and heteronormativity. I think part of that work begins with people in the privileged spaces of the academy calling into question our complicity in advancing the colonial legacy of research practices that, among other things, establish knowledge hierarchies that objectify people and their life experiences. This type of questioning permeated the conversations that happened at the Fall 2017 CIES Symposium. I hope this volume of essays inspires similar conversations globally and into the future.

References

Boyce Davies, C. (2003). Introduction. In C. Boyce Davies, M. Gadsby, & C. Peterson (Eds.), *Decolonizing the academy: African diaspora studies* (pp. ix–xvi). Trenton, NJ: Africa World Press Inc.

Campbell, M. L. (2016). Intersectionality, policy-oriented research and the social relations of knowing. *Gender, Work & Organization, 23*(3), 248–260.

Parker, P. S. (forthcoming). *Ella Baker's catalytic leadership approach: A primer on community engagement and communication for social justice leadership*.

Parker, P. S., Holland, D., Dennison, J., Smith, S. H., & Jackson, M. (2017). Decolonizing the academy: Lessons from the graduate certificate in participatory research at the University of North Carolina at Chapel Hill. *Qualitative Inquiry,* 24(7), 464–477.

Parker, P. S., Oceguera, E., Sanchez, J., & Mumby, D. K. (2011). Intersecting differences: Organizing (ourselves) for social justice research with people in vulnerable communities. In D. K. Mumby (Ed.), *Reframing difference in organizational communication studies: Research, pedagogy, practice.* Thousand Oaks, CA: Sage.

Parker, P. S., Smith, S. H., & Dennison, J. (2017). Decolonising the classroom. *Gender Studies,* 20(3), 233–247.

Ransby, B. (2003). *Ella Baker and the Black freedom movement: A radical democratic vision.* Chapel Hill, NC: University of North Carolina Press.

Smith, D. E. (1987). *The everyday world as problematic: A feminist sociology.* Toronto: University of Toronto Press.

Smith, L. T. (2013). *Decolonizing methodologies: research and indigenous peoples.* London: Zed Books Ltd.

Wallerstein, N. B., & Duran, B. (2006). Using community-based participatory research to address health disparities. *Health Promotion Practice,* 7(3), 312–323.

CHAPTER 12

Knowledge Hierarchies and Interviewing Methods in Cambodia: Strategies for Collaborative Interpretation

Kelly Grace and Sothy Eng

Abstract

Work with interpreters in focus group discussions and individual interviews warrants a consideration of the ways that these methodologies create, sustain or dismantle knowledge hierarchies in comparative and international education (CIE) research. Although power and knowledge hierarchies are examined within the researcher/participant dynamic, interpreters' role in qualitative research is less explored. Drawing on the extensive experience of the authors in conducting interviews and focus group research in Cambodia, this chapter considers the collaborative role between researchers and interpreters in interviewing methods. In particular, it focuses on how collaborative methods of interpretation can be used to transform knowledge hierarchies and embrace interpreter local knowledge in the qualitative research process. The strategies outlined include decolonizing interpreter training, the co-construction of meaning with interpreters and taking a backseat in the interpretation research process. These strategies aim to support researchers and interpreters involved in cross-cultural CIE research in the dismantling of power hierarchies in qualitative research.

Keywords

power and knowledge hierarchies – collaboration – interviewing – local knowledge – decolonization – comparative and international education

1   Introduction

Qualitative methods such as interviews and focus groups aim to create deep contextual meaning from the language of participants (Brinkmann & Kvale,

2015). Issues of power and knowledge hierarchies between researcher and participant are well-documented (Fairclough, 1989; Hoffman, 2007; Wang, 2006), and research in qualitative methods illustrates the impact of translation and interpretation on the quality of data (Esposito, 2001; Saldanha & O'Brien, 2014; Temple & Edwards, 2002). Much of this research considers skills, techniques, and approaches needed to develop quality data using these qualitative methods, and the potential power hierarchies between researcher, researched and interpreters. While power hierarchies in research are acknowledged, and discussed in the literature (Smith, 2013), the use of interviews and focus group discussions as tools for decolonizing the research process is less explored. Additionally, the possibilities for invoking indigenous worldviews to inform and reframe the interview process (Chilisa, 2011) remains underutilized. A rich body of research exists examining participatory methods that highlight participant knowledge and voice in Comparative and International Education (CIE), however this research deviates from this literature in that it focuses on decolonizing methods in CIE research by focusing on the role of the interpreter. Little is written about the role of interpreters in the propagation or deconstruction of power and knowledge hierarchies in cross-language research through in interviews and focus group discussions. This is particularly relevant in contexts such as Cambodia, where national development, and the use of INGOs and NGOs in the development of the education system, has spurred an influx of international research using Western frameworks and approaches.

This chapter examines the challenges associated with traditional approaches to the researcher/interpreter relationship, arguing that a transformation of the knowledge hierarchies requires a collaborative relationship between researcher and interpreter. We contend that this transformation requires an examination of the process of dismantling knowledge hierarchy in interviews by being aware of researcher identity, conversational dynamics, and co-construction of meaning with interpreters during and after the interview process. These strategies draw from the extensive experience of the authors in conducting interviews and leading groups of student researchers in Cambodia. Additionally, they address issues of interpreter training, co-construction of meaning, and "taking a backseat" in the interviewing process. Decolonizing interpreter training requires skillful navigation to ensure that interpreters provide accurate translations but are not pressured to provide direct translations which alienate their own cultural knowledge and nuanced linguistic capacities. Co-constructing meaning lies at the heart of the qualitative research interpretivist paradigm, which undertakes the central endeavour of understanding the subjective human experience (Guba and Lincoln, 1989) and asserts that reality is socially constructed (Bogdan and Biklen, 1998). While there are a number of interpretivist paradigms, we use this broad understanding of interpretivist paradigm and assert that including interpreters in the co-construction of human experience conveyed in interviews and focus groups supports the decolonizing of these methods of data collection. This deviates from a positivist paradigm approach which relies on the assumption of measurable entities and facts (Kivunja & Kuyini, 2017). Finally, this chapter addresses the power hierarchy that can be inadvertently propagated between researcher and interpreter. This includes examples of situations in which a researcher may fight to control the interview process and resist the benefit of dismantling knowledge hierarchies that comes from relinquishing control in the interpretation/translation process. This chapter expands/adds to the literature on CIE research methods by outlining inclusive and decolonizing practices when working with interpreters in qualitative interviews and focus group discussions, thereby addressing inequitable knowledge hierarchies within the research process. These practices draw from specific research projects in education, and in particular gender and education, that we undertook in Cambodia, which are highlighted in the chapter to exemplify the development of collaborative approaches to interviews and focus groups.

Positionality in post-colonial contexts remains a significant issue in CIE, as the field works to disentangle its own colonial past and to consider how the field can move forward with the decolonization of theories and methodologies in CIE (Crossley & Tickly, 2004; Takayama, Sriprakash, & Connell, 2017). In this work, we consider two aspects of decolonization of theories and methods that are prominent in the literature and particularly relevant to our work with focus group and individual interviews, namely the privileging of local knowledge in the research process and critically examining assumptions regarding knowledge and power (Smith, 2013). While engaging in qualitative field work with CIE students and researchers, the authors struggled with limited practical strategies for addressing power hierarchies and incorporating local knowledge when conducting interviews and working with interpreters in qualitative research. To this end, current practices, as they are addressed in the literature, often do not support students and researchers in privileging local knowledge of interpreters, creating a collaborative approach to interpretation and interviewing, and examining assumptions regarding who has power over knowledge production (Quinn, 1998). The involvement of interpreters in cross-language focus groups and individual interviews provides a unique opportunity to consider decolonizing qualitative methods in the field of CIE, by examining the authors' experiences and outlining our attempts to interrogate and dismantle our own colonial practices.

Three persistent issues in translation in interviews include: "hierarchies of language power, situated language epistemologies of researchers, and issues around naming and speaking for people seen as 'other'" (Temple & Young, 2004, p. 162). Therefore, understanding the role of the interpreter in the interview process is particularly important when students and researchers are conducting interviews and focus group discussions in languages other than their own mother tongue. An understanding of the interpreter's role within interviews and the relationships between researcher, interpreter, and participant is also crucial in accessing participant knowledge and in transforming the knowledge hierarchy that exists between the three parties. Researchers who view interpreters as mere conduits of language risk alienating themselves from participants, remaining ignorant of sociocultural and linguistic nuances that are critical to a deep understanding of the participants' experiences, and thus create dynamics which disempower interpreters and participants.

2 Interrogating the Positivist Research Paradigm

In recent decades, the field of CIE has critiqued the dominant positivist paradigm of research seeking "objective" approaches to research by undertaking critical methodologies that interrogate dominant discourses in education research and methods (Klees, 2008; Wiseman & Anderson, 2016). In particular, research in the field of CIE has embraced understandings of whose knowledge is privileged, examination of the role of researcher reflexivity, and the use of methodologies to disrupt the dominant paradigm (Baily, Shah, & Call-Cummings, 2016). Through our work in CIE, we came to question our approach to data collection with interpreters, realizing the colonizing nature of our procedure that was unconsciously driven by (a) our presumed superior Western knowledge, (b) objectivity in the language translation and the felt superiority of the English language, and (c) the dominant positivist paradigm embedded in research practices with the intent of endorsing comparative data and analyses. This is our main point of argument that while it has been common that the research in CIE field is endorsing comparative data and analysis, growing interrogation of cross-national data and the acceptance of interpretivist paradigms allow researchers in the field of CIE to expand their research inquiries and methodologies in a way that is decolonizing and deliberating in which this edited book intends to address.

This reflection allows us as researchers to be aware of our social and educational position during the research and data collection process in relation to our interpreters who most of the time consider us to be "the experts" and are ready to take any orders and instructions as given. It also provides an opportunity for us as researchers to humanize our interpreters in a way that integrates their experience and cultural knowledge into the interview sessions. With this reflection, we seek to overcome our entrenched beliefs of objectivity by being more flexible, more collaborative, and supportive of our interpreter's effort in their translation work. In doing this, we seek to create an environment conducive to participant expression and supported by the smooth and dynamic interactions between the researchers, interpreters, and participants.

3 Researcher Identities

The approaches to interpreter participation in interviews and focus groups outlined in this chapter draw from the experiences of the authors and their consideration of their positionality. Their reflections and experiences led to the development of what we call decolonizing interviewing tools. The first author is a white, female graduate student educated in the United States, who does not speak Khmer, the dominant language in Cambodia, and has been traveling to Cambodia conducting interviews and focus groups for four years. The second author is a Cambodian male, educated in Phnom Penh, Cambodia, who is currently a professor in the United States. The second author served as an interpreter for researchers in Cambodia before beginning a career conducting research in Cambodia more than a decade ago. Through a university program in CIE, which supports graduate student research in Cambodian schools, the authors began working together on research projects where interpreters provided translation support.

Over the course of more than fifty individual interviews and focus group discussions, we recognized the need to develop interviewing methods that privilege the local knowledge of interpreters and develop a collaborative approach towards interpretation and translation. As a graduate student new to research, the first author labored under the mistaken notion that the researcher had to "be in charge" and seen as the "expert" throughout the interview process. I was under the assumption that "good data" (i.e. reliable and valid in the positivist sense) in qualitative research was unfiltered through the experiences of interpreters, and therefore must include only the verbatim translation of participants words. Without realizing it, I was operating under a positivist assumption, brought about by previous training and coursework, which became increasingly problematic as I conducted interviews through an interpreter. Additionally, I believed that interpreters were charged with one role: to translate from English to Khmer and Khmer to English verbatim so as to not interfere with the data collection process. This interference assumed that, first, language has an unbiased and verbatim English counterpart that is shared by all interpreters, and second, that variation from verbatim translation introduces an inherently negative bias that should be avoided. It became clear that adherence to a belief of the interpreter as an unbiased tool was unrealistic and dehumanizing, and that important contextual, cultural and local understandings were missing by excluding interpreter knowledge and experiences. As we reflected on our identity as researchers conducting research in an international, cross language setting, we began to develop decolonizing methods of ensuring that interpreter knowledge was regarded as essential, valuable, and that they were included in the process of constructing meaning, as they understood it, from the data.

4 Dismantling Knowledge Hierarchies in Interviews

Although Temple and Young (2004) highlight important and persistent issues in interpretation and translation relating to knowledge hierarchies, including "the hierarchies of language power, situated language epistemologies of researchers, and issues around naming and speaking for people seen as 'other'" (p. 162), solutions to or suggestions for dismantling these knowledge hierarchies in decolonizing the researcher/interpreter roles were not provided. Decolonizing interviewing practices speaks to Spivak's (1992) concept of power differentials between languages and countries, and her 'politics of translation' which views language as the process of meaning-construction. This suggests that postcolonial translation no longer need "be as 'indistinguishable' as possible from the native English speaker" (p. 187). While some argue that verbatim interpretation is necessary for validity of the data (Essén, Jonsdotter, Hovelius, Gudmundsson, Sjöberg, Friedman, & Östergren, 2000; Phillips, 1960), Squires (2009) advises against the "invisibility" of interpreters, by engaging them as mere conduits of language and ignoring the experiences and knowledge that they bring to interpretation. Studies have examined the potential for interpreters' roles in qualitative research which were "non-hierarchical" (Adamson & Donovan, 2002; Turner, 2010), including interpreters in the data analysis and interpretation as well as a comparison of situated knowledges in interviews. Yet there is little mention, beyond discussions with interpreters, of methodological approaches associated with dismantling knowledge hierarchies, which legitimizes and prioritizes the researcher and researcher knowledge.

The interpreter as an "object' is a concern to researchers attempting to decolonize qualitative research in the Global South. Viewing interpreters as an impediment or conduit for "good data" effectively diminishes, or potentially fully excludes, interpreters as human beings with experiences, knowledge and, in some cases, research skills acquired in their field. Edwards (2012) cautions against the abuse of power and privilege in interviewing with interpreters by positioning oneself as "the researcher" and interpreters as mere conduits of language. She acknowledges the role of interpreters as gatekeepers and suggests that the treatment of interpreters as objects betrays the trust of local communities and reinforces dominant knowledge hierarchies that are as threatening to trustworthiness (Lincoln and Guba, 1988) as inaccurate linguistic interpretations. Of further concern, yet rarely addressed, is the abuse of power, and the abuse of interpreters, in the research process. This is of particular concern in Cambodia, where international non-governmental organizations (INGOs) and nongovernment organizations (NGOs) proliferate, often without consideration of the impact of the research process on local communities, including participants and interpreters within these communities.

In Cambodia, INGOs and NGOs often provide social services, programs and resources that the government is unable to provide. In post-war reconstruction, INGOs proliferated and today Cambodia has the highest number of NGOs in proportion to its population in the world (Frewer, 2013). At the NGO level, there is often a pressure for a project to produce outcomes satisfactory to donors that usually leads to NGOs putting time and efforts on trying to please donors more than exploring solutions to the problems faced those who are in a real need (Nunnenkamp & Ohler, 2012). This pressure can result in the inflexibility of the research process where interpreters are involved in the data collection process along with international experts or consultants. And at the community level where people receive the service and are selected as research participants, they may feel obligated to respond to the researchers in a way that is pleasing and grateful for what is being implemented in their villages. Bawole (2015), in his study in a community project planning in Ghana, found that "although community members were engaged in project planning processes in many respects, these engagements were limited to endorsing pre-prepared plans, decisions, and mundane aspects of the project. The engagements were largely tokenistic, rhetorical, and to garnish legitimacy, and lacked the key elements of empowerment which promoted downward accountability" (p. 920). And where research is involved, the interpreters have a sense of what participants actually feel because of their familiarity with the local cultural context, but due to the inflexibility and expectation from the researchers, they are more likely to ignore these cultural nuances expressed by the participants.

Interpreters are often instructed by researchers to translate everything, word by word and exactly as mentioned by the participants. This can create tension on the part of interpreters, as direct translation in some contexts is difficult. Furthermore, interpreters hired from within a local community often feel a responsibility to represent the participants with full acknowledgement of their dignity and privacy when some participants' responses may be perceived by other members of the group and/or interpreters, as too taboo or embarrassing, and to this end may summarize long responses from the participants. The summary usually causes frustration for the researchers who expect the whole response to be translated verbatim, and the assumption of interpreter incompetence creates tension between researcher and interpreter. Good relationships and trust between the two parties may dissolve at this point and the richness of and the quality of data can be lost as interpreters focus on the length of the translation at the expense of quality in order to appease the researcher and avoid negative judgement. In addition, the tension between the researchers and the interpreters can be felt easily by the participants who could become reserved about sharing openly. Building relationships and gaining trust with the interpreters allows them to incorporate not only their skills and cultural knowledge into the research, but also their motivation to facilitate a smooth and dynamic response from the participants.

5   Collaborative Interpretation: A Tripartite Approach

In our experience, as researchers and a former interpreter in Cambodia, in order to understand participant meaning and create quality qualitative data, an active approach to the dismantling of knowledge hierarchies and decolonization of research, particularly in the Cambodian context, is needed. As a result of our experiences in qualitative research in Cambodian education, we recognize the benefits and challenges of these methodologies. Consequently, we began to methodically approach our relationship with interpreters, particularly through training practices, the collaborative possibilities in the co-construction of meaning with interpreters, and what it meant to "take a backseat", or relinquish control to interpreters, in the research and interpretation process during qualitative interviews. A truly collaborative approach to interpretation in qualitative interviews must go beyond discussions of "power" with interpreters and serve to dismantle embedded interpreter and researcher knowledge hierarchies. Using strategies such as toolbox meetings before interviews and peer debriefing after interviews places researchers and interpreters at the center of the co-construction of meaning and yields rich, contextualized and inclusive data. While these strategies were developed across a number of education projects implemented at schools in Cambodia, we found that several projects related to gender and education challenged our understanding of the role of interpreters in interviews and focus groups. In particular, three qualitative projects examining gender equity in early childhood education and in secondary schools and a project examining barriers to post-secondary achievement for female graduates, provided some of the material and experiences used in developing and implementing these strategies. Over the course of these projects we worked with several interpreters. With one interpreter, we had a long-standing relationship through his work as a program manager at a local NGO. This program manager recommended other interpreters. When possible we worked with the same interpreters across multiple projects to support our working relationship with them and to provide constancy in the interview process.

6   Decolonizing Interpreter Consultations

Prior to interviews, we held brief interpreter consultations to ensure that purpose, objective, and approaches to interpretation in research were clearly outlined. We found that many interpreters had worked as English guides or did informal interpretations and were therefore unaware of the requirements of qualitative research, which included translating and documenting participants' exact words. The need for more than a summary was a challenge to interpreter training, and we sought to strike a balance between data that represented participants' views, beliefs and experiences, but also allowed interpreters to engage local knowledge, for example, in the form of probing questions and clarifications that would be missed if the researcher were to insist on verbatim translations or minimize the interactions between interpreters and participants.

This training, however, did not consist of a mere transfer of knowledge regarding research and the research topic but instead consisted of a collaborative conversation surrounding researcher and interpreter own understandings of gender, particularly in their own contexts. We used transcripts from our previous research projects conducted at a local NGO in Siem Reap to examine contextual gender vocabulary and to explore differences in meaning regarding challenging and highly contextualized Khmer words and phrases, or cultural conceptions and expectations that were new to the researcher. Discussion of these concepts, for example the Cambodian poem Chbab Srey, or rules for girls, allowed interpreters to bring their own contextual knowledge of gender, discuss the researchers' potential conflicting meanings or understandings, and to build a connection between the researcher, interpreter and the content of the interviews.

The deconstruction of contextualized meanings and local knowledge served two purposes in the processes of decolonizing what counted as knowledge in interviews. The first was to break down interpreters' beliefs regarding the researcher as the sole proprietor of expertise and knowledge, and allowed space to move beyond the common misconception that the interpreter held only language translation skills. An example includes an interpreter that we will call Dara. Dara worked as a gender equity manager at a local NGO-run school, where he had developed a local Khmer gender equity curriculum within this role. From this role, he developed an extensive knowledge of gender and the Cambodian context. Dara also had experience in translation and interpretation. I held the assumption that he would freely share this local knowledge while providing an interpretation that accurately conveyed participants' meaning. After the first interview, it became clear that Dara, despite his extensive experience, unintentionally was working from the belief of the researchers' "superior position". But, as a researcher who does not speak Khmer, the ability to capture particular Khmer phrases and cultural nuances surrounding the social construct of gender was challenging. It was from this experience, as we went back through the first transcript of the interview before moving to the second, that the need to dismantle the notion of the privileged knowledge of the researcher was apparent. In subsequent trainings, this became a focal point of discussion in attempting to examine the assumption of the researcher and interpreter that all knowledge, save linguistic knowledge, stemmed from the researcher. As we came across examples of interpreter knowledge in the transcripts, we discussed the importance of this knowledge to the research process.

A second purpose of using previous transcripts with interpreters, in addition to shifting researcher/interpreter understanding of what is legitimate knowledge, was to build rapport with the interpreter and accommodate interpreter local knowledge in the interview process. While the process described above was a technical piece to interpreter training, it also served in relationship building and creating a safe space for interpreters to engage and share their own knowledge. With rapport established between researcher and interpreter, coupled with the explicit acknowledgement that local knowledge is imperative to the co-construction of meaning, interpreters were asked/invited to participate in consultations before and after the interviews to further engage the interpreter in the interview process.

Discussions related to asking for clarification, probing, and privileging local knowledge, while adhering to practices which assure quality data proved to be vital. We found it necessary to involve interpreters in creating a balance in which the researcher is in a learner position as a result of the interpreter's knowledge, but is also remains informed on the content of the interview and is able to cooperate with the interpreter to ensure that what is communicated is both sensitively conveyed and germane to the research goals. Interpreter knowledge is critical in cross-language interviews, however, we have also had experiences in which data quality and participant experience were compromised when interpreters injected opinions which can make participants uncomfortable or which are inherently problematic by introducing, for example, inequitable attitudes and beliefs regarding gender in interviews. We have also had experiences in which data are lost, as interpreters engage with participants, but do not keep the researcher informed of the conversation and have forgotten previous content or have not fully translated participant responses. A balance was accomplished by creating a shared understanding of the importance of conveying participant data in a reliable and trustworthy manner, and that all parties served the common goal of co-creating meaning together, with no one excluded from the conversation for extensive periods of time. Practically this was addressed with the simple practice of notifying the researcher that the interpreter would be clarifying or probing, how they would be clarifying and probing, giving brief feedback to the researcher along the path of clarification and probing, and keeping notes written notes in English of what was being discussed so that the researcher could read along with the interpreters' conversation with participants.

While phases of clarifying and probing should remain fairly brief so that researcher and interpreter are moving along collaboratively, often the process takes time and falters when the researcher intervenes. Interpreter knowledge is then incorporated into the translation for the researcher, clearly demarcated as such by the interpreter. The most difficult part of the process is two-fold: first, ensuring that no data are lost in the process. It is imparted that everything still gets interpreted and relayed to the researcher verbatim, which can be a balancing act for the interpreter. Second, the researcher must adapt to a vacuum of information that is created through the interpretation process, yet interject for clarification if the researcher feels that the interpreting has gone for too long without a check-in. It is particularly helpful to have a second interpreter as well, both for note taking, clarification between interpreters and between interpreter and researcher, and, as will be discussed, for collaborative co-construction of meaning.

7 Co-Constructing Meaning with Interpreter Knowledge

In addition to interpreter training, interviews were constructed with the opportunity for interpreters to support the co-construction of meaning to include local knowledge. This began with a "toolbox" meeting before the interviews.

Toolbox meetings, commonly used in businesses to discuss safety and build rapport with employees, were an opportunity for interpreters to address questions surrounding the interview process, offer thoughts regarding previous interview strengths and challenges, and give voice to the interpreter process, as they experienced the contextual nuances and understandings surrounding the topics. While previous research has approached issues of power through "discussions" (Edwards, 2013), toolbox meetings provided more than just an opportunity to discuss the positionality of researchers and interpreters. This approach provided a forum for interpreter voice.

This process was initially unfamiliar to interpreters, as assumptions regarding the role of interpreters was entrenched in an understanding of what constitutes "good research". Particularly difficult was developing an understanding that while interpreters should provide local knowledge and understanding, that interpreter biases needed to also be challenged. This was particularly important in focus groups and interviews surrounding gender. This required rapport between researcher and interpreter in order to honestly challenge biases held by both interpreter and researcher. Another approach that we found useful was having a second interpreter, originally intended as an observer, whose role was to note behaviors, language exchanges, and cultural cues that might be missed during the interview. This second individual, who was also Khmer, participated in interpretation, and supported the unpacking of rich cultural concepts, and challenged interpreter bias or misinterpretations. This provided another layer of co-construction of meaning, and helped ensure accuracy of interpretation, which was particularly useful when contextual concepts were particularly meaning-laden and difficult to convey. The observer provided notes, which often served as secondary transcripts, to check for meaning and understanding along with the initial intent of providing body language cues and aspects of the interviews.

This approach was not flawless, and the original intent of the observer (to take observational notes), was not as fruitful as the opportunity for concurrent co-construction of meaning during and after interviews. This option was also costly. However, it was only after the first interview, when interpreter, observer, and researcher came together to discuss the interview, did we realize how valuable it was to have the opportunity to look through the notes of the observer and discuss participant meaning and opportunities for privileging local knowledge. During one interview with former high school students, this approach presented an opportunity for interpreter and observer to discuss graduates' discussions of family obligations and how the graduate viewed her "duties" to take care of parents and siblings. For women in Cambodia, this is a difficult balancing act, as the financial responsibility of aging parents and younger siblings falls to daughters. While this obligation is seen as an honorable role, the toll that it takes on girls and their educational opportunities is an issue.

During the interview, the observer pointed out conflicting meanings regarding experiences of family obligations, and interpreter and observer began to discuss, amongst themselves, and with the participant, clarification of these obligations. This was an important conversation as the interpreter was female and the observer was male. The researcher was briefed on the clarification and the disagreement regarding meaning during the clarification. After clarification, interpreter, observer and participant came to an understanding that represented the participant's experiences. Through clarification during interviews between interpreter and observer, and discussions between interpreter, observer, and researcher after the interview, the complex feelings and expectations related to daughters' role in families was clearly examined and everyone- researcher, interpreters and participant- arrived a deeper understanding of the nuances of this role, and how women dealt with its implications for their educational outcomes based on the participant's experience. This aspect of girls' Cambodian education could have easily been overlooked had the interpreter remained unchallenged in her own assumptions regarding girls' obligations.

7.1   *Taking a Backseat*

Researcher positionality may not be a typical topic of discussion with interpreters. However, we found that once the subject of whose knowledge was privileged in the interview/interpretation process were broached, the entire process flowed more smoothly. The difficulty, as a researcher who does not speak Khmer and who was entrenched in her own position as "researcher", i.e. the one with legitimate knowledge, was in allowing the time and space for the perceived silence that is part of the interpretation process when one does not speak the language of participants. The feeling of loss of control, while sitting in a vacuum of language and communication, can be maddening. Even with a sense of trust and rapport with interpreters and observers, the need to control the situation was overwhelming and frustrating. This need for control is legitimate, as trustworthiness of the findings remains a concern and is ultimately the researcher's responsibility.

The ability to "take a backseat" in the interviewing process is a balancing act. To "take a backseat" is to recognize and concede to the fluidity of power, roles and knowledge production between researcher, interpreter and participants in the interview process, to honor the time and space needed for interpretation and construction of meaning, and to embrace the importance of local knowledge. The ability to manage times when the researcher takes a secondary role is important in allowing interpreters and participants to arrive at meaning and understanding. Regular check-ins during the interpretation process, for example if the interpretation is going on for more than a few minutes without debriefing the researcher, can ensure that the researcher stays abreast on the information being conveyed, yet also allows interpreters to grasp dense meanings and understandings. This seems like a simple concept, yet probing with questions for and eliciting brief summaries from the interpreter is a delicate act that can disrupt important rapport and communication with the participant.

Also important is to remain engaged in the interpretation, even when the researcher does not know the language, and therefore, does not understand what is being discussed. This decreases the likelihood that the researcher will be forgotten in the process and also maintains the researcher, interpreter, and participant rapport. During interpretation participants can forget that the researcher does not understand the language and then engages both researcher and interpreter in the communication. It is important for participants to be "heard" by both interpreter and researcher, even if the researcher can only engage the participant through engaged body language. Taking a backseat does not mean total disengagement during the interpretation process, but instead requires careful navigation of the interview process without needlessly distracting interpreter and participant discussion. With researcher and interpreter providing directions, but allowing control of the process to fluidly shift amongst all involved in the interview process, this process brings voice and visibility to interpreters and participants and allows consensus on meaning-making by collaboratively constructing knowledge without privileging researcher knowledge.

Finally, learning at least a rudimentary level of the language can support researchers in "taking a backseat". While this is not always possible, this serves two purposes. First, introducing yourself in the local language, and being able to engage on a basic level of conversation during introductions builds rapport with participants. Second, the vacuum of communication discussed above dissipates when the researcher can listen for the few words that she knows and internally engage with participants' responses. The process of actively listening, even when the researcher can only understand basic phrases, eases discomfort and the desire to interrupt and control, increases trust between interpreter and researcher, and allows the researcher to engage in the interpretation and meaning making in small ways during the interview. This engagement can be as simple as probing during the appropriate time with questions such as 'I heard that she is talking about family here, and we know the importance of girls' family obligations and education. Can you tell me what she is saying about family?" The answer may or may not be important in the analysis of the final data, but the researcher, interpreter and participant are all then engaged in the interview and interpretation process, even if only briefly and once or twice during the entire interview. While learning basic levels of the local language may not always be possible, it is helpful in reducing researcher anxiety, allows the researcher to play a supporting role in the interview process, and gives space for interpreter local knowledge and meaning construction.

8   Conclusion

The central thesis of this chapter suggests building a collaborative role for interpreters in interviews and focus groups to support the dismantling of knowledge hierarchies and interrogate positivist paradigms in CIE research. We argue that the rigidity in the data collection process related to the positivist paradigm on the unobtainable goal of unbiased and verbatim data collection and analysis, reflects and reinforces the colonization of traditional research paradigms – the knowledge hierarchy and English-language primacy of the researchers, related to their identity, in an international, cross-language context. Relying on our years of experience in conducting qualitative research in a cross-language setting in Cambodia, we propose that in order to yield reliable, contextually relevant responses from participants leading to meaningful data, researchers must understand the important and collaborative role of interpreters, and allow such dynamic in the interview process.

We argue that interpreters are more than a conduit to the knowledge that researchers produce; however, with pressure and tension during the translation as a result of rigidity or inflexibility of the researchers, such as insisting on immediate and verbatim translation, translation materials are not as meaningful and in some cases less accurate. This rigid approach reflects the researchers' fixation on remaining objective, as well as effectively dehumanizing attitudes and behaviors toward interpreters as they assume a superior knowledge hierarchy and the power of English language, toward the interpreters. In this way, interpreters are treated as objects or "Other" whose knowledge and expertise are irrelevant or invalid. In this chapter, we suggest that researchers (a) meet with interpreters and construct a holistic scope of the study and their collaborative role in creating data, (b) co-construct meaning with the interpreters during and after the interview sessions, and (c) take a backseat while facilitating the conversations during the interview sessions (see Figure 12.1).

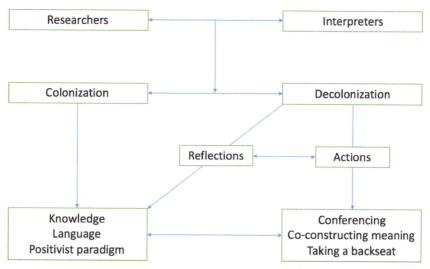

FIGURE 12.1   Decolonizing concepts between researchers and interpreters

Decolonizing practices in data collection, and research in general, requires researchers to reflect on their own identity (for example, the presumed superior education and language that they speak), and the paradigms in which their fields are embedded and practiced, and to take action towards working in equal partnership with the interpreters. This reflection develops awareness of the researcher's social and educational position in relation to the interpreters while their actions allow them to decolonize their practice during the data collection. Through reflections and subsequent actions, what Freire (1970) calls "praxis," true transformation of knowledge can occur, leading to the liberation of the researchers from a traditionally oppressive role, and the attainment of knowledge that is inclusive for all human beings, and the humanization of interpreters and participants in the research process.

References

Baily, S., Shah, P., & Call-Cummings, M. (2016). Reframing the center: New directions in qualitative methodology in international comparative education. In A. W. Wisemen & E. Anderson (Eds), *Annual review of comparative and international education 2015* (pp. 139–164). Oxford: Emerald Group Publishing Limited.

Baldwin, R. G. (1996). Faculty career stages and implications for professional development. In D. Finnegan, D. Webster, & Z. F. Gamson (Eds.), *Faculty and faculty issues in colleges and universities* (2nd ed.). Boston, MA: Pearson Custom Publishing.

Bawole, J. N., & Langnel, Z. (2016). Downward accountability of NGOs in community project planning in Ghana. *Development in Practice, 26*(7), 920–932.

Bogdan, R. C., & Biklen, S. K. (1998). *Qualitative research in education: An introduction to theory and methods.* Needham Heights, MA: Allyn and Bacon.

Brinkmann, S., & Kvale, S. (2015). *Interviews: Learning the craft of qualitative research interviewing.* Thousand Oaks, CA: Sage.

Chilisa, B. (2011). *Indigenous research methodologies.* Thousand Oaks, CA: Sage.

Crossley, M., & Tikly, L. (2004). Postcolonial perspectives and comparative and international research in education: A critical introduction. *Comparative Education, 40*(2), 147–156.

Edwards, R. (2013). Power and trust: An academic researcher's perspective on working with interpreters as gatekeepers. *International Journal of Social Research Methodology, 16*(6), 503–514.

Esposito, N. (2001). From meaning to meaning: The influence of translation techniques on non-English focus group research. *Qualitative Health Research, 11*(4), 568–579.

Essén, B., Jonsdotter, S., Hovelius, B., Gudmundsson, S., Sjöberg, N. O., Friedman, J., & Östergren, P. O. (2000). Qualitative study of pregnancy and childbirth experiences in Somalian women resident in Sweden. *British Journal of Obstetrics and Gynaecology, 107,* 1507–1512.

Fairclough, N. (1989). *Language and power.* London: Longman.

Freire, P. (1970). *Pedagogy of the oppressed* (pp. 65–80, M. B. Ramos, Trans.). New York, NY: Continuum.

Frewer, T. (2013). Doing NGO work: The politics of being 'civil society' and promoting 'good governance' in Cambodia. *Australian Geographer, 44*(1), 97–114.

Guba, E. G., & Lincoln, Y. S. (1994). Competing paradigms in qualitative research. In N. K. Denzin & Y. S. Lincoln (Eds.), *Handbook of qualitative research* (3rd ed., pp. 105–117). Thousand Oaks, CA: Sage.

Hoffman, E. (2007). Open-ended interviews, power, and emotional labour. *Journal of Contemporary Ethnography, 36*(3), 318–346.

Kivunja, C., & Kuyini, A. B. (2017). Understanding and applying research paradigms in educational contexts. *International Journal of Higher Education, 6*(5), 26–41.

Klees, S. J. (2008). Reflections on theory, method, and practice in comparative and international education. *Comparative Education Review, 52*(3), 301–328.

Mora, J., & Diaz, D. (2004). *Latino social policy: A participatory research model.* New York, NY: Haworth Press.

Morison, S. E. (1936). *Harvard college in the seventeenth century.* Cambridge, MA: Harvard University Press.

Saldanha, G., & O'Brien, S. (2014). *Research methodologies in translation studies.* London: Routledge.

Smith, L. T. (2013). *Decolonizing methodologies: Research and indigenous peoples*. London: Zed Books Ltd.

Squires, A. (2009). Methodological challenges in cross-language qualitative research: A research review. *International Journal of Nursing Studies, 46*(2), 277–287.

Takayama, K., Sriprakash, A., & Connell, R. (2017). Toward a postcolonial comparative and international education. *Comparative Education Review, 61*(S1), S1–S24.

Temple, B., & Edwards, R. (2002). Interpreters/translators and cross-language research: Reflexivity and border crossings. *International Journal of Qualitative Methods, 1*(2), 1–12.

Temple, B., & Young, A. (2004). Qualitative research and translation dilemmas. *Qualitative Research, 4*(2), 161–178.

Turner, S. (2010). Research note: The silenced assistant. Reflections of invisible interpreters and research assistants. *Asia Pacific Viewpoint, 51*(2), 206–219.

Wang, J. (2006). Questions and the exercise of power. *Discourse and Society, 17*(4), 529–548.

CHAPTER 13

Amplifying the Voices of People with Disabilities in Comparative and International Education Research with PhotoVoice Methodology

Alisha M. Braun

Abstract

Despite the increased attention to inclusion and diversity in comparative and international education policy and practice, the voices of people with disabilities often remain unheard or are silenced by dominant hegemonic discourses. To promote and enact a socially just and transformative ethos grounded in ethical participatory engagement between researchers and the researched, the stories and narratives of people with disabilities should actively be supported by the research methodologies we employ. PhotoVoice is an alternative methodology designed to realize this aim of amplifying the voices of marginalized communities in the research process and literature. This chapter explores the application of PhotoVoice methodology to the field of comparative and international education in the study of disability. Ghana is used as a single-country case in the Global South to illustrate the application of this methodology when researching the inclusion of students with disabilities. The research exemplar illustrates the types of findings that PhotoVoice methodology can offer the field and limitations to consider.

Keywords

photovoice methodology – disability – inclusion – Global South – Ghana – participatory action research – marginalization – comparative and international education

1   Introduction

"Nothing about Us without Us!" When reimagining the methods and methodologies used in comparative and international research, we should be reminded of this slogan that characterized the disability rights movement of the 1990s. These empowering words rallied by prominent disability activists around the world such as Michael Masutha and William Rowland in South Africa and James Charlton in the United States express the conviction of people with disabilities that they have the right to full and direct participation in policy and social issues that concern them. We can apply this slogan to comparative and international educational research to foster true inclusion and equal representation in research on and for people with disabilities. Despite the increased attention to inclusion and diversity in comparative and international education policy and practice, the voices of people with disabilities often remain unheard or are silenced by dominant hegemonic discourses. Literature on the inclusion of students with disabilities is commonly saturated with the voices and perspectives of educators, particularly in the Global South (e.g., Kuyini, Yeboah, Das, Alhassan, & Mangope, 2016; Nketsia & Salviita, 2013). To promote and enact a socially just and transformative ethos grounded in ethical participatory engagement between researchers and the researched, the stories and narratives of people with disabilities should actively be supported by the research methodologies we employ. PhotoVoice is an alternative methodology designed to realize this aim of amplifying the voices of marginalized communities in the research process and literature. This chapter explores the application of PhotoVoice methodology to the field of comparative and international education in the study of disability. Ghana is used as a single-country case in the Global South to illustrate the application of this methodology when researching the inclusion of students with disabilities.

To contextualize disability within comparative and international education discourse and scholarship, the chapter begins by introducing the term disability and provides a brief overview of the limited yet rising presence of disability in international education development policy agendas and in mainstream comparative and international education research literature. A justification of the need for a greater representation of the voices of people with disabilities within comparative and international education research is provided and scholars are encouraged to consider adopting this methodology as one way of fostering a more inclusive research space for all. A recently conducted study by the author and her research colleagues on access to higher education for students with mobility disabilities in Ghana closes the chapter as an exemplar to illustrate how PhotoVoice can be used to highlight the types of findings this methodology can offer the field and limitations to consider. Connections to the use of PhotoVoice research in the Global South in general and in Ghana specifically are embedded throughout the chapter to emphasize the value of using this methodology in these national and regional contexts.

2 Disability and Voice

2.1 *Linguistically Representing and Defining Disability*

A brief discussion of the linguistic representation and corresponding definition of the term disability is provided, given that the emphasis of this chapter is on using PhotoVoice methodology to amplify the voices of people with disabilities in comparative and international education discourse. There is no standard or uniform way of writing the term disability, however field-driven and personal choice differences are emerging in the use of a backslash, parenthesis, or other alternative ways of writing the term disability. These alternative linguistic representations are often intended to both visually and theoretically draw attention to the intersecting yet contextually defined boundaries between disability and ability. For example, disability studies scholar Goodley (2014) uses the term *dis/ability* to promote the reconceptualization of the categories of disability and ability, as well as the corresponding processes of disablism and ableism operating within a neoliberal social and political context. Similarly, feminist disability studies theorist Garland-Thomson (2009) uses the term *ability/disability system* to differentiate the culturally fabricated fictions of disability and ability on the basis of bodily variations that correspond to unequal distributions of power, status and resources within a social and architectural environment. Alternatively, instead of using a backslash, other scholars use parenthesis in their linguistic representation of disability. For example, Schalk (2017) uses the term *(dis)ability* to designate the socially constructed system of norms that categorizes, ranks, and values bodyminds based on the historically and culturally bound concepts of disability and ability. Schalk (2017) explains her preference to use the curve of the parenthesis in (dis)ability, rather than the hard, distinct line of the backslash in dis/ability or disability/ability, as the curve visually highlights the uneven, contestable, and context dependent nature of the boundaries between disability and ability.

In this chapter, disability is understood as a complex social construction that is historically, politically, socially, culturally, and economically context dependent. The term disability is used throughout this chapter to reflect the institutionalized use of the label for students who are identified by educational systems around the world as having a disability. In so doing, the chapter aims to bring attention to what Schuelka (2015) terms the paradox of inclusion, or the construction of labels of difference to better include. In the promotion of educational equity, social justice and inclusion, sociocultural labels like disability can serve a divisive role as markers of marginalization and difference, yet at the same time can serve a unifying advocacy role by increasing the visibility of groups considered to be outside of sociocultural norms. Regardless of whether conventional or alternative linguistic representations and related definitions of disability are used, those considering using PhotoVoice methodology to amplify the voices of people with disabilities in comparative and international research are encouraged to be thoughtful and clear in their approach given the complexities in the use of the term disability.

2.2   The Presence of Disability in Comparative and International Education

The visibility of disability on the global educational policy stage has gradually increased in recent years. The issue of access to education for people with disabilities in particular has risen to the international policy priority agenda as the global inclusive education movement continues to gain momentum. The United Nations' Convention on the Rights of Persons with Disabilities (CRPD) (UN, 2006) has been instrumental in the global inclusive education movement with its promotion of equal access to all levels of education for people with disabilities. Many nation states have endorsed this inclusive education policy directive by signing and ratifying the CRPD and adopting their own national inclusive education policies. To date, 161 countries or regional integration organizations have signed the convention and 92 of these have also signed its optional protocol (UN, 2018). Ghana, the site of this chapter's application, is among these countries, having signed both the convention and optional protocol in 2007, as well as ratified the convention and protocol in 2012 (UN, 2018). In addition to making these commitments to inclusive education at the global policy level, in May of 2016 Ghana launched a national Inclusive Education Policy dedicated to transforming the existing educational system into an inclusive system that educates learners with disabilities in mainstream schools through supports such as financial prioritization and strategic planning (Ministry of Education, 2016).

In addition to disability-focused policy directives like the UN CRPD and national inclusive education policies, disability and inclusive education are increasingly becoming reflected in broader international educational development agendas. A brief comparison of the current education UN Sustainable Development Goals (SDGS) with their Millennium Development Goals (MDGS) predecessor illustrates this upward trend of the attention being paid to disability in the international development arena. The UN Millennium Development Goals (MDGS) and Education for All (EFA) framework focused international development efforts on the issue of increasing access to education for disadvantaged populations with their universal primary education and gender parity indicators and targets from the late 1990s to 2015 (Ahmed, 2014). As we have left the MDG-EFA era, the international development emphasis on access to education is being replaced by an emphasis on quality education. Beginning in 1990, and accelerating to the 2015 MDG deadline, critique and attention has turned to learning quality (McGrath, 2014). A major criticism of the MDG-EFA framework was its failure to sufficiently address learning, which is at the core of the educational experience (Adams, 2012). While efforts during the MDG-EFA era were focused on getting children into school, less attention was paid to learning in school or the acquisition of knowledge and skills that enable children to live productive, healthy, safe lives.

To rectify these purported shortcomings, the UN Sustainable Development Goals (SDGS; UN, 2015) that are currently driving the post-2015 international education development agenda carry forth a renewed focus on access to quality education. SDG Goal 4 for quality education is designed to "ensure inclusive and quality education for all" (UN, 2015, p. 14). Furthermore, to situate disability within the international education development agenda, it is important to point out that disability is explicitly mentioned in two of the ten SDG Goal 4 targets. These include Target 4.5 with regard to ensuring equal access to all levels of education for the vulnerable, including people with disabilities, as well as Target 4.8 to build and upgrade education facilities that are disability-sensitive and inclusive.

Complimenting this gradual upward trend concerning the presence of disability in global educational policy discourse, the presence of disability within comparative and international education scholarship is limited, albeit slowly increasing over time. A comprehensive literature review by Brown (2014) analysing the presence of research on disability across four leading comparative and international education academic research journals, namely the *Comparative Education Review*, *International Journal of Educational Development*, *Comparative Education*, and *Compare: A Journal of Comparative Education*, documented the limited number of studies published on students with disabilities from the year 2000 to 2013. While the overall percentage of comparative education journal articles published on disability out of the total number of articles published in the field's leading journals during that time period was a mere 1.08%, the graphical distribution of the number of comparative education articles on disability published by year illustrated an upward trend (Brown, 2014). Figure 13.1 shows an updated extension of Brown's analysis to capture more recent activity by incorporating articles published in the field's leading journals on disability through 2018. Despite variations across years, the general trendline is in the positive direction, implying that the historically marginalized and overlooked population of people with disabilities is slowly gaining an increased presence in comparative education literature.

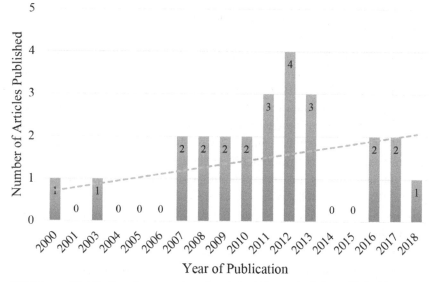

FIGURE 13.1 Distribution of comparative education articles on disability published by year

While it is encouraging to see disability's rising visibility within comparative and international research and the international development agendas that often motivate and guide research endeavours, continued work is needed to build upon this trend. People with disabilities have a heightened risk of educational marginalization and as a result are especially likely to be neglected or overlooked, particularly in the current international educational development context focused on quality education. This focus on excellence in policy and research may generate new concerns about equity because vulnerable and marginalized children are likely to be left behind in a system driven solely by learning outcomes. The United Nations Educational, Scientific and Cultural Organization (UNESCO, 2010) considers disability to be "one of the least visible but most potent factors in educational marginalization" (p. 181). For this marginalized population, concerns of equity are paramount given that children and adolescents with disabilities routinely have significantly lower school attendance and completion rates compared to peers without disabilities, especially in the Global South. For example, the primary school completion rate is 10% lower for girls with disabilities compared to girls without disabilities in 11 sub-Saharan African countries[1] and the disability gap for boys is 13% (Wodon, Male, Montenegro, and Nayihouba, 2018). Further research to address these educational injustices and exclusions on the basis of disability is essential to disrupt the reproduction of hierarchical educational inequity.

2.3 The Power of Voice and Participation

Beyond encouraging comparative and international education scholars to continue contributing scholarship on disability to further enhance the visibility of this marginalized population in the field, a key motivation for this chapter relates to the power of voice. Scholars from various disciplines have focused on issues of power, voice, and the representation of marginalized and historically silenced populations over the past two decades (Clifford & Marcus, 1986; Fine, 1998; Luttrell, 2010, as cited in Shah, 2015). This body of research emphasizes a participatory research by explicitly including the voices and perspectives of women and children into research and policy discourse (Corsaro & Miller, 1992; Clark, 1999; Luttrell, 2010, as cited in Shah, 2015). However, even when historically marginalized participants' voices and perspectives are included, those with disabilities are still largely ignored.

Despite disability's emerging presence and representation in shifting international educational equity discourse for comparative and international education, the voices of people with disabilities themselves are rarely featured in the literature. Instead, literature on access to education for students with disabilities remains dominated by the voices and perspectives of educators. For example, in Ghana, the vast majority of studies focus on teacher attitudes towards inclusive education and disability (Agbenyega, 2007; Kuyini et al., 2016; Nketsia & Saloviita, 2013; Ntuli & Traore, 2013; Obi, Mamah, & Avoke, 2007). While the perspectives of educators are undoubtedly essential to consider for the successful implementation of inclusive education policy in Ghana and other countries in the Global South, it is also important that voices of people with disabilities for whom these educational policies are intended to serve are also reflected in the literature. Sharing the stories and narratives of people with disabilities trying to navigate educational systems can help comparative and international educational researchers, practitioners and policymakers better understand first-hand experiences to inform how best to meet their unique needs and make inclusion a reality.

To do so, the field of comparative and international education can learn from other fields such as disability studies and health care that have incorporated the voices and active participation of people with disabilities in their research epistemologies (Hammel et al., 2008; Kehayia et al., 2014; Minkler et al., 2002). These fields experienced a paradigm shift during the Disability Rights Movement in the 1990s that influenced how research is conducted with people with disabilities in a more participatory and egalitarian manner, thereby acknowledging the importance of including people with disabilities in research that concerns them (Dassah, Aldersy, & Norman, 2017). This paradigm shift and its ensuing approach of involving people with disabilities as coresearchers complements the ongoing call in the field of comparative and international education for more participatory action research (e.g., Cooper, 2006; Crossley, 2010; Sallah, 2014). PhotoVoice research with people with disabilities is often used as a methodology within a participatory action research approach and will be explained in more detail in the following section.

3   PhotoVoice Methodology

PhotoVoice is a promising methodology that can enable the field of comparative and international education to open up safer, more inclusive spaces for the voices of people with disabilities to be heard in research that informs international educational development conversations.

3.1   *Methodological Overview and Disciplinary Origins*

PhotoVoice is a unique qualitative methodology that combines (1) photo taking, (2) interviews, and/or (3) writing about the content of the images (Dassah et al., 2017). These three components of the research methodology process are carried out by the participants who are often coresearchers themselves to capture personal experiences related to the topic of study in both visual and narrative forms. It is important to highlight this active role of participants as coresearchers in PhotoVoice methodology due to its onto-epistemological underpinnings in participatory action research, which differs from other research approaches that use image-intensive data where the roles of participants may be less participatory (see Onto-Epistemological Underpinnings section for more details). The three stages of this research approach often build upon one another in an iterative or sequential fashion, as the photographs that are taken using PhotoVoice methodology typically serve as a catalyst for further critical discussion about the research topic. Additionally, the photographs taken using this methodology can be useful for people with limited research experience or education, such as people with disabilities, to help shape a research conversation about salient issues in their local community (Dassah et al., 2017). In PhotoVoice methodology, not only does a photograph have the power to serve as a form of data in its own right that can be disseminated to give voice to the photographer in a visual form, but it also has the power to facilitate the interviewing and writing phases of the research process, thereby eliciting spoken and written narrative forms of voice that can also be disseminated. The multimodal utility of photographs when conducting and disseminating research within a PhotoVoice approach is a unique aspect and strength of this methodology, particularly when aspiring to create inclusive research spaces for the voices and narratives of people with disabilities to be heard.

PhotoVoice was originally designed to gain knowledge on Yunnan Chinese women's experiences (Wang and Burris, 1997) and has since been adapted by different disciplines to be used with various marginalized groups, including community rehabilitation and disability studies (Lal, Jarus, & Suto, 2012). In the field of comparative and international education, scholars have advocated for the increased use of participatory qualitative methods such as PhotoVoice to engage student and teacher voices on the ground in educational development (Lehtomäki et al., 2014), as well as to challenge dominant hegemonic discourses and contest epistemological issues of what can be known and how (Bailey, Shah, and Call-Cummings, 2015). While comparative and international educational research has used PhotoVoice methodology with marginalized student populations such as rural adolescent girls in India (Shah, 2015) and rural secondary students in Kenya (Milligan, 2016), disability as a category of marginalization remains largely absent.

3.2   Onto-Epistemological Underpinnings

PhotoVoice embodies the ethos of participatory action research by assuming that research participants are experts about the issues experienced in their local communities and should be actively involved in the production of knowledge about their contexts (Bisung et al., 2015; Castleden, Garvin, and First Nation, 2008; Wang and Burris, 1997). Accordingly, when using PhotoVoice methodology with people with disabilities, an inherent assumption underlying such an approach is that people with disabilities themselves are experts about the issues they are experiencing in their local communities, and thus have the right to be actively involved in producing knowledge about their experiences and contexts. Furthermore, the abovementioned accessibility element of the methodology utilizing photographs to catalyse research conversations coupled with its participant-cantered approach lends itself for use by people with disabilities. Bringing together the participant-centered knowledge production and analysis elements of the approach, PhotoVoice research has the power to present alternative perspectives and knowledge to challenge dominant hegemonic discourses, serving as both an analytic heuristic as well as a method of empowerment itself (Bailey et al., 2015; Shah, 2015).

To promote the empowerment of researched populations as experts and equals, extensive reviews of the PhotoVoice methodology since its inception in 1997 advocate for the importance of privileging participant voice at all stages of the research process (Catalani & Minkler, 2010; Dassah, 2017; Evans-Agnew & Rosemberg, 2016; Hergenrather, Rhodes, Cowan, Bardoshi, & Pula, 2009; Lal et al., 2012; Sanon, Evans-Agnew, & Boutain, 2014). Consistent with a participatory action research approach, it is recommended that participants serve as coresearchers or equal partners in the research problem identification, design and methodology, data collection, data analysis, and dissemination of the findings phases of the project (Castleden et al., 2008; Whyte, 1991). A unique way that coresearchers can disseminate and facilitate critical dialogue about community issues beyond traditional academic dissemination in books and journal article publications is via public art exhibitions of the photographs, as recommended by the PhotoVoice developers Wang and Burris (1997). Applying these participatory action research techniques to equalize power between the researchers and coresearchers when using PhotoVoice methodology in comparative and international education research can facilitate more inclusive research spaces for people with disabilities in the field.

4 PhotoVoice with People with Disabilities in the Global South

Beyond acknowledging the utility of PhotoVoice methodology with people with disabilities globally, existing literature suggests that this methodology is especially needed in the Global South. A recent literature review conducted by Dassah and colleagues (2017) on PhotoVoice calls for more research using this methodology with people with disabilities in the Global South because the methodology has the potential to empower marginalized groups. Stigma often serves as a barrier to full participation in PhotoVoice projects as coresearchers, and stigma is often experienced by people with disabilities in communities in the Global South to a greater degree compared to other world regions (Booyens, Van Pletzen, & Lorenzo, 2015). Furthermore, the potential utility of PhotoVoice in the Global South is more pronounced from a disability empowerment and advocacy standpoint due to the fact that people with disabilities in the Global South are often regarded as the poorest and most marginalized in the world (WHO, 2011). PhotoVoice methodology holds particular promise to help overcome the pronounced social exclusion and stigma experienced by people with disabilities in the Global South by inviting people with disabilities to participate in studies as coresearchers and providing a safe and supportive global avenue for their voices to be heard in comparative and international education literature.

4.1 *Research Exemplar*
To highlight the utility of PhotoVoice methodology for comparative and international education research, an example procedure and select findings related to exclusion and stigma from research conducted with people with disabilities in Ghana follows. Challenges encountered in the research are then discussed in connection to existing literature.

In a recent study by Braun and Naami (in press), PhotoVoice methodology is used to highlight the stories of students with mobility disabilities about the access barriers encountered in their daily lives navigating the postsecondary environment in Ghana. The goals of the study are to feature the voices of students with disabilities, seeking not only to identify barriers experienced firsthand when accessing the postsecondary environment, but also the emotional and academic impact of student experiences to provide a rich understanding of their educational journey to inform inclusive education policy and practice.

To accomplish these goals, the exploratory study was conducted as part of a larger study on accessibility challenges that people with physical mobility disabilities encounter in their daily lives in the Accra metropolis of Ghana. From the larger sample of 10 adults with mobility disabilities, the exemplar study focuses on the lived experiences of 2 students attending tertiary higher education institutions. Both postsecondary students are 26-year-old males. Evans is in his final year studying social work at a large public university and uses a wheelchair, while Felix is in his final year studying accounting at a mid-size public technical university and does not use any assistive devices for his mobility disability, which he describes as a hunchback.[2] Consistent with the participatory action research assumption mentioned previously that research participants are experts about the issues experienced in their local communities and should be actively involved in the production of knowledge about their contexts (Bisung et al., 2015; Castleden, Garvin, and First Nation, 2008; Wang and Burris, 1997), an underlying assumption of this study is that Felix and Evans are experts about the accessibility of postsecondary institutions in Accra, Ghana because they have to personally navigate and overcome challenges accessing various spaces and places within the physical environment as they go about their daily lives studying at the library, attending lectures, visiting instructors during office hours, eating at the cafeteria, using the bathroom facilities, mailing a letter at the campus post office, moving about their dormitory, and so on. Asking postsecondary administrators, educators, service staff or peers without disabilities about the physical accessibility of the campus would fail to capture first-hand lived experience and would likely miss some powerful insights that can only be gained from personal experience.

In accordance with the PhotoVoice tradition (Palibroda, Krieg, Murdock, & Havelock, 2009; Wang & Burris, 1997), coresearchers participated in two full-day workshops. In the first workshop, professional photographers and the lead researchers trained coresearchers in basic photography, research ethics, photo captioning, narration, and analysis of the content of the photos. Examples of places and things to look for when taking photographs to convey challenges with physical access barriers were discussed. The coresearchers were then each given a camera to take photos and journal their experiences for two months. In the second workshop, the content and context of the photographs taken were discussed in focus groups, as well as the meanings and messages attached to the photos, which were then related to the coresearchers' collective experiences. The 'SHOWeD' framework (Palibroda et al., 2009; Wang, 1999) was used to facilitate discussion and critical analysis of the content of the photographs with the following questions: What do you See here? What is really Happening here? How does this relate to Our lives? Why does this strength or problem/concern exist? What can we Do about it? The second workshop was audio-taped with coresearchers' permission and transcribed.[3]

Considering the emotional impact of experiences accessing the postsecondary educational environment, one finding that emerged from the photography and narrative data is the relative positioning of people with disabilities as being 'less than' in relation to their social roles as adults and as people. During focus group discussions about photographs taken, coresearchers frequently referred to their displeasure of being infantilized when they had to rely on others (e.g., fellow students, university staff) to help them move around campus. For example, Felix shares, "I feel ashamed whenever they hold my hand as a child although I am an adult. But, if they don't hold my hands, I cannot climb or descend the stairs". Likewise, Evans remarks, "I am not a child, but they always carried me as such ... I feel infantilized".

Beyond feeling excluded from the social category of 'adult' and being relegated to 'child' status, coresearchers also express feeling excluded from the social conception of 'person' or 'human'. To explain with an example, Evans aptly captions one of his narrations of a memory being carried upstairs by his classmates as, "I am a Person, Not an Object to Carry". The experience of having to be carried not only makes him feel like a child (i.e., infantilized) as explained above, but represents a form of objectification that denies him of his personhood.

The following narration and corresponding photograph in Figure 13.2 captioned by Felix as "I am not a car" provides another example of one's personhood being invalidated:

> This is the main entrance to university. It is a turning start entrance which I cannot use due to my condition. It is difficult to push through and risky as well. The security men at the entrance sometimes ask me to use the entrance for cars, which is more accessible, but I do not feel good about it because I am a human being and I should use the entrance for people and not the one for cars. I feel I am being treated unfairly by the university management by not providing an accessible entrance.

FIGURE 13.2   "I am not a car". Turn stall campus entrance gate in use

It is especially symbolic that the location where Felix's sense of personhood is challenged is the entrance to the university. If Felix feels inhuman and 'less than' when he enters the postsecondary campus, it is critical to question how that sets the stage for his daily experience and feelings of inclusion. Upon critically reflecting on the photographs through the PhotoVoice research process, Felix and Evans have the opportunity to reclaim the power that is lost by feeling like a child or an object by asserting their position in society as adults and as humans.

5   Challenges and Unintended Consequences in Context

PhotoVoice is often seen as an empowering, emancipatory method, but it is important for researchers to maintain awareness and foresight about potential challenges and unintended consequences associated with the method. For example, Call-Cummings and Martinez (2016) share the unintended consequences of their PhotoVoice study perpetuating and further entrenching oppressive relationships in the community with historically marginalized populations. To avoid such unintended consequences, Wang (2003, 2006) recommends that PhotoVoice be used as a first step in participatory research for needs assessment and planning purposes, rather than a last step exposing community members' deficiencies. People with disabilities are often socially perceived in a deficit-driven manner (e.g., see earlier discussion of dis/ability at beginning of chapter), so are increasingly susceptible in this regard. Given the focus of the research exemplar on highlighting the disabling elements of the external physical learning environment as opposed to situating deficiency and disability internally within a person, researchers aimed to reduce the potential of reinforcing oppressive community relationships.

Relatedly, Wang and Redwood-Jones (2001) caution PhotoVoice researchers to be sensitive to issues related to invasion of privacy, recruitment, representation, participation ownership and advocacy. Again, given the vulnerable position of people with disabilities in society, these ethical concerns are especially relevant when using PhotoVoice methodology with people with disabilities. In the exemplar study, special attention was paid to the expressed desires of our co-researchers to remain anonymous by using pseudonyms in all resultant research publications from the project. In contrast, coresearchers in other studies may wish to be identified by name for disability advocacy or personal ownership purposes. It is important to have open, authentic conversations throughout the PhotoVoice research process about these sorts of ethical decisions to ensure that everyone's rights are being respected.

Additional practical challenges related to adapting PhotoVoice methodology to meet the unique needs and abilities of coresearchers with disabilities in the research exemplar will now be highlighted and connected to existing literature. While some scholars express concern about the lack of a "uniform regimented structure" in PhotoVoice methodology (e.g., Sutton-Brown, 2014, p. 171), this can also be viewed as a strength of the method. To explain, the lack of a uniform structure provides the opportunity for flexibility and adaptation, which can be particularly beneficial when working with coresearchers with diverse physical and cognitive abilities. Previous research establishes that PhotoVoice should be tailored to address the developmental needs and capacities of coresearchers (Strack, 2004), such as adjusting the length and number of workshops (Warne, Snyder, & Gadin, 2012). Furthermore, coresearchers may not be familiar with the technical or artistic aspects of photography, so training in the use of equipment and techniques should be provided (Woodgate, Zurba, & Tennet, 2017; Lenette & Boddy, 2013). In the research exemplar study, similar adjustments to enhance the length and depth of photography training were made to accommodate the abilities and backgrounds of our coresearchers. It also became apparent during the research process that our coresearchers needed additional support completing their written narratives, so scribes were used to pen some of the coresearchers' spoken narratives. When conducting PhotoVoice research with people with disabilities, it is important to maintain flexibility throughout the research process so that adaptations can be made to meet the needs and capabilities of coresearcher and cultivate a truly inclusive, participatory research space.

Despite these methodological limitations and challenges, the above research case exemplar illustrates how the combined use of photographs and narration afforded by PhotoVoice methodology can augment critical discussion in postsecondary students with disabilities about issues of exclusion and educational access as they work through the research process. The methodology provides a multimodal visual and narrative way for their stories to be shared and disseminated to local and global community members. Further research utilizing PhotoVoice methodology in comparative and international educational research with people with disabilities is needed to continue to amplify additional voices and perspectives to enhance the representation of this marginalized population in global policy conversations about disability and equal access to education.

6 Conclusion

In closing, PhotoVoice methodology is an underutilized comparative and international education research practice that can promote and enact a socially just and transformative ethos anchored by an ethic of participatory engagement between researchers and the researched to feature the voices of people with disabilities more prominently in comparative and international education discourse. This chapter's country-specific case analysis of the inclusion of students with disabilities in Ghana within a cross-national discussion of relevant literature emphasizes the value and need for PhotoVoice research with people with disabilities to share their stories and narratives, particularly in the Global South. This is consistent with the current call in the field of comparative and international education to reshape the traditional flow of global knowledge production and exchange from the Global North to the Global South. Historically, the global diffusion of educational ideals has mostly flowed in a unidirectional North-South manner (Anderson-Levitt & Alimasi, 2001; Steiner-Khamsi, 2010). The field's desire to disrupt this pattern is evident in recent calls for papers in its leading journals and academic conferences (e.g., the 2018 Comparative and International Education Society annual conference theme was Re-mapping Global Education: South-North Dialogue). Not only does PhotoVoice methodology have the potential to amplify the voices of the poorest and most marginalized population of the world, but in so doing it further reinforces the field's broader aspiration to re-map and re-envision its historically rooted hierarchical regional divisions and inequities. Even with its limitations, PhotoVoice can address the underrepresentation and silencing of people with disabilities in comparative and international scholarship, practice, and policy.

Note

1 The 11 countries analyzed for disability gaps in educational attainment are: Burkina Faso, Ethiopia, Ghana, Kenya, Liberia, Mali, Malawi, Mozambique, South Africa, South Sudan, and Zambia.
2 Pseudonyms are used throughout to protect participant confidentiality.
3 Ethical clearance for all data collection procedures was obtained from the University of Ghana Office of Research Innovation and Development Ethics Committee for Humanities (approval #ECH 027/17-18).

References

Adams, A. M. (2012). *The education link: Why learning is central to the post 2015 global development agenda* (Working Paper 8). Washington, DC: The Brookings Institution.

Agbenyega, J. (2007). Examining teachers' concerns and attitudes to inclusive education in Ghana. *International Journal of Whole Schooling, 3*(1), 41–56.

Ahmed, M. (2014). Squaring the circle: EFA in the post-2015 global agenda. *International Journal of Educational Development, 39*, 64–69.

Anderson-Levitt, K., & Alimasi, N. (2001). Are pedagogical ideals embraced or imposed? The case of reading instruction in the Republic of Guinea. In B. A. U. Levinson & M. Sutton (Eds.), *Policy as practice: Toward a comparative sociocultural analysis of educational policy* (pp. 33–58). Westport, CT: Ablex.

Antonio, A., Astin, H., & Cress, C. (2000). Community service in higher education: A look at the nation's faculty. *Review of Higher Education, 23*(4), 373–398.

Baily, S., Shah, P., & Call-Cummings, M. (2016). Reframing the center: New directions in qualitative methodology in international comparative education. In A. Wiseman & E. Anderson (Eds.), *Annual review of comparative and international education 2015* (pp. 139–164). (International Perspectives on Education and Society Series). Bingley: Emerald Group Publishing.

Baldwin, R. G. (1996). Faculty career stages and implications for professional development. In D. Finnegan, D. Webster, & Z. F. Gamson (Eds.), *Faculty and faculty issues in colleges and universities* (2nd ed.). Boston, MA: Pearson Custom Publishing.

Bisung, E., Elliott, S., Abudho, B., Schuster-Wallace, C., & Karanha, D. (2015). Dreaming of toilets: Using photovoice to explore knowledge, attitudes and practices around water-health linkages in rural Kenya. *Health and Place, 31*, 208–215.

Braun, A. M. B., & Naami, A. (in press). Access to higher education in Ghana: Examining experiences through the lens of students with mobility disabilities. *International Journal of Disability, Development and Education*.

Booyens, M., Van Pletzen, E., & Lorenzo, T. (2015). The complexity of rural contexts experienced by community disability workers in three southern African countries. *African Journal of Disability, 4*(1), 1–9.

Brown, A. M. B. (2014). Situating disability within comparative education: A review of the literature. *Global Education Review, 1*(1), 56–75.

Call-Cummings, M., & Martinez, S. (2016). Consciousness-raising or unintentionally oppressive? Potential negative consequences of photovoice. *The Qualitative Report, 21*(5), 798–810.

Castleden, H., Garvin, T., & First Nation, H. (2008). Modifying photovoice for community-based participatory Indigenous research. *Social Science and Medicine, 66*, 1393–1405.

Catalani, C., & Minkler, M. (2010). Photovoice: A review of the literature in health and public health. *Health Education and Behavior, 37*, 424–451.

Clark, C. (1999). The autodriven interview: A photographic viewfinder into children's experience. *Visual Sociology, 14*(1–2), 39–50.

Clifford, J., & Marcus, G. (1986). *Writing culture: The poetics and politics of ethnography*. Berkeley, CA: University of California Press.

Cooper, E. (2006). What do we know about out-of-school youths? How participatory action research can work for young refugees in camps. *Compare: A Journal of Comparative and International Education, 35*(4), 463–477.

Corsaro, W., & Miller, P. (Eds.). (1992). *Interpretive approaches to children's socialization*. San Francisco, CA: Jossey-Bass.

Crossley, M. (2010). Bridging cultures and traditions in the reconceptualization of comparative and international education. *Comparative Education, 36*(3), 319–332.

Dassah, E., Aldersey, H. M., & Norman, K. E. (2017). Photovoice and persons with physical disabilities: A scoping review of the literature. *Qualitative Health Research, 27*(9), 1412–1422.

Evans-Agnew, R. A., & Rosemberg, M. S. (2016). Questioning photovoice research: Whose voice? *Qualitative Health Research, 26*, 1019–1030.

Fine, M. (1998). Working the hyphens: Reinventing self and other in qualitative research. In N. Denzin & Y. Lincoln (Eds.), *The landscape of qualitative research: Theories and issues* (pp. 130–155). Thousand Oaks, CA: Sage.

Garland-Thomson, R. (2009). Integrating disability, transforming feminist theory. In R. Warhol-Down & H. D. Price (Eds.), *Feminism Redux: An anthology of literary theory and criticism* (pp. 487–513). New Brunswick, NJ: Rutgers University Press.

Goodley, D. (2014). *Dis/Ability studies: Theorising disablism and ableism* (1st ed.) New York, NY: Routledge.

Hammel, J., Magasi, S., Heinemann, A., Whiteneck, G., Bogner, J., & Rodreguez, E. (2008). What does participation mean? An insider perspective from people with disabilities. *Disability and Rehabilitation, 30*, 1445–1460.

Hergenrather, K. C., Rhodes, S. D., Cowan, C. A., Bardhoshi, G., & Pula, S. (2009). Photovoice as community-based participatory research: A qualitative review. *American Journal of Health Behavior, 33*, 686–698.

Kehayia, E., Swaine, B., Longo, C., Ahmed, S., Archambault, P., Fung, J., ... Poldma, T. (2014). Creating a rehabilitation living lab to optimize participation and inclusion for persons with physical disabilities. *European Journal of Disability Research, 8*, 151–157.

Kuyini, A. B., Yeboah, K. A., Das, A. K., Alhassan, A. M., & Mangope, B. (2016). Ghanaian teachers: Competencies perceived as important for inclusive education. *International Journal of Inclusive Education, 20*(10), 1009–1023.

Lal, S., Jarus, T., & Suto, M. (2012). A scoping review of the photovoice method: Implications for occupational therapy research. *Canadian Journal of Occupational Therapy, 79*, 181–190.

Lehtomäki, E., Janhonen-Abruquah, H., Tuomi, M. T., Okkolin, M., Posti-Ahokas, H., & Palojoki, P. (2014). Research to engage voices on the ground in educational development. *International Journal of Educational Development, 35*, 37–43.

Lenette, C., & Boddy, J. (2013). Visual ethnography and refugee women: Nuanced understandings of lived experiences. *Qualitative Research Journal, 13*(1), 72–89.

Luttrell, W. (2010). A camera is a big responsibility: A lens for analysing children's visual voices. *Visual Studies, 23*(3), 224–237.

McGrath, S. (2014). The post-2015 debate and the place of education in development thinking. *International Journal of Educational Development, 39*, 4–11.

Milligan, L. (2016). Insider-outsider-inbetweener? Research positioning, participative methods and cross-cultural educational research. *Compare: A Journal of Comparative and International Education, 46*(2), 235–250.

Minkler, M., Fadem, P., Perry, M., Blum, K., Moore, L., & Rogers, J. (2002). Ethical dilemmas in participatory action research: A case study from the disability community. *Health Education and Behavior, 29*, 14–29.

Morison, S. E. (1936). *Harvard College in the seventeenth century*. Cambridge, MA: Harvard University Press.

Nketsia, W., & Saloviita, T. (2013). Pre-service teachers' views on inclusive education in Ghana. *Journal of Education for Teaching, 39*(4), 429–441.

Ntuli, E., & Traore, M. (2013). A study of Ghanaian early childhood teachers' perceptions about inclusive education. *The Journal of the International Association of Special Education, 14*(1), 50–57.

Obi, F., Mamah, V., & Avoke, K. (2007). Inclusive education in an emerging country: The state of teacher preparedness in Ghana. *Journal of International Special Needs Education, 10*.

Palibroda, B., Krieg, B., Murdock, L., & Havelock, J. (2009). *A practical guide to photovoice: Sharing pictures, telling stories and changing communities*. Winnipeg: Prairie Women's Health Centre of Excellence.

Sallah, M. (2014). Participatory action research with 'minority communities' and the complexities of emancipatory tensions: Intersectionality and cultural affinity. *Research in Comparative and International Education, 9*(4), 402–411.

Sanon, M., Evans-Agnew, R. A., & Boutain, D. M. (2014). An exploration of photovoice research studies from 2008 to 2013. *Nursing Inquiry, 21*, 212–226.

Schalk, S. (2017). Critical disability studies as methodology. *Lateral: Journal of Cultural Studies Association, 6*(1).

Schuelka, M. J. (2015). The evolving construction and conceptualisation of disability in Bhutan. *Disability and Society, 30*(6), 820–833.

Shah, P. (2015). Spaces to speak: Photovoice and the reimagination of girls' education in India. *Comparative Education Review, 59*(1), 50–70.

Steiner-Khamsi, G. (2010). The politics and economics of comparison. *Comparative Education Review, 54*(3), 323–342.

United Nations. (2006). *Convention on the rights of persons with disabilities* (UN Document A/RES/61/106). New York, NY: Author.

United Nations. (2015). *Transforming our world: The 2030 agenda for sustainable development* (UN Document A/RES/70/1). New York, NY: Author.

United Nations. (2018). *Convention on the rights of persons with disabilities.* Retrieved from the UN Treaties Collection website https://treaties.un.org/doc/Publication/MTDSG/Volume%20I/Chapter%20IV/IV-15.en.pdf

United Nations Educational, Scientific and Cultural Organization. (2010). *Education for all global monitoring report 2010: Reaching the marginalized.* Paris: Author.

Wang, C. C. (1999). Photovoice: A participatory action research strategy applied to women's health. *Journal of Women's Health, 8*(2), 185–192.

Wang, C. C. (2003). Using photovoice as a participatory assessment and issue selection tool: A case study with the homeless in Ann Arbor. In M. Minkler & N. Wallerstein (Eds.), *Community-based participatory research for health* (pp. 179–196). San Francisco, CA: Jossey-Bass.

Wang, C. C. (2006). Youth participation in photovoice as a strategy for community change. *Journal of Community Practice, 14*(1–2), 147–161.

Wang, C., & Burris, M. A. (1997). Photovoice: Concept, methodology, and use for participatory needs assessment. *Health Education and Behaviour, 24*(3), 369–387.

Wang, C. C., & Redwood-Jones, Y. A. (2001). Photovoice ethics: Perspectives from Flint Photovoice. *Health Education and Behaviour, 28*(5), 560–572.

Whyte, W. F. (1991). *Participatory action research.* Newbury Park, CA: Sage.

Wodon, Q., Male, C., Montenegro, C., & Nayihouba, A. (2018). *The challenge of inclusive education in Sub-Saharan Africa: The price of exclusion* (Disability and education series). Washington, DC: The World Bank.

Woodgate, R. L., Zurba, M., & Tennet, P. (2017). Worth a thousand words? Advantages, challenges and opportunities in working with photovoice as a qualitative research method with youth and their families. *Forum: Qualitative Social Research, 18*(1).

PART 4

Implications for Methodology: Towards More Equitable Futures

CHAPTER 14

Implications for Methodology: Towards More Equitable Futures

Supriya Baily, Betsy M. Scotto-Lavino and Meagan Call-Cummings

Abstract

In this chapter we frame the future of CIE research at a time of conflicting and intersecting ideas. Where do we want CIE research to go? At the symposium, speakers debated the complexity of quality, rigor, impact, and ethics as those issues pertained to new developments in the field. Over the past twenty years we see shifts in methodological approaches to move beyond the narrower definitions of empiricism and science. This chapter continues this call for methodological and onto-epistemological imagination to ask novice and experienced scholars to expand our definitions of quality and to seek out methods to diversify audiences, values, and outcomes. We push researchers to ask themselves if it is possible to engage with researcher reflexivity and the decolonization of methods while conducting research that is seen as 'scientific' and has the impacts we – and those to whom we are answerable, desire? Finally, we explore how our various ontological and epistemological identities and subjectivities find a space in the development, implementation, and dissemination of research. We argue that scholars must push the system in equitable directions by agreeing that *impact* can be broader than citation figures and by reflecting the transformation of individual or community lived experiences.

Keywords

future – methodological diversity – equity – decolonization – innovation

1   Introduction

The struggle to understand depends on both the way in which the messenger frames their message and the translation of this message to the receiver. For too long, the world has operated in single frames, where structures of power have established primacy both as the arbiter of knowledge and the exporter of what ought to be considered excellent. These structures, which include but are not limited to patriarchy, race, linguistic dominance, and colonization, support a world where knowledge generation and dissemination has predominantly been male, white, English speaking, and colonial. In a context where these structures continue to dominate, at times and in ways that do harm to others, the challenge has been to create space for alternative forms of knowledge. Unfortunately, due to the overwhelming influence of those structures across not only those who live in those frames but for those who are denied space within those frames, the very nature of the value of other ways of knowing is deemed suspicious or doubtful.

This was the foundation for our question at the symposium and in this final section of the book: what does the future of comparative and international education (CIE) research look like? As policymakers, practitioners, and scholars, where do we want CIE research to go? Plenary speakers debated the complexity of quality, rigor, impact, and ethics as they saw those issues pertain to new developments in the field. Over the past twenty years we have seen shifts in methodological approaches that attempt to move beyond the narrower definitions of empiricism and science and the pursuit of objectivity and neutrality as the gold standard. We have witnessed the embrace of new ontoepistemological approaches, fresh methodological designs, and innovative and increasingly technology-savvy tools. Scholars are more willing to take risks with their research and to push against more traditional, positivist notions of what knowledges should be honored, valued, and rewarded, creating an urgency to reconceptualize quality in this landscape while also ensuring that our research is meaningful and useful.

As we continue to contemplate our initial questions, the contributions of plenary speakers at the symposium, and the chapters included in this section, we find ourselves still grappling with how CIE moves on from here. We echo Art Bochner's (2000) "desire to create new and more interesting ways to talk about the work that many of us are doing" (p. 267) as we continue to push against and yet feel ourselves enveloped and constrained by dominant criteria, concepts, and definitions:

> In our hearts, if not in our minds, we know that the phenomena we study are messy, complicated, uncertain, and soft. Somewhere along the line, we became convinced that these qualities were signs of inferiority, which we should not expose. It appeared safer to keep the untidiness of our work to ourselves, rather than run the risk of having our word belittled

as 'unscientific' or 'unscholarly'. We seem uncommonly neurotic in our fear of having our little secret discovered, so we hide behind the terminology of the academic language games we've learned to play, gaining some advantage by knowing when and how to say 'validity', 'reliability', 'grounded', and the like. Traditionally, we have worried much more about how we are judged as 'scientists' by other scientists than about whether our work is useful, insightful, or meaningful – and to whom. We get preoccupied with rigor but are neglectful of imagination. (Bochner, 2000, p. 267)

In an effort to productively respond to this call for methodological and onto-epistemological imagination, we ask, how do we expand our definitions of quality? To what extent do methods complement or compete in terms of audience, value, and outcome? Is it possible to engage with researcher reflexivity and the decolonization of methods while conducting research that is seen as 'scientific' and that has the impacts we – and those to whom we are answerable (Patel, 2016) – desire? And most critically, how do our various ontological and epistemological identities and subjectivities find a space in the development, implementation, and dissemination of research?

This was something that Lesley Bartlett (2017) posited in her approach to these ideas. She shared at the symposium:

> We have what historian of science Theodore Porter (1996) called a "trust in numbers" that has encouraged us to avoid the politics of measurement (much as Ferguson [1994] described) and ignore what Radhika Gorur (2016) calls the performativity of international assessments. Further, because CIE is a "big tent" field, with multiple disciplines represented, we seem to have tacitly agreed not to question the politics of each other's methods.

We also draw from Peter Demerath's (2017) ideas, as he argued at the symposium:

> We need to push for complementarity between diverse forms of knowledge production. All the while we need to seek to have broader impacts beyond academia, heeding Norma Gonzalez's 2005 observation that, "We can't influence educational communities if we produce knowledge only for colleagues".

Finally, bringing in ideas from scholars who do not call comparative and international education their home discipline, Lilliana Saldaña (2017) returned to the central notion of the influence research must have on social justice in education:

> For Chicana/o scholars in education, research is about healing from historical trauma and colonial wounds, affirming our existence in curricula, and dignifying our humanity in the face of settler-colonial practices that continue to inflict linguistic, epistemic, and cultural violence in our schools and communities (Tuhiwai Smith, 2012).

If we agree with Demerath's (2017) point, that research must be written for a broader audience, and our work must be digested by more than just a small subsection of our peers, and we are aligned with Saldaña's (2017) call that research must offer restorative justice to marginalized communities, the collective we, searching for greater equity in broadening the ways of knowing, can begin to advocate for those shifts in our own work as researchers. Offering novice researchers a chance to write, both as academics to further their career and more accessibly for the broader public, can be institutionally supported. Scholars can push the system in equitable directions by agreeing that *impact* can be broader than citation figures and by reflecting the transformation of individual or community lived experiences.

2 Countering Hegemony in CIE Research

The counter narratives that are emerging, across so many intersections of identity, push back against the 'hegemony of the metropole' (Connell, 2010). For Connell, the 'metropole' is the term used to identify those capital-rich countries in North America and Europe, oftentimes, former imperialist powers that are connected to the nexus of military, economic and cultural supremacy. Connell finds this "hegemony of the metropole is a tangible reality for researchers everywhere else in the world" (p. 608). This is the argument that Ghaffar-Kucher makes in her chapter, that with the one-directional flow of information, will researchers ever truly be able to decolonize the structures that are supported and sustained? We would add that the intersection of power between economic, military, and cultural supremacies does not necessarily mean that knowledge produced in certain local contexts does not also sustain and support hegemonic knowledges. Similarly, frames of patriarchy, class, language, and ideologies can produce their own loco-hegemons as well.

As we contemplate how CIE moves forward, we appreciate the centrality of power and acknowledge the dynamic, fluid, and situated personal and material entanglements (Barad, 2007) that make this conversation so complex. At the same time, we agree with our plenary speakers – and with, we are sure, many if not all symposium audience members and presenters – that in order to move forward in ethical and response-able (Battiste, 2013) ways, we must first root out and make explicit our subjectivities and collectively confront and interrupt the violence caused by accepted, depoliticized methodological practices and orientations. Confrontation requires accurate recognition of the opposing force. Have we accurately recognized the forces we are resisting? Connell, Collyer, Maia and Morrell (2017) contend that the erroneous use of the words "knowledge system" emphasizes "boundaries and closure" and "a static, consensual picture of knowledge formations, rather than a dynamic and internally conflictual picture" (p. 25). This faulty conceptualization produces practices that reproduce power dynamics. McGarry (2016) puts this another way:

> Power and knowledge are inextricably linked, knowledge should be seen as a dynamic product of the power relations governing the specific context in which is produced (Foucault, 1977, p. 194). It follows therefore, that a failure to understand the power relations characterizing the research process must necessarily lead to a misconception of the knowledge generated through the process. (p. 341)

Edward's chapter in this volume, detailing the flawed logic on which most quantitative studies are based, exemplifies the danger of this misconception going unchecked. Ghaffar-Kucher's chapter, a critique and challenge to the power structures that determine the flow of information from the "Minority North" to the "Majority South", allows us to imagine an alternate reality of bidirectional information flow. These pieces demonstrate the potential of an individual researcher to chip away at established beliefs and norms, creating space for new methods and conceptions to emerge when understanding that the relations between power and research are both acute and continuously evolving through researcher self-awareness, intentionality, and accountability.

In the same vein, researchers can use reflexivity to "legitimize, validate, and question research practices and representations" (Pillow, 2003, p. 175). Milner (2007) highlights the critical step of reflexivity to avoid the, "dangers (that) can emerge when and if researchers do not engage in processes that can circumvent misinterpretations, misinformation, and misrepresentations of individuals, communities, institutions and systems" (p. 388). Milner (2007) provides a framework of self-reflection to better understand one's positionality as integral to remediating these dangers. This framework is comprised of three parts:

- An examination of the self to "bring to awareness and consciousness known (seen), unknown (unseen), and unanticipated (unforeseen) issues, perspectives, epistemologies, and positions";
- An examination of the research in terms of others around them and involved in the research; and finally,
- Action that bridges both reflection and representation, where "researchers and participants engage in reflection together" in order to prevent one perspective dominating the interpretation (Milner, 2007, pp. 395–396).

While training in researcher reflexivity has expanded in influence, Hằng, DeCoster, Gombin-Sperling, and Reedy point out in this volume that,

> The emerging normativity of reflexivity cannot be taken for granted as victory. For us, there have been many moments of discomfort with the ways that we are being taught about this practice. Much of the attention seems to be on establishing the importance of reflexivity, which leaves the actual process less examined.

Examining reflexivity, highlighting our biases, privileges, and power as researchers, and moving beyond the need to define a single, knowable truth, are all goals we hope researchers would seek to consider as they think about methodology in their work.

3 Concluding Thoughts

So can we argue that the future of comparative and international education research is determined by more fluidity in the methods, purposes, dissemination, and *value* of research? Can we hone the quality of knowledge production with greater awareness of our prejudices and deeper reflection on our motivations for why and how we conduct research? This struggle to understand positionality is shared by researchers across disciplines with varying expertise. Earl (2017) describes wrestling with her positionality and candidly shares her own discomfort with the process despite being a more experienced researcher:

> Understanding how to create critical distance from the happenings witnessed whilst attempting to assist the movement from the position of a researcher and academic activist ... is not an easy place to live, and this kind of work often stands at one side or the other of the interstice between hope and despair, solidarity and frustration, and love and bitterness. (p. 130)

In understanding the imperial/colonial metamorphosis, Mignolo (2013), argues for an allegiance of the whole world to participate in the decolonial process which cannot be a project of a "linear narrative of modernity (rather) a radical *undoing* of modernity/coloniality in order to build a world of differences without hierarchies: a polycentric rather than a unipolar world" (p. 111, emphasis in original). Are we up for this challenge? Are we, as researchers, scholars, knowledge producers and consumers, willing to better understand the power we hold and to undo some of our own frames in order to make space for other forms of knowledge and to engage with other types of researchers? Ones who might test our own onto-epistemological beliefs and with whom we might not find any common ground? Are we ready for that future?

References

Barad, K. (2007). *Meeting the universe halfway: Quantum physics and the entanglement of matter and meaning.* Durham, NC: Duke University Press.

Bartlett, L. (2017, October). Symposium statement. In *Proceedings of the 2nd Comparative and International Education Symposium: Interrogating and Innovating CIE Research.* Arlington, VA: George Mason University. Retrieved from https://cehd.gmu.edu/2017symposium/

Battiste, M. (2013). *Decolonizing education: Nourishing the learning spirit.* Saskatoon: Purich Publishing Limited.

Bochner, A. P. (2000). Criteria against ourselves. *Qualitative Inquiry, 6,* 266–272. doi:10.1177/107780040000600209

Connell, R. (2010). Kartini's children: On the need for thinking gender and education together on a world scale. *Gender and Education, 22,* 603–615.

Connell, R., Collyer, F., Maia, J., & Morrell, R. (2017). Toward a global sociology of knowledge: Post-colonial realities and intellectual practices. *International Sociology, 32,* 21–37.

Demerath, P. (2017, October). New frontiers in ethnographic and comparative education research: The relational turn and emotion culture. In *Conference Proceedings of the 2nd Comparative and International Education Symposium: Interrogating and Innovating CIE Research.* Arlington, VA: George Mason University. Retrieved from https://cehd.gmu.edu/2017symposium/

Earl, C. (2017). The researcher as cognitive activist and the mutually useful conversation. *Power and Education, 9,* 129–144. doi:10.1177/1757743817714281

Ferguson, J. (1994). *The anti-politics machine: Development, depoliticization, and bureaucratic power in Lesotho.* Minneapolis, MN: University of Minnesota Press.

Foucault, M. (1977). *Discipline and punish: The birth of the prison.* London: Allen Lane.

Gonzalez, N. (2005). *Anthropology and education: Reflections on the field*. Paper presented at invited session of the American Anthropological Association Annual Meeting, San Francisco, CA.

Gorur, R. (2016). Seeing like PISA: A cautionary tale about the performativity of international assessments. *European Educational Research Journal, 15,* 598–616. doi:10.1177/1474904116658299

McGarry, O. (2016). Repositioning the research encounter: Exploring power dynamics and positionality in youth research. *International Journal of Social Research Methodology, 19,* 339–354.

Mignolo, W. (2013). Imperial/colonial metamorphosis: A decolonial narrative, from the Ottoman Sultanate and Spanish Empire to the US and the EU. In G. Huggan (Ed.), *The Oxford handbook of postcolonial studies.* Oxford: Oxford University Press.

Milner, H. (2007). Race, culture, and researcher positionality: Working through dangers seen, unseen, and unforeseen. *Educational Researcher, 36,* 388–400. doi:10.3102/0013189X07309471

Patel, L. (2016). *Decolonizing educational research: From ownership to answerability.* New York, NY: Routledge.

Pillow, W. (2003). Confession, catharsis, or cure? Rethinking the uses of reflexivity as methodological power in qualitative research. *International Journal of Qualitative Studies in Education, 16,* 175–196. doi:10.1080/0951839032000060635

Porter, T. M. (1996). *Trust in numbers: The pursuit of objectivity in science and public life.* Princeton, NJ: Princeton University Press.

Saldaña, L. P. (2017, October). Symposium statement. In *Conference Proceedings of the 2nd Comparative and International Education Symposium: Interrogating and Innovating CIE Research.* Arlington, VA: George Mason University. Retrieved from https://cehd.gmu.edu/2017symposium/

Tuhiwai Smith, L. (2012). *Decolonizing methodologies: Research and indigenous peoples* (2nd ed.). London: Zed Books.

CHAPTER 15

CIE Methodology and Possibilities of Other Futures

Ameena Ghaffar-Kucher

Abstract

In this chapter, Ghaffar-Kucher explores the possibilities of decolonizing academia and the fields of comparative and international educational development specifically. To do so, she provides tangible steps that researchers and practitioners in the field of CIE (and International Educational Development more specifically) can take to destabilize dominant forms of knowledge production, an important corrective actions that moves us in the direction of decolonization. These steps are centered around pushing back against the dominant trends in CIE research in terms of data, methods, conceptual frameworks and location of research.

Keywords

decolonization – colonialism – post-colonialism – academia – knowledge – data – research – methodology

> *when you take away the punctuation*
> he says of
> lines lifted from the documents about
> military-occupied land
> its acreage and location
> *you take away its finality*
> *opening the possibility of other futures*
>   F. VOELTZ (Body of Work/When You Take Away the Punctuation
>   quoting *Craig Santos Perez, Chamuru scholar and poet*)

1 Introduction

Of late, there has been a great deal of discourse in academia more generally, and the field of Comparative and International Education (CIE) specifically, around "decolonizing" our research, our teaching, and our practice. Attempts around this decolonizing include paying attention to whom we cite, what we assign our students to read, and how we engage with our research participants and partners. The growing calls to decolonize the CIE field are not surprising given the colonial roots of the CIE sub-fields of comparative education (CE) and international educational development (IED), which have grown in tandem with "the development of capitalism as a global economic system" (Roy, Negrón-Gonzales, Opoku-Agyemang, & Talwalker, 2016, p. 9).

With its colonial roots and Eurocentric economic worldview, the field of IED in particular leaves little room for other ways of knowing, seeing or hearing the world. Instead, it leads us to dividing the world into binary categories, pitted as polar opposites of haves and have-nots[1]: first and third; developed and developing; east and west; north and south; metropole and satellite. Our knowledge flow is one directional: from the Minority World or Global North, downwards to the Majority World or Global South. Given this unidirectional knowledge flow, our methodologies are also limited. We are so deeply entrenched in our ways of knowing, seeing, hearing, understanding, and feeling the world that there is little room for us to think otherwise that could actually lead to any semblance of decolonization. Even the framing of the 2017 CIES Symposium that has brought together several of the authors in this volume – with words like decolonization, scientific, rigor – are entrenched in a particular way of knowing the world. This particular worldview has largely been informed by colonialism and "western" (read: white, Christian, cis-male, heterosexual, Eurocentric) epistemologies and ontologies.

While the rhetoric and some preliminary actions are there, in my view, we are falling short of any genuine decolonization efforts. In this chapter, I explain why I believe that decolonization is not within our grasp – at least not in the near future. Instead, I propose tangible steps that researchers and practitioners in the field of CIE (and International Educational Development more specifically) can take to destabilize dominant forms of knowledge production, an important corrective action that moves us in the direction of decolonization. These steps are centered around pushing back against the dominant trends in CIE research in terms of data, methods, conceptual frameworks and location of research. I begin with discussing my understandings of decolonization.

2 Decolonizing or Destabilizing?

My main point of contention in this essay is that we[2] – members of the Global North academy – are not ready to decolonize CIE research. To understand why I do not believe decolonization is within our reach requires us to first have some semblance of a definition of colonialism – a term that has eluded a clear understanding. Horvarth (1972) defined colonialism simply as "a form of domination – the control of individuals or groups over territories and behavior of other ... the idea of domination is closely related to the concept of power" (p. 46). Loomba (1998) takes a more critical view and not only distinguishes between different eras of colonialism, but also links modern colonialism to capitalism. Specifically, she defines colonialism as "the forcible takeover of land and economy, and, in the case of European colonialism, a restructuring of non-capitalist economies in order to fuel European capitalism" (p. 40). The word "decolonization", then, in one sense can be understood as the "undoing" of colonialism.

To genuinely decolonize CIE research would thus require a systemic overhaul of the current academic system, which thrives on hierarchies and intense competition for grant money, publications, and promotions (see Ghaffar-Kucher, 2016), and the belief in a "homogeneous domain of knowledge" (Connell, 2014, p. 211). To genuinely decolonize our work would also require some serious reparation on our part, as a way to concede the power and authority that we have taken and at times been bestowed with (as a result of colonial encounters). In terms of tangible actions (within academia at least), these reparations would mean putting our third-world thought partners as first author, no matter who has done the bulk of the work. It would mean publishing in journals of and from the Global South, even if these are not recognized by our tenure committees in the academy. It would mean engaging in theories from the periphery, even if they do not fit in with our current forms of knowledge and theorizing. It would mean writing publications in languages other than English. It would mean changing how we disseminate information, not just in terms of "open access" and more accessible writing and languages, but also other forms of dissemination – storytelling, movie making, plays, poetry, spoken word – and acknowledging or "counting" these as legitimate and scholarly. It would mean changing the standards of what we consider to be valid data, even if it means taking risks and exploring the metaphysical, the fantastic, and the unobservable.

In suggesting these reparations as part of the decolonizing process, by no means am I suggesting that we "go back" to pre-colonial times or that this would even help undo colonialism. This of course is an impossible task given the messy entanglements and damage resulting from hundreds of years of European colonialism. Rather, decolonization should mean creating a post-colonial and post-European form of humanism, which would push back on the categories and binary thinking that have plagued European enlightenment thought (Maldonado-Torres, 2004; Nayar, 2011). Instead, it would move us to a place where difference is both recognized and respected (Nayar, 2011). And yet despite our best intentions, I do not believe that we will decolonize CIE research anytime soon, mostly because the reparations – as described above – would take far more responsibility than we are willing, or perhaps able, to take on. Further, power is always conditioned and when those in power give away their power, they can also just as easily take it back. Decolonization cannot happen from above. At the same time, the expectation for those "below" to do this work is yet another form of colonization. As Puawai Cairns, head of the Mātauranga collection at Te Papa Tongarewa (Museum of New Zealand) wonders, "Why did we – as the colonized subject – have to do all the work to repair ourselves and go through a painful and laborious process of reconstruction, while colonization continued on its merry way (contrary to popular perception, there is no post- in colonization)?" (Cairns, 2018, para. 7). This then leaves us at a difficult juncture – who is to do this work? De Sousa Santos (2018) suggests that in fact, this reinterpreting of the world as it is changing is a collective work and calls for solidarity from "rearguard intellectuals [from the North], intellectuals that contribute with their knowledge to strengthening the social struggles against domination and oppression to which they are committed" (p. ix).

Thus, while decolonization might not be within our reach, what those of us in positions of comparative power can do is work with those in/from/of the Global South to destabilize the Global North as the vanguards of intellectual knowledge in an attempt to move towards a post-colonial, anti-colonial, and post-European form of humanism, a humanism grounded in the ethics of mutual recognition and respect, and one that absolves itself from dualistic thinking, and the positioning of the 'west' above 'all the rest'. In this 'new humanism', groups that have been colonized would be able to 'restory' and hence restore themselves and their communities (see Cairns, 2018). This restorying must be acknowledged, recognized, and supported by all. What I offer in this piece are a few thoughts regarding this destabilizing that builds off work in CIE that has already started in this regard (Andreotti, 2011; Baily, Shah, & Call-Cummings, 2016; de Sousa Santos, 2007; Takayama, Sriprakash, & Connell, 2016; Mercer, Mohan, & Power, 2003). I begin with considering the question, what counts as data?

3   Recounting Data

My first thought – and perhaps this is the most obvious, is around methodological pluralism – different questions need different kinds of methods. And here, I do not simply mean both qualitative and quantitative research. Rather, I am interested in exploding the boundaries of what we count as 'knowledge'. Our ways of knowing the world are grounded in empiricism and a particular understanding of "science". This "science" is what Nyamnjoh (2012) describes as one that has,

> tended to celebrate dichotomies, dualisms, teleologies and analogies, dismissing anything that does not make sense in Cartesian or behaviourist terms, confining to religion and metaphysics what it cannot explain and disqualifying as non-scientific more inclusive epistemologies. This epistemology's logic is simple and problematic: it sacrifices pluriversity for university and imposes a one best way of attaining singular and universal truth. (p. 131)

This dominant perspective that Nyamnjoh critiques renders our views of science and of what "counts" as data in very narrow terms. The prize is empirical, tangible, measurable evidence – evidence that can be sanitized and packaged neatly into numbers and charts or even stories told in a particular way. What is needed is a broadening not only of methodological tools and ways of knowing, but more importantly, expanding the notion of what is considered data, including methods and sources that might strike us as invalid, unreliable, anecdotal, and unobservable. Drawing on Nyamnjoh once again, "The real is not only what is observable or what makes cognitive sense; it is also the invisible, the emotional, the sentimental, the intuitive and the inexplicable" (pp. 131–132). Part of the problem why we have been so limited in this regard is that we are so entrenched in our particular way of knowing the world that to even try to understand the world differently is almost an impossible task since anything we view is through a western post-enlightenment paradigm. And yet there are other ways to think about the world as scholars in this volume exemplify. This brings me to my next point on our capacity as researchers.

4   Building Our Own Capacities

In response to the oft-cited question that Gayatri Chakravorty Spivak asked over three decades ago, "Can the sub-altern speak?", Raeywen Connell (2007) replied, "Yes they can, but can the metropole hear?"[3] Many of us currently lack the capacity to hear – not just to listen but to hear, to think, or do our work differently than what is familiar or known to us.

Much of the work in the fields of Comparative Education and especially International Educational Development is around 'technical assistance' and 'capacity building'. While 'local' people's capacities to be 'productive' is rarely questioned (though that has not historically always been the case), or the fact that they may have 'valuable funds of knowledge' that need to be tapped into and understood, these capacities and funds of knowledge are only deemed valuable when they fit into our frames of reference. As de Sousa Santos (2007) reminds us, "having been overspecialized by a form of knowledge that knows by creating *order* in nature as well as in society, we cannot easily practice or even imagine a form of knowledge that knows by creating *solidarity* both in nature and in society" (p. 428, emphasis added).

To destabilize IED and CE methodology would thus require us to move beyond sharing our knowledge with others and teaching them the skills we know (or building their 'capacity'), to instead re-examine our own ways of knowing and its limits and to open our minds to other ontologies and epistemologies. Though Spivak might argue that this is an impossible task, I am more optimistic and agree with Andreotti (2011) that such a "self-reflective 'epistemology of seeing'" (and hearing) would aid in the creation of knowledge through solidarity rather than one "of ordering and control" (p. 391).

5   Flipping the Frames of Our Conceptual Frameworks

Not only do we need different methods and ways of seeing the world, we must also begin to think about different kinds of questions that CIE research can focus on as a way to destabilize the hold of the Global North. We need to flip our frames of reference around by asking what Ananya Roy (2003) refers to as "third world questions of the first world", and in doing so, examine injustice here in the 'Global North' from a southern perspective. In other words, we need to encourage researchers to turn their gaze to the Global North and understand the Global North from southern perspectives. As Connell (2014) reminds us,

> The role of the periphery is to supply data, and later to apply knowledge in the form of technology and method. The role of the metropole, as well as producing data, is to collate and process data, producing theory (including methodology) and developing applications which are later

exported to the periphery. (p. 211, see also Connell, 2007 for an excellent introduction to Southern theories)

Flipping this script is not an attempt to necessarily increase the knowledge about the Global North and to strengthen its grip on global knowledge, but to be able to destabilize the Global North as the metropole. It would further have the added benefit for IED researchers to understand the implications of northern policies and practices on southern states.

Take the example of poverty. We are living in what those in the burgeoning field of Critical Poverty Studies refer to as 'the Age of Poverty' (Roy et al., 2016). This may seem a strange thing to contend in a world where absolute wealth is at its zenith. This is because our knowledge of poverty comes from our definition of poverty as an absence of wealth; consequently, the location of our studies have always been in the periphery. This obsession with poverty is not new. Almost thirty years ago, Arturo Escobar (1997) noted,

> The perception of poverty on a global scale 'was nothing more than the result of a comparative statistical operation, the first of which was carried out only in 1940' (Sachs, 1990, p. 9). Almost by fiat, two-thirds of the world's peoples were transformed into poor subjects when the World Bank defined as poor those countries with an annual per capita income below $100. And if the problem was one of insufficient income, the solution was clearly economic growth. (p. 23)

To summarize Escobar's point: we have come to understand poverty as an absence of wealth and the silver bullet is capitalism. And yet, the poverty that we choose to "see" is almost always located elsewhere. The whole premise of the development project has been to a large degree an attempt to recreate the Global South in the powerful Global North's image. By this I mean the ways in which Development has essentially been an attempt to bring all countries in the world into a system of co-dependency using neoliberal tools of the capitalist, free-market economy, with English as the linguistic handmaiden to capitalism. Yet, despite now 70 years of 'the development project', the wealth gap has only grown – not just in the Global South but within the North itself. If capitalism is the solution, why are we seeing this tremendous growth in poverty across the globe, including within the Metropole?

Moreover, drawing on the work of the Palestinian poet Mourid Barghouti, Chimamanda Adichie reminds us in her brilliant 2009 Ted Talk, "The Danger of a Single Story", that,

> If you want to dispossess a people, the simplest way to do it is to tell their story and to start with, 'secondly'. Start the story with the arrows of the Native Americans, and not with the arrival of the British, and you have an entirely different story.

Start the story with extreme poverty and not with the advent of global capitalism, and you have an entirely different story. The point I wish to make is that the story of contemporary poverty that we hear not only renders the West's role as entirely invisible in the creation of this very poverty, but also makes invisible the problems of poverty and inequality within the Global North itself. Poverty in the Global North needs to be studied from a CIE/IED perspective as much as poverty elsewhere.

6 Locating CIE Research

Related to the questions we must ask is my final point regarding the location of our research. There are two essential areas of research that CIE researchers should consider, and they lie at two extremes: one at the heart of the capitalist enterprise in the metropoles as mentioned above, and the other at those corners of the earth where capitalism has not yet extended its reach. Let me start with the first. As mentioned earlier, for too long, CIE researchers – especially those who study International Educational Development – have studied educational development in the periphery. Much of our fascination with the periphery has been grounded in questions of poverty, particularly the education of those at the "bottom of the pyramid", the poorest of the poor (Prahalad, 2010). However, it is important to remember that poverty is not inevitable, it is actively constructed (Escobar, 1995; Roy et al., 2016). Moreover, poverty is a relational concept (Roy et al., 2016) – what it means to be poor in Philadelphia in the United States, the city where I currently live, is vastly different from what it means to be poor in Karachi, Pakistan, my city of birth. Questions of poverty are usually questions of injustice. And these questions of injustice are almost always intimately tied with the capitalist enterprise.

Remarkably, while the first goal in the new SDGs is to end poverty, the onus of that herculean task falls on the poorest nations of the world with the assistance of the richest countries. Yet, the solution to end poverty is not necessarily with the poor but with the rich themselves whose insatiable desires are creating an unprecedented wealth gap both within and across borders. Why then are we not studying consumption? Understanding the effects of our own consumption on the creation of poverty might generate more solutions than comparing poverty in Caracas with Calcutta. It is time to turn our gaze to the core and understand how the spread of capitalism and the Global North's dependency on the Global South (for cheap labor and resources) is tied to the creation of poverty, and which then affects the kinds of schooling made available (or that is affordable) in the Majority World. On the other hand, we also need to study those places "beyond capitalism's reach" as Gidwani (2008, p. 218) argues, in order to discover alternatives to capitalism (which tends to be linear and deterministic), which would in turn provide yet another entry point to imagine and advocate for other forms of education, modernity and development – ones that actually will lead us to a more equitable future.

Acknowledgements

I would like to thank Supriya Baily for encouraging me to write this piece, and Magali García-Pletsch and Hye Min Chung for their helpful comments.

Notes

1. All of the terms used to describe groups of nations are problematic in one way or the other and so throughout this piece, I use these terms interchangeably as a heuristic device, not as absolute categories.
2. I acknowledge that while I am a child of the Global South, my privileged life experiences and current position at an elite university in the United States, coupled with my education, which has rendered the Global South invisible when it comes to theory, has in fact removed me from my third-world roots. My positioning gives me a degree of privilege and authority (though comparatively less than my white colleagues) that is not afforded to my colleagues in the Majority World. Thus, I position myself with those in power. To present myself otherwise would be disingenuous.
3. Spivak herself argues that the subaltern cannot speak because of the political and discursive identities within historically determinate systems of political and economic representation that have failed to hear – which is Connolly's exact point.

References

Adichie, C. (2009, July). *The danger of a single story* [Video file]. Retrieved from https://www.ted.com/talks/chimamanda_adichie_the_danger_of_a_single_story

Andreotti, V. (2011). (Towards) decoloniality and diversality in global citizenship education. *Globalisation, Societies and Education, 9*(3–4), 381–397. https://doi.org/10.1080/14767724.2011.605323

Baily, S., Shah, P., & Call-Cummings, M. (2016). Reframing the center: New directions in qualitative methodology in international comparative education. In A. W. Wiseman & E. Anderson (Eds.), *Annual review of comparative and international education 2015 (International perspectives on education and society* (Vol. 28, pp. 139–164). Bingley: Emerald Group Publishing Limited. https://doi.org/10.1108/S1479-367920150000028022

Cairns, P. (2018, December 17). Decolonisation: We aren't going to save you [Blog post]. *American alliance of museums*. Retrieved January 15, 2019, from https://www.aam-us.org/2018/12/17/decolonisation-we-arent-going-to-save-you/

CIES Symposium. (2017). Overview. In *CIES Symposium 2017: Interrogating and innovating CIE research.* https://cehd.gmu.edu/2017symposium/

Connell, R. (2007). *Southern theory: The global dynamics of knowledge in social science.* Cambridge: Polity.

Connell, R. (2014). Using southern theory: Decolonizing social thought in theory, research and application. *Planning Theory, 13*(2), 210–223. doi:10.1177/1473095213499216

de Sousa Santos, B. (Ed.). (2007). *Cognitive justice in a global world: Prudent knowledges for a decent life.* Lanham, MD: Lexington Books.

de Sousa Santos, B. (2018). *The end of the cognitive empire: The coming of age of epistemologies of the South.* Durham, NC: Duke University Press.

Escobar, A. (1995). *Encountering development: The making and unmaking of the Third World.* Princeton, NJ: Princeton University Press.

Ghaffar-Kucher, A. (2017). Love & labor in academia: Dear faculty members who mentor doctoral students of color. In M. Harris, S. L. Sellers, O. Clerge, & F. W. Gooding Jr. (Eds.), *Stories from the front of the room: How higher education faculty of color overcome challenges and thrive in the academy.* Lanham, MD: Rowman & Littlefield.

Gidwani, V. K. (2008). *Capital interrupted: Agrarian development and the politics of work in India.* Minneapolis, MN: University of Minnesota Press.

Horvarth, R. J. (1972). A current definition of colonialism. *Current Anthropology, 13*(1), 45–57. doi:10.1086/201248

Loomba, A. (2015). *The new critical idiom: Colonialism/postcolonialism* (3rd ed.). London: Routledge.

Maldonado-Torres, N. (2004). The topology of being and the geopolitics of knowledge, *City, 8*(1), 29–56. doi:10.1080/1360481042000199787

Mercer, C., Mohan, G., & Power, M. (2003). Towards a critical political geography of African development. *Geoforum, 34*(4), 419–436. doi:10.1016/s0016-7185(03)00045-9

Nayar, P. K. (2011). Frantz Fanon: Toward a postcolonial humanism. *The IUP Journal of Commonwealth Literature, 3*(1), 21–35. https://ssrn.com/abstract=1788033

Nyamnjoh, F. B. (2012). 'Potted plants in greenhouses': A critical reflection on the resilience of colonial education in Africa. *Journal of Asian and African Studies, 47*(2), 129–154. doi:10.1177/0021909611417240

Prahalad, C. K. (2010). *The fortune at the bottom of the pyramid: Eradicating poverty through profits.* Upper Saddle River, NJ: Wharton School Publishing.

Roy, A. (2003). Paradigms of propertied citizenship: Transnational techniques of analysis. *Urban Affairs Review, 38*(4), 463–491. https://doi.org/10.1177/1078087402250356

Roy, A., Negrón-Gonzales, G., Opoku-Agyemang, K., & Talwalker, C. (2016). *Encountering poverty: Thinking and acting in an unequal world.* Oakland, CA: University of California Press.

Spivak, G. (1988). Can the sub-altern speak? In C. Nelson & L. Grossberg (Eds.), *Marxism and the interpretation of culture* (pp. 271–313). Urbana, IL: University of Illinois Press.

Takayama, K., Sriprakash, A., & Connell, R. (2016). Toward a postcolonial comparative and international education. *Comparative Education Review, 61*(S2). doi:10.1086/690455

Voeltz, F. (2012, April 25). Body of work/when you take away punctuation [Blog post]. *Detail Collector.* Retrieved September 4, 2017, from
https://frantelope.wordpress.com/2012/04/25/body-of-work-when-you-take-away-punctuation/

CHAPTER 16

The "Significance" of Epistemicide: Unpacking the Problematic Statistical Foundations of Knowledge Production in Global Education Governance

D. Brent Edwards Jr.

Abstract

The present chapter takes aim at the research methods that undergird 'evidence-based policy', particularly as they are used in the realm of global education governance. It does so by unpacking the foundational practices and assumptions of the statistical methods that are commonly employed to inform such research. The research practices critiqued here are those that serve as the basis for determining (a) 'what works' in education policy, (b) 'best practices', and (c) which variables are associated with influencing outcomes of interest. Since the goal of much quantitative research in the service of global governance is to directly inform policy and practice, the present chapter represents a challenge to the dominant approaches to knowledge production in the field of global education policy. It can thus be seen as an attempt to contribute to the rich literature that has emerged in recent decades that not only critiques the basis and application of quantitative methods, but which also critiques the historical foundations of those methods.

Keywords

epistemicide – quantitative methods – impact evaluations – regression analysis – randomized controlled trials – evidence-based policy – best practices – hypothesis testing – normal curve – p values

1 Introduction

The present chapter takes aim at the research methods that undergird "evidence-based policy", particularly as they are used in the realm of global education governance. It does so by unpacking the foundational practices and assumptions of the statistical methods that are commonly employed to inform such research. The research practices critiqued here are those that serve as the basis for determining (a) "what works" in education policy, (b) "best practices", and (c) which variables are associated with influencing outcomes of interest. Since the goal of much quantitative research in the service of global governance is to directly inform policy and practice, the present chapter represents a challenge to the dominant approaches to knowledge production in the field of global education policy. It can thus be seen as an attempt to contribute to the rich literature that has emerged in recent decades that not only critiques the basis and application of quantitative methods (e.g., Deaton & Cartwright, 2016; Dumas & Anderson, 2014; Erickson & Gutierrez, 2002; Klees, 2016; Luecke & McGinn, 1975; Pogrow, 2017; Walters, Lareau, & Ranis, 2009), but which also critiques the historical foundations of those methods (e.g., Grosfoguel, 2013; Kaomea, 2015; Shahjahan, 2011; Smith, 1999).

The importance of unpacking the research foundations of evidence-based policy stems, in part, from the fact that the wisdom of both evidence-based policy and the underlying methods have tended to be rarely questioned. In the current context of education politics, the name of the game is for reform to be guided by research that is seen as rigorous and objective and which is able to speak to causal relations (i.e., research which is able to say what causes the observed outcomes) (Walter et al., 2009). However, as this chapter makes clear, research which espouses to embody these characteristics is based on foundations that lead one to question the feasibility of this endeavor.

An additional reason to clarify the problematic research foundations of evidence-based policy is because these methods contribute to epistemicide, where epistemicide refers to the exclusion or elimination of other ways of knowing (de Sousa Santos, 2007; Hall & Tandon, 2017). Here, the point is that dominant methods of knowledge production – which for centuries have been Western, positivist, and quantitative in nature – are valorized while non-dominant forms – which for centuries have been Indigenous, have centered alternative ontologies, and, frequently, have been qualitative in nature – are devalued if not entirely ignored (Grosfoguel, 2013; Shahjahan, 2011; Smith, 1999). These dynamics have been particularly evident since the 1800s, in the context of modern state bureaucracy, where the art of governing has relied on the ability to collect and manipulate quantitative data on various aspects of society and economy (Porter, 1995). In more contemporary times, i.e., in the post-WWII context, these methods have been adopted and extended as governments and international organizations have sought to take the politics out of policymaking by relying on the policy sciences, which are rooted in the application of sophisticated quantitative methods to analyze and respond to social, political, and economic issues (Fischer, 2007; Klees & Edwards, 2014). Thus, as one contribution to a growing literature that is critical of quantitative and Western research, the goal here is to push back against the epistemicide that is perpetrated by the methods of evidence-based policy. Arguing against the use and abuse of these methods is more effective if one can clearly spell out their limitations.

So, what, then, are the statistical foundations that this chapter calls into question? Stated directly, the focus is on the practices and assumptions related to hypothesis testing, p values, the normal curve, and the reporting and interpretation of effect sizes. While these issues may seem esoteric or technical – and while, to some extent, they may be – it is argued here that their relevance cannot be understated. Indeed, as will become clear, each of the aforementioned issues is at the core of the evidence-based policy enterprise, and, in particular, at the core of the production of impact evaluations, the most highly regarded form of quantitative investigation employed in evidence-based policy research (more will be said about impact evaluations in the next section). By extension, the critiques offered here cut to the core of the knowledge production practices that drive education reform politics in the global education policy field. More broadly, and more damningly, the critiques leveled here against the issues mentioned above are also applicable to all forms of quantitative research that attempt to identify what variable or program is associated with outcomes of interest in statistically significant terms, where statistical significance has become the main criteria for determining if a quantitative research finding should be taken seriously. As will be seen, this chapter addresses dominant methods in their own terms in addition to offering historical and ontological critiques.

To give some idea of the gravity of the critique offered, consider that, without the practices discussed here, it would not be possible, for example, for the World Bank to say which of its reforms 'work'. Neither would it be possible for the Organization for Economic Cooperation and Development (OECD) to say which practices are associated with higher scores on its well-known assessment of student learning, known as the Program for International Student Assessment (PISA). Likewise, non-governmental organizations could not, in statistical sense, confidently identify the effects of their programs on outcome indicators, while researchers could not arrive at seemingly definitive findings about the relationships among student, family, school, and community characteristics, for example. Without the benefit of commonly accepted criteria for revealing associations and impact, the foundation of 'credible' knowledge production methods is called into question.

The implication, then, is that the significance of this chapter derives from the fact that it offers a critique of the 'significance' on which the methods and popularity of quantitative research, the policy sciences, and evidence-based policy have been built over the past one hundred plus years – to the exclusion of other forms of research and other ways of knowing. However, although the practices and assumptions critiqued here are relevant to much quantitative research, the discussion focuses primarily on the relation of these practices to the methods used for producing policy-relevant research (i.e., the methods that are invoked for identifying "what works" and "best practices") in the context of global education governance, first, because of the exceptional level of influence of these methods in this area and, second, in hopes of informing actors (i.e., researchers and others) in the global governance of education of the limitations of these practices, practices which are often taken for granted.

The remainder of the chapter proceeds, first, by characterizing the primary set of research methods that are used in support of evidence-based policy, with these methods falling under the label of impact evaluation. In that they are perceived by many as the most credible form of research for producing policy-relevant knowledge, impact evaluations are the spearhead of epistemicide in education policy research and thus offer a particularly salient point of entry for addressing the underlying concerns related to statistical significance. After characterizing impact evaluation, the subsequent (and most substantive) section of turns to an in-depth engagement with the practices and assumptions related to hypothesis testing, p values, and the normal curve. In concluding, the final section reflects on the implications of the critique and argues that, while the assessment offered here of each of the issues of interest is critical, the combined critique encourages one to rethink their faith in the practices and assumptions that surround statistical significance and the possibility of these practices for revealing meaningful connections among variables.

2   Evidence-Based Policy Research and Impact Evaluations

To push back against evidence-based policy means to push back against what is called impact evaluation since the latter is the foundation of – or at least the most highly preferred form of research for justifying – the former. The reason for the privileged position of impact evaluation, and reason for which it is referred to as the gold standard of research by proponents (Castillo & Wagner, 2013), has to do with the fact that it claims to reveal causal relations (Gertler, Martinez, Premand, Rawlings, & Vermeersch, 2016). If policymakers, organizations or others are going to rely on research to inform their decisions, they want to be sure that the informational basis of their decisions directly justifies the chosen path of reform. In that impact evaluation is portrayed as being able to connect policy or programmatic experiments to outcomes, they are seen as particularly desirable. In the language of quantitative research, the defining characteristic of impact evaluation is that they uncover attribution, that is, the extent to which changes in outcomes of interest can be attributed to participation in an intervention (e.g., some policy, program, pedagogy, etc.).

While impact evaluations can be carried out through a variety of methods, only the essential characteristics of the most common approaches will be discussed here. Since the goal of the remaining sections of this chapter is to unpack the problematic foundations of the underlying statistical practices and assumptions, it is only essential here that one has a general understanding of how impact evaluations work. With that in mind, there are two approaches of interest. One is based on regression analysis; the other is based on randomization.

Regression analysis is a statistical approach that attempts to identify the effect of various independent variables (on one side of the equation) on a dependent variable (on the other side). Typically, the independent variable of interest in an impact evaluation is some intervention or treatment, for example, some policy, program, project, or pedagogy, whereas the dependent variable of interest in a given study can take a number of forms, for example, test scores, student retention, teacher attendance, etc. The other independent variables included in the equation are used to account for all the other factors that can influence the dependent variable. In the end, statistical procedures and statistical assumptions are followed that attempt to indicate whether changes in the observed outcomes are likely to be the result of the treatment (i.e., variable) being examined. (In quantitative research more generally, researchers seek to determine if any number of variables [e.g., gender, ethnicity, age, socio-economic status, etc.] is associated with outcomes of interest, not only a given treatment or reform program.)

As noted above, the second approach to impact evaluation is grounded in randomization. The term for this approach is randomized control trial (RCT). Here, as opposed to developing complex equations wherein one tries to account for all relevant factors that can affect outcomes, the strategy is to randomly assign participants to treatment and control groups, with the idea being that, if sample sizes are large enough, "the randomized assignment mechanism will ensure that any characteristic of the population will transfer to both the treatment group and the comparison group" (Gertler et al., 2016, p. 98). Put differently: through randomization, the treatment and control groups should be identical, both in terms of their observed and unobserved characteristics (Gertler et al., 2016). The implication, in theory, then, is that one can compare the average outcomes of interest for the two groups to see if the intervention had an overall positive impact. However, as with regression analysis, numerical tests are necessary to see if the differences in the outcomes of the two groups are meaningful in a statistical sense.

Although the above comments highlight the centrality of practices related to statistical significance when it comes to impact evaluation and quantitative research more generally, these comments also contrast with the focus of extant literature on impact evaluations. That is, despite the fact that impact evaluations can – and do – influence education reform trends globally, there is scant literature that brings a critical lens to their underlying foundations. What critical literature does exist has examined (a) their role within the politics of global education policy, (b) the political-organizational pressures that influence their conduct and interpretation, and (c) the methodological practices (but not statistical foundations) that undergird them (Carnoy, 2015; Edwards, 2019; Klees, 2016; Klees & Edwards, 2014; Lubienski, Weitzel, & Lubienski, 2009; Pogrow, 2017; Steiner-Khamsi, 2012; Verger, Edwards, Kosar-Altinyelken, 2014; Verger, Fontdevila, Rogan, & Gurney, forthcoming). The present chapter thus seeks to probe deeper than previous literature by examining the statistical practices and assumptions that generally go unquestioned but which fundamentally serve as the basis for making meaning of the studies on which they are based.

3   Problematic Practices and Foundational Assumptions

Aside from the general points above, there are additional dimensions of a more technical nature along which impact evaluations should be critically understood. These technical aspects relate to the computation, assumptions, and reporting of certain statistics – statistics which indicate if the related variables should be interpreted as contributing significantly to the outcomes of interest. What is fascinating is that the procedures and practices discussed below have serious weaknesses and limitations that call into question the meaningfulness of the impact evaluation enterprise. The first section focuses on issues associated with hypothesis testing (the procedure used to determine statistical significance) while the second section shifts to issues related to p values and the normal distribution. As will be explained, these latter two items serve as the philosophical and statistical foundation for hypothesis testing. The final section turns to the questionable ways that statistical effects are manipulated and reported by researchers.

3.1 Hypothesis Testing: The Influence of Sample Size and the "Crud" Factor

As noted above, the foundation of RCTs is the idea that the means for the outcome of interest of the control and treatment groups can be compared to see if the intervention made a difference, for example, by producing higher average test scores in the treatment group. To make this determination, a statistical test is set up that is intended to indicate "how often differences as large or larger than the differences we found would occur as a result of chance or sampling [error]" (Carver, 1978, p. 380). The point of departure for this test is the assumption that there is no difference in means, which, if true, supports the claim that the intervention had no effect. This point of departure is known as the null hypothesis, the opposite of which is the research hypothesis that states that there is a difference in means.

The test most often used to make a decision about the null hypothesis is known as the t-test. The values produced by the t-test are associated with different levels of probability (known as p values). If the t-test statistic is sufficiently large, the null hypothesis is rejected in favor of the research hypothesis.[1] Typically, if the t-test suggests that the probability is 5% or less that results would be found as large or larger than the ones in the study as a result of chance or sampling error, then the differences are labeled statistically significant. By extension, the results are also taken as support that the intervention "worked", since "sampling, or chance, is no longer considered a good (i.e., likely) explanation for the cause of the difference between the means" (Carver, 1978, p. 380).

One problem with the t-test and other similar tests is that they are very sensitive to sample size. This is easy to understand when one notes how the t-test is constructed. To that end, the overall t-statistic is defined as a fraction:

$$\frac{\text{Effect}}{\text{Standard error of the effect estimate}}$$

The "effect" in the numerator is simply the difference in the treatment and control means (i.e., treatment mean − control mean). Thus, one way to get a large t-statistic (and thus a result that is deemed statistically significant) is if the program is actually effective in improving the outcome for the treatment group (and thereby increasing the size of the numerator). However, even if the difference in means is very small (which should raise questions about the practical significance of the results), one can still arrive at a t-statistic that indicates statistical significance by affecting the denominator of the t-statistic (i.e., the standard error).

The standard error in the denominator of the above fraction gives some measure of the variation (i.e., standard deviation) around the mean of the individual results (e.g., individual test scores) for the treatment and control groups. That is, it speaks to the distribution of the results in these groups. With that in mind, it can be mentioned that the standard error is itself a fraction (or, more technically, in the case of the two-sample t-test, the addition of two fractions) that boils down to:

$$\frac{\text{Standard deviation of the means}}{\text{Square root of sample sizes}}$$

The practical implication of the standard error definition is that one can greatly affect the interpretation of the overall results of a study by increasing the sample sizes of the treatment and control groups. To put this statement in relation to the comments in the preceding paragraph, if one increases the sample size, the value of the standard error gets smaller, which then impacts the value that results from the first fraction above, that is, from the definition of the t-statistic, by making it larger. And as stated previously, larger t-statistics are associated with smaller probabilities that results as large or larger than those obtained would occur due to chance or sampling error. At the point when such a probability dips below the 5% threshold, it is customary for researchers to interpret the results as statistically significant, as also noted above.

The sensitivity of hypothesis testing to sample size is well known and has been criticized by many scholars (e.g., Boruch, Rindskopf, Anderson, Amidjaya, & Jansson, 1979; Carver, 1978, 1993; Deaton & Cartwright, 2016; Klees, 2016; Levine, Weber, Hullett, Park, & Lindsey, 2008). As Levine et al. (2008) put it, sample size sensitivity "can lead to dismissing potentially important findings when a sample is small and embracing trivial effects with large samples" (p. 176). Of course, as sample size increases, the outcome means and the standard deviations of the samples will stabilize (i.e., will become less sensitive to the addition of new participants), which leads to more confidence (or more reliability) in the t-statistic, but this doesn't change the fact that researchers can ensure statistical significance for minute differences in means if they have large enough samples. Moreover, there are no clear rules on how large is a large enough sample, nor for how small is too small to have faith in a statistically significant result (Deaton & Cartwright, 2016). Thus, while sample size is a crucial issue, there is no consensus on how to address its risks. For our purposes, the point is to be aware of the fact that practically dubious results of RCTs can show up as statistically significant because of large sample sizes and, vice versa, that potentially meaningful differences may not register as statistically significant because of small samples.

While the comments above focused on RCTs, parallel comments can be made with regard to hypothesis testing when using regression analysis as a form of impact evaluation (and, more generally, when using regression analysis to explore the relationships among variables). The same test statistic and the same logic apply to the determination of statistical significance of individual variables (or, more specifically, their regression coefficients). The difference is that – when it comes to the "effect" portion of the t-statistic definition mentioned above – the focus is on the dummy variable that represents program participation (as opposed to the difference in outcome means). One looks to see if the independent variable of interest (participation in the intervention) has an impact on the dependent variable (e.g., test scores) that is greater than zero (i.e., one looks to see if the relationship between this variable and the outcome variable is not zero), while holding all other variables constant. In other words, in the hypothesis test for determining statistical significance, one compares the mean of the (coefficient of the) intervention participation variable with zero in order to see if the intervention contributes to explaining changes in the value of the outcome variable (or at least is associated with these changes) (Uriel, 2013). More technically speaking, researchers hope to reject the null hypothesis that the (coefficient of the) intervention participation dummy variable is equal to zero – and, as with the difference in means in RCTs, they want to make such a decision based on a low probability that results as large or larger than those obtained would occur due to chance or sampling error. For our purposes, though, the problem remains that statistical significance for the intervention variable depends on sample size since the hypothesis test for statistical significance still includes sample size in the denominator.

In practice, impact evaluation advocates suggest making sample size decisions through a particular procedure. For example, the handbook produced by the World Bank on impact evaluations does not suggest specific sample sizes; instead the authors suggest the use of "power calculations" (Gertler et al., 2016), a procedure which, based on certain assumptions (related to projected effect size and p value – more on the latter below), will tell you the sample size needed to have "a specified probability of declaring as significant a particular difference or effect" (Johnson, 1999, p. 767). In other words, power calculations can be used to tell a researcher the sample size needed to ensure a high probability that a particular effect size registers as statistically significant. This characteristic of power analysis can lead to further skepticism of impact evaluations since researchers can reverse engineer the sample size needed to have a good likelihood of arriving at a statistically significant result.[2]

Stepping back, one must also recognize that, beyond specific calculations, statistical significance is based on the assumption that data are normally distributed. For this reason, the next section turns to a critical discussion of the normal curve.

3.2   P Values and the Normal Curve

More needs to be said about p values to shed light on its technical and historical issues. It was noted at the beginning of the section above that the t-statistic is associated with probabilities – i.e., p values – that indicate whether or not the null hypothesis should be rejected; however, the relationship between the t-statistic and the null hypothesis as well as the assumptions that underlie the p values should be further clarified. There are fundamental issues here that go to the heart of the impact evaluation enterprise and, indeed, to the heart of quantitative research more generally, since statistical significance is so central to making meaning of quantitative results.

First, I return to the definition of the p value. While it is sometimes assumed that a p value can be interpreted as the probability that the results observed were due to chance, or the probability of getting the results based on the data gathered, this is not the case. That is, a p value of 5% (or 0.05) does not mean that, based on the data collected, there is a 1 in 20 chance of getting a particular result; rather, it means the opposite. As Carver (1978) writes, the p value "is a number which tells us the *proportion of the time* that we can expect to find mean differences as large or larger" than what was found if we were to repeat the study procedures (p. 380, emphasis added). Put differently, if X difference is found in the means in two groups, a p value of 0.05 says that we will find a difference as large or larger than X *in 5% of cases* "when sampling a pair of means from the same population" (p. 381).

However, in any given study or impact evaluation we typically only have one set of means from which to make a decision, and we have no way of knowing what the other cases would produce. This fact leads to the observation that the interpretation of a p value amounts to making a decision regarding statistical significance based on "hypothetical alternative scenarios" (Nuzzo, 2015, p. 1). As Nuzzo (2015) further, and quite damningly, elaborates:

> The p-value summarizes how often results at least as extreme as those observed would show up if the study were repeated an infinite number of times when in fact only pure random chance was at work. … This means that the p-value is a statement about imaginary data in hypothetical study replications, not a statement about actual conclusions in any given study. Instead of being a "scientific lie detector" that can get at the truth

of a particular scientific finding, the p-value is more of an "alternative reality machine" that lets researchers compare their results with what random chance would hypothetically produce. (para. 1)

With the increased scrutiny of p values in recent years, at least one journal (*Basic and Applied Social Psychology*) decided, as of 2015, that it would no longer accept studies that employ them. This is a radical move given that p values have been commonly used in practically all areas of research over approximately the past 100 years (Fendler & Muzzafar, 2008; Gigerenzer et al., 1989). The significance of this break from precedent is further underscored when one considers that p values have been used in at least three million scientific papers (Nuzzo, 2015). In a move with direct relevance for impact evaluations, even the American Statistical Association now advises that "scientific conclusions and business or policy decisions should not be based on only whether a p-value passes a specific threshold" (Novella, 2016, p. 4).

The above recommendation makes sense when one recalls that p values are simply used to reject (or not) the null hypothesis that there is no difference in the two values being compared. In the case of an RCT, even when we reject the null hypothesis that the two means are equal, all we are saying is that there is a high probability that the means are not the same; we cannot say why this is the case. Further to the point, Greenland et al. (2016) highlight an issue which is frequently overlooked: "the P value tests all the assumptions about how the data were generated (the entire model), not just the targeted hypothesis it is supposed to test (such as a null hypothesis)" (p. 339). That is to say, "not only does a P value not tell us whether the hypothesis targeted for testing is true or not; it says nothing specifically related to that hypothesis unless we can be completely assured that every other assumption used for its computation is correct" (p. 339). The range of assumptions includes not only those conditions mentioned earlier in the chapter in relation to regression analysis but also such issues as correctly following data collection protocols. Thus, the fact of rejecting the null hypothesis does not necessarily support the theory or policy of interest (Meehl, 1986). Moreover, just because a p value suggests that the means are different, this does not immediately imply that the difference is "substantial, or beneficial, enough to be of practical importance" – a conclusion for which more information would be needed (Pogrow, 2017, p. 7; see later section on interpreting and reporting effects for more on this point).

For the second issue, it is necessary to go beyond the interpretation of p values as probabilities to critique as well the underlying basis for those probabilities. Simply put, the distribution against which p values are judged is assumed to have a standard normal distribution (or bell curve shape). On the basis of this assumed distribution, individual values (such as mean differences in RCTs or individual variable coefficients in regression analysis) are judged to be more or less likely based on their distance from the hypothetical mean of the parent population. Thus, in impact evaluations, is it assumed that all social variables have normal distributions and that it makes sense to judge statistical significance on the probability that a given result would not occur – except by chance or sampling error – in the majority of cases.

One problem with the practice of making decisions on the grounds of the normal distribution is that it was not created to be applied in the social sciences. Initially, the normal distribution emerged in the 18th century as a way to describe probabilities associated with coin tossing (Fendler & Muzaffar, 2008). It also developed from the work of astronomers, who used the normal distribution as a way of assessing measurement error in determining the positions of heavenly bodies (Gigerenzer et al., 1989). It was only adopted in the social sciences in the 19th century with the development of modern nations, the growth of governmental bureaucracies, and the desire to use statistics "as a technology by which government offices could rationalize systems of population management, diagnosis, and intervention" (Fendler & Muzaffar, 2008, p. 72). Although initially seen as scandalous and although there was initially significant pushback, the "transformation in the understanding of [the] normal distribution from a statement about the regularities of arithmetical probability to an insight into the workings of society" was gradually accepted in the second half of the 19th century (Fendler & Muzaffar, 2008, p. 71).

The shortcoming of this wholesale adoption, however, is that it meant not only the importation of technique but also the imposition of interpretation. As Gigerenzer et al. (1989) relate:

> When Adolphe Quetelet applied the curve describing observational errors in astronomy to social statistics, he took over the substance as well as the form; the interpretation as well as the technique. If astronomers understood the normal distribution as a scattering of observations around the mean, true value for, say, the position of a comet, then social statisticians must understand the same distribution as a scattering of nature's 'errors' around the mean 'true' value for, say, the moral condition of a nation. (p. 272)

The appropriation of this technique by psychology in the late 1800s and 1900s meant that the normal distribution was also applied to such things as cleverness, wit, and civility (Fendler & Muzaffar, 2008). In so doing, the underlying assumption was that "nature aimed at a fixed [i.e., average] point in forming human beings, but made a certain frequency of errors" (Goertzel, n.d., p. 3).

However, despite its widespread use, there has long been recognition from researchers that data often do not reflect the normal distribution. As Berkson stated in 1938: "It is practically certain that any series of real observations does not actually follow a normal curve with absolute exactitude in all respects" (p. 526). Separately, Goertzel (n.d.) comments that "social life ... is not a lottery, and there is no reason to expect sociological variables to be normally distributed" (p. 14). Even Karl Pearson, one of the founders of modern statistics "sought to move statistics away from the tendency to assume that data are distributed according to the normal curve, and to this end he defined a whole family of curves, of which the normal was only one special case" (Gigerenzer et al., 1989, p. 113).

Recent research by O'Boyle and Aguinis (2012) has convincingly demonstrated the need to take the aforementioned admonitions seriously. Here, the authors conducted studies that looked across five professional fields – including researchers, entertainers, politicians, and athletes – and found, based on 198 samples with 633,263 participants, that performance is not normally distributed, in particular, because the samples regularly included extreme values.[3] In that this study looked at individual performance, the results, arguably, are particularly salient for education, where teachers, students, and principals are often evaluated individually. Furthermore, in that impact evaluations in education often look at outcomes on tests of student knowledge, it should be mentioned that such tests, by design, will produce results that are approximately normal, even though the underlying variable of interest (i.e., student knowledge) is not (Goertzel, n.d.).[4] To that end, it is debatable what the underlying variable is that tests of student knowledge measure. Is it knowledge? Scholastic aptitude? Intelligence? The larger point, though, is that the practice of assuming normality of outcomes, including those assessed in impact evaluations, is highly questionable (Deaton & Cartwright, 2016).

The implication of the above is that the body of knowledge that has been developed through previous impact evaluations and through all studies based on statistical significance may not mean much of anything if the underlying basis for judging statistical significance does not reflect the actual distribution of data, or, in the case of achievement tests, does not reflect the distribution of the underlying variable of interest. More generally, for any type of distribution, one can question the wisdom of using probability tests for judging the likelihood of an outcome, since doing so assumes that social phenomena occur with some form of mathematical regularity and that it makes sense to judge current and future events against an assumed distribution regardless of context (Fendler & Muzaffar, 2008; Klees, 2016; Meehl, 1978). In practice, researchers ignore or are unaware of the evolution of the use of the normal distribution. Rather than be preoccupied with such issues, they may eliminate extreme values from the dataset in order to make their distributions conform to the assumption of 'normality'. Thus, there is reason to believe that normal distributions do not always occur naturally and, where we are presented with them, it may be because of researcher manipulation to create (or to hide) a statistically significant result.

4 Conclusions

This chapter has endeavored to shine light on the problematic foundations for determining statistical and practical significance in quantitative research. The critiques offered relate to the procedures for hypothesis testing (sensitive as they are to sample size and the "crud" factor), the definition of p values (misunderstood as they are to give more useful information than they do), and the practice of using the standard normal distribution (inappropriately applied as it is to the analysis of all social variables). Taken together, the practices and assumptions questioned in this chapter represent core aspects of the widely accepted foundations of quantitative research.

But why is such a critique necessary in a book on "interrogating and innovating comparative and international education"? The answer is: because statistical significance is the bedrock of those research practices that seek to influence reform trends in education globally. That is, not only is statistical significance the common criteria for determining if two variables have a meaningful relationship, but, more specifically, it is the most essential characteristic of research that is taken seriously by policymakers, reformers, and policy entrepreneurs – where this research takes the form of impact evaluations and attempts to identify the effect of a given intervention (e.g., a policy, program, or pedagogy) on particular outcomes of interest (e.g., test scores, attendance, retention, etc.). As such, the practices discussed here are arguably among the most important when it comes to interrogating the foundations of research related to comparative and international education.

A few examples underscore the centrality of statistical significance to research in global education governance. Consider that, without statistical significance, international organizations such as the World Bank and the Organization for Economic Cooperation and Development would not be able to crunch the numbers in their vast datasets (using regression analysis) to determine which factors are associated with improved educational outcomes across countries. Likewise, researchers – such as those at the influential Jameel Poverty Action Lab at the Massachusetts Institute of Technology – would not be able to employ RCTs to determine if some innovation "worked" to enhance a particular indicator. And practitioners engaged in various settings around the world would not be able, based on either regression analysis or RCTs, to identify "best practices" that are presumed to produce positive results regardless of context.

The key implication of the critiques in this chapter is that the methods in question are no more credible than other forms of research, and, indeed, are arguably less so. To that end, one of the primary goals is to assist in opening space for alternatives – alternative methods, alternative politics of education, and alternative ontologies. There is a new wave of research in comparative and international education (see, e.g., Shahjahan, 2017) which, from the perspective of the present author, is seen as a welcome development in that it draws attention to the possibility and importance of ways of knowing and being in the world that break from the positivist paradigm. While others – cited at the outset of this chapter – have critiqued positivist research and its current offspring of impact evaluation on ontological and methodological grounds as well as for the ways that these methods have been employed historically to the detriment of marginalized and less-powerful groups, it is hoped that the present chapter has contributed something when it comes to critically understanding the statistical practices and assumptions that undergird dominant quantitative approaches to producing knowledge in the context of global education governance.

Notes

1 The language of rejecting the null hypothesis might sound odd, but as Steidl, Hayes, and Schauber (1997) remind us: "In the framework of the hypothetico-deductive method, research hypotheses can never be proven; rather, they can only be disproved (rejected) with the tools of statistical inference" (p. 271).
2 An additional issue not discussed here is the way that technical issues related, e.g., to correlation among variables affects which variables often spuriously appear as significant. See Edwards (2018, ch. 2) for more. Relatedly, see Pogrow (2017) for more on how effects are often inappropriately reported and interpreted.
3 O'Boyle and Aguinis (2012) suggest instead the use of the Paretian (power law) distribution.
4 On test results and normality, Goertzel (n.d.) explains: "If a large number of people fill out a typical multiple choice test such as the Scholastic Aptitude Test (or a typical

sociological questionnaire with precoded responses such as 'strongly agree, agree') at random using a perfect die, the scores are very likely to be normally distributed. This is true because many more combinations of response give a sum that is close to the theoretical mean than give a score that is close to either extreme" (p. 6).

References

Berkson, J. (1938). Some difficulties of interpretation encountered in the application of the chi-square test. *Journal of the American Statistical Association, 33*(203), 526–536. doi:10.1080/01621459.1938.10502329

Boruch, R., Rindskopf, D., Anderson, P., Amidjaya, I., & Jansson, D. (1979). Randomized experiments for evaluating and planning local programs: A summary on appropriateness and feasibility. *Public Administration Review, 39*(1), 36–40. doi:10.2307/3110376

Carnoy, M. (2015). *International test score comparisons and educational policy: A review of the critiques*. Boulder, CO: National Education Policy Center. Retrieved from http://nepc.colorado.edu/publication/international-test-scores

Carver, R. (1978). The case against statistical significance testing. *Harvard Educational Review, 48*(3), 378–399. doi:10.17763/haer.48.3.t490261645281841

Carver, R. (1993). The case against statistical significance testing, revisited. *The Journal of Experimental Education, 61*(4), 287–292. doi:10.1080/00220973.1993.10806591

Castillo, N., & Wagner, D. (2013). Gold standard? The use of randomized controlled trials for international educational policy. *Comparative Education Review, 58*(1), 166–173.

Cohen, J. (1988). *Statistical power analysis for the behavioral sciences*. Hillsdale, NJ: Lawrence Erlbaum.

de Sousa Santos, B. (2007). Beyond abyssal thinking: From global lines to ecologies of knowledge. *Review, 30*(1), 45–89. http://www.jstor.org/stable/40241677

Deaton, A., & Cartwright, N. (2016). *Understanding and misunderstanding randomized controlled trials* (NBER Working Paper No. 22595). Retrieved from http://www.nber.org/papers/w22595

Dumas, M., & Anderson, G. (2014). Qualitative research as policy knowledge: Framing policy problems and transforming education from the ground up. *Education Policy Analysis Archives, 22*(11), 1–24. http://dx.doi.org/10.14507/epaa.v22n11.2014

Durlak, J. (2009). How to select, calculate, and interpret effect sizes. *Journal of Pediatric Psychology, 34*(9), 917–928. doi:10.1093/jpepsy/jsp004

Edwards Jr., D. B. (2018). *Global education policy, impact evaluations, and alternatives: The political economy of knowledge production*. New York, NY: Palgrave MacMillan.

Edwards, D. (2019). Best practices from best methods? Big data and the limitations of impact evaluation in the global governance of education. In T. Jules & F. Salajan

(Eds.), *The educational intelligent economy: Big data, artificial intelligence, machine learning and the internet of things in education* (pp. 69–85). Bingley, UK: Emerald Publishing Limited. https://doi.org/10.1108/S1479-367920190000038005

Erickson, F., & Gutierrez, K. (2002). Culture, rigor, and science in educational research. *Educational Researcher, 31*(8), 21–24. doi:10.3102/0013189x031008021

Fendler, L., & Muzzafar, I. (2008). The history of the bell curve: Sorting and the idea of normal. *Educational Theory, 58*(1), 63–82. doi:10.1111/j.1741-5446.2007.0276.x

Fischer, F. (2007). Policy analysis in critical perspective: The epistemics of discursive practices. *Critical Policy Studies, 1*(1), 97–109. doi:10.1080/19460171.2007.9518510

Gertler, P., Martinez, S., Premand, P., Rawlings, L., & Vermeersch, C. (2016). *Impact evaluation in practice* (2nd ed.). Washington, DC: World Bank.

Gigerenzer, G., Swijtink, Z., Porter, T., Datson, L., Beatty, J., & Kruger, L. (1989). *The empire of chance: How probability changed science and everyday life*. New York, NY: Cambridge University Press.

Goertzel, T. (n.d.). *The myth of the bell curve*. Retrieved from http://crab.rutgers.edu/~goertzel/normalcurve.htm

Greenland, S., Senn, S., Rothman, K., Carlin, J., Poole, C., Goodman, S., & Altman, D. (2016). Statistical tests, P values, confidence intervals, and power: A guide to misinterpretations. *European Journal of Epidemiology, 31*(4), 337–350. doi:10.1007/s10654-016-0149-3

Grosfoguel, R. (2013). The structure of knowledge in Westernized universities: Epistemic racism/sexism and the four genocides/epistemicides of the long 16th century. *Human Architecture, 11*(1), 73–90.

Hall, B. L., & Tandon, R. (2017). Decolonization of knowledge, epistemicide, participatory research, and higher education. *Research for All, 1*(1), 6–19. doi:10.18546/RFA.01.1.02

Jimenez, E., & Sawada, Y. (1999). Do community-managed schools work? An evaluation of El Salvador's EDUCO program. *The World Bank Economic Review, 13*(3), 415–441. https://doi.org/10.1093/wber/13.3.415

Johnson, D. (1999). The insignificance of statistical significance testing. *Journal of Wildlife Management, 63*(3), 763–772. doi:10.2307/3802789

Kaomea, J. (2015). Qualitative analysis as Ho'oku'iku'i or Bricolage: Teaching emancipatory indigenous research in postcolonial Hawaii. *Qualitative Inquiry, 22*(2), 1–8. doi:10.1177/1077800415620222

Klees, S. (2016). Inferences from regression analysis: Are they valid? *Real-world Economics Review, 74*, 85–97. Retrieved from http://www.paecon.net/PAEReview/issue74/Klees74.pdf

Klees, S., & Edwards Jr., D. B. (2014). Knowledge production and technologies of governance. In T. Fenwick, E. Mangez, & J. Ozga (Eds.), *World yearbook of education:*

2014. *Governing knowledge: Comparison, knowledge-based technologies and expertise in the regulation of education* (pp. 31–43). New York, NY: Routledge.

Levine, T., Weber, R., Hullett, C., Park, H., & Lindsey, L. (2008). A critical assessment of null hypothesis significance testing in quantitative communication research. *Human Communication Research, 34*(2), 171–187. doi:10.1111/j.1468-2958.2008.00317.x

Lubienski, C., Weitzel, P., & Lubienski, S. (2009). Is there a 'consensus' on school choice and achievement? Advocacy research and the emerging political economy of knowledge production. *Educational Policy, 23*(1), 161–193. doi:10.1177/0895904808328532

Luecke, D., & McGinn, N. (1975). Regression analyses and education production functions: Can they be trusted? *Harvard Educational Review, 45*(3), 325–350. doi:10.17763/haer.45.3.661951r044l05128

Meehl, P. (1978). Theoretical risks and tabular asterisks: Sir Karl, Sir Ronald, and the slow progress of soft psychology. *Journal of Consulting and Clinical Psychology, 46*(4), 806–834. doi:10.1016/j.appsy.2004.02.001

Meehl, P. (1986). What social scientists don't understand. In D. Fiske & R. Shweder (Eds.), *Metatheory in social science: Pluralisms and subjectivities* (pp. 315–338). Chicago, IL: University of Chicago.

Novella, S. (2016). P value under fire. *Science-Based Medicine.* Retrieved from https://sciencebasedmedicine.org/p-value-under-fire/

Nuzzo, R. (2015). Scientists perturbed by loss of stat tools to sift research fudge from fact. *Scientific American.* Retrieved from https://www.scientificamerican.com/article/scientists-perturbed-by-loss-of-stat-tools-to-sift-research-fudge-from-fact/

O'Boyle, E., & Aguinis, H. (2012). The best and the rest: Revisiting the norm of normality of individual performance. *Personnel Psychology, 65*(1), 79–119. doi:10.5465/ambpp.2011.65869128

Pogrow, S. (2017). The failure of the U.S. education research establishment to identify effective practices: Beware effective practices policies. *Education Policy Analysis Archives, 25*(5), 1–19. Retrieved from https://epaa.asu.edu/ojs/article/view/2517

Porter, T. (1995). *Trust in numbers: The pursuit of objectivity in science and public life.* Princeton, NJ: Princeton University Press.

Shahjahan, R. A. (2011). Decolonizing the evidence-based education and policy movement: Revealing the colonial vestiges in educational policy, research, and neoliberal reform. *Journal of Education Policy, 26*(2), 181–206. doi:10.1080/02680939.2010.508176

Shahjahan, R. A. (2017, October). Making the "invisible" visible in CIE research: Ontology, temporality and affective economies. In *Proceedings of the 2nd Comparative and International Education Symposium: Interrogating and Innovating CIE Research.* Arlington, VA: George Mason University. Retrieved from https://cehd.gmu.edu/2017symposium/

Smith, L. T. (1999). *Decolonizing methodologies: Research and Indigenous peoples.* London: Zed Books.

Steidl, R., Hayes, J., & Schauber, E. (1997). Statistical power analysis in wildlife research. *The Journal of Wildlife Management, 61*(2), 270–279. doi:10.2307/3802582

Steiner-Khamsi, G. (2012). For all by all? The World Bank's global framework for education. In S. Klees, J., Samoff, & N. Stromquist (Eds.), *The World Bank and education* (pp. 3–20). Rotterdam, The Netherlands: Sense Publishers.

Uriel, E. (2013). *Hypothesis testing in the multiple regression model*. Retrieved from https://www.semanticscholar.org/paper/Hypothesis-testing-in-the-multiple-regression-model-Uriel/4bd039f9ec7d50cfdbab3b15173f0c1330ad9386

Verger, A., Edwards Jr., D. B., & Kosar-Altinyelken, H. (2014). Learning from all? The World Bank, aid agencies and the construction of hegemony in education for development. *Comparative Education, 50*(4), 1–19. doi:10.1080/03050068.2014.918713

Verger, A., Fontdevila, C., Rogan, R., & Gurney, T. (forthcoming). Manufacturing an illusory consensus? A bibliometric analysis of the international debate on education privatisation. *International Journal of Educational Development*.

Walters, P., A. Lareau, & Ranis, S. (Eds.). (2009). *Education research on trial: Policy reform and the call for scientific rigor*. New York, NY: Routledge.

CHAPTER 17

Continuing the Conversation: Towards a Model of Collective Critical Reflection in CIE Research

Lê Minh Hằng, Brendan DeCoster, Jeremy R. Gombin-Sperling and Timothy D. Reedy

Abstract

A key part in reimagining comparative and international education (CIE) qualitative research is making sure that emerging researchers are supported in engaging in reflexivity, or methodological practices that promote self-awareness, humility, and questioning. Although reflexivity has become more normative in recent years, there is room to go beyond its common manifestation of the positionality statement. In this chapter, we present a collaborative process of critical reflection in which we engaged during and after a short-term research study abroad program in Cuba. By critical reflection, we refer to a series of dialogical processes dedicated to uncovering the power dynamics of knowledge production, including researcher biases, disciplinary tendencies, relations between researcher and researched, our shortcomings, and the logic of coloniality embedded in comparative international education research. We discuss the value of collaborative critical reflection, the steps we engaged in, and the conditions enabling us to continue this process. Although our reflection stems from a specific study abroad program, these practices can support other short-term research endeavours and other emerging scholars in the field who are grappling with the complexity of research, the pressures of being a doctoral student, and the ethics of knowledge production.

Keywords

reflexivity – critical reflection – emerging scholar(s) – international research – collaboration – short-term

1 Introduction

In February 2017, we embarked on a one-week international research program to Cuba. Our program was the product of a longstanding partnership between a group of scholars and educators in the United States and the *Asociación de Pedagogos de Cuba* (APC, Association of Cuban Educators). This exchange program aimed to foster an environment of mutual learning with a sincere interest in bettering U.S.-Cuban relations despite the ongoing U.S blockade. Throughout the week, we participated in lectures, workshops, and roundtables with Cuban colleagues and discussed a variety of issues and challenges in the education systems on both sides. In addition, the U.S. participants designed and carried out their own qualitative research projects on various aspects of the Cuban education system.

Reflection was a key aspect of the program, and it was built into all stages of the experience. During these reflection activities, we often honed in on the tension between the critical framing, pedagogy, and goals of this research/ study abroad trip and the broader proliferation of short-term international research programs that allow graduate students to conduct extractive research projects, often in a country to which students have had limited to no exposure (Schroeder, Wood, Galiardi, & Koehn, 2009). This is perhaps a reflection of the broader tensions within our field of comparative and international education (CIE) as a whole: even as the call to decolonize CIE research grows louder, this work still takes place within the boundaries of academic structures propped up by settler colonialism and propelled by neoliberal capitalism (Tuck & Yang, 2012). The academy continues to reward our productivity and efficiency rather than encourage a process of inquiry grounded in self-reflection, humility, and concern for the impact our research has on the communities abroad with whom we work. Failure to engage in self-reflective practice – what we refer to as *reflexivity* – has often led to the prioritization of knowledge extraction from communities abroad, while overlooking our complicity as academics in the reproduction of colonial power dynamics (Sobe, 2017).

Yet training in reflexivity also is becoming part of the expectations the academy has for us as doctoral students (Sriprakash & Mukhopadhyay, 2015). This is a valuable development, but in acknowledgment of the ways with which the academy has appropriated alternative and resistance knowledge paradigms into the dominant Western-centric onto-epistemic grammar (Shahjahan, Ramirez, & Andreotti, 2017; Tuck & Yang, 2012), the emerging normativity of reflexivity cannot be taken for granted as a victory. For us, there have been many moments of discomfort with the ways that we are being taught about this practice. Much of the attention seems to be on establishing the importance of reflexivity, which leaves the actual process less examined. As scholars-in-training, we continue to grapple with the question of how we engage in reflexivity, and more importantly, how we engage in reflexivity without being complicit in the coloniality of research (Call-Cummings, Dennis, & Martinez, 2018; Mignolo, 2011).

In this chapter, we present a collaborative critical reflection process that we engaged in before, during, and after our experience in Cuba as an effort to engage with these questions of reflexivity. We focus this chapter around what we refer to as emerging researchers, i.e. doctoral students in the earlier years of their programs. While we would argue that this framework applies to researchers at all levels, we focus on emerging researchers as a reflection of our own positionality and in order to highlight the importance of institutionalizing these practices as early as possible in the training of future scholars. We also want to acknowledge that this collaborative critical reflection process was a messy and imperfect one that we pieced together along the way. In the beginning, we largely pursued reflexivity as an uncritical activity of unpacking our biases and positionalities as researchers; yet through continual return to this exercise as a group, we began to realize the value of systematic and collective critical reflection as a way to move beyond self-centric reflexivity (Pillow, 2003). The process described here is not meant to be viewed as a panacea for combating the limitations of short-term international field research nor as a declaration of a methodological 'best practice'. Rather, we hope to provide a framework that can be adapted and employed by other emerging researchers who wish to disrupt the coloniality of research as well as to further the conversation on methodologies that could embody an ethic of global social justice.

2   Short-Term International Programs

As short-term international programs involving institutions in the Global North traveling to the Global South become more popular, they continue to reproduce postcolonial power hierarchies based on dynamics of knowledge extraction, whether intentionally or not (Hernández-Acosta, 2015; Smith, 1999; Mignolo, 2011). Extraction is further exacerbated by the current academic structure of 'publish or perish', with the quantity of publications increasingly serving as a key indicator of or proxy for one's worth as a scholar (De Bellis, 2009). In the case of short-term research programs such as the one in which we participated in Cuba, there is a structural incentive to actively seek out ways to 'cash in' and produce publishable research as quickly and effectively as possible. This situation collectively reflects the ever-growing influence of neoliberal principles in international higher education, which value the ability of emerging researchers to produce endlessly rather than to assess the systems of power in which they operate, the privileges they possess, and the impact of their actions (Martin & Griffiths, 2012).

Yet these issues are rarely addressed. Many programs do not ask students to engage with the more complicated and potentially harmful aspects of international research (Schroeder et al., 2009). One of the ways through which the extractive nature of short-term programs goes unchecked is through what Elliot (2015) labels the 'doing good' complex of study abroad. When we discuss international experience, we primarily frame it as a positive endeavor of gaining knowledge about the world, developing intercultural competence, and contributing to some abstract global good, without diving into the more critical questions of who benefits and who does not (Elliot, 2015). Arguably, this 'do good' complex reproduces the colonial assumption that the civilizing force from White empires and their current iterations in the international development apparatus was and is still needed and welcomed (Rahman, 2009).

International research programs like the one we participated in are operating within the consequences of this history. Without exposure to critical reflexive practice, many students go through their programs without questioning these narratives (Endres & Gould, 2009). The lack of critical reflection allows programs to operate on the false notion that participants are entitled to extract knowledge from the host community or even that extraction is the desired outcome (Mitchell, Donahue, & Young-Law, 2012). This is not to undermine the agency of students or host communities in interrupting these dynamics; however, it is important to note how these practices are entrenched in the culture of short-term research abroad initiatives.

We argue, therefore, that in order to recalibrate the expectations of participants and to eliminate any grandiose notions of becoming the White savior, we must implement a more engaging and critical process of reflection in international research projects (Kortegast & Boisfontaine, 2015). Opening up uncomfortable but necessary conversations on the power, impact, and the possibilities of research are essential practices that ground the goals and expectations of programs, while also bringing the question of impact in its full nuance to the forefront of the researchers' consciousness.

3 On Reflexivity

On the surface, the rise of reflexivity as a normative methodological discourse (Sriprakash & Mukhopadhyay, 2015) would provide the perfect opportunity to bring critical reflection into short-term research programs. Yet, there is still much disagreement in how we conceptualize reflexivity in academia (D'Cruz, Gillingham, & Melendez, 2007). More often than not, researchers see reflexivity as a mere acknowledgment of one's social identities (e.g., race, gender, sexuality, etc.) and positionality, with little self-interrogation into how the possession of such experiences influences research questions, methodological decisions, and data interpretation and analysis (D'Cruz et al., 2005). While there are scholars working as we are to complicate the idea of reflexivity (Pillow, 2003; Yarwood, Ogilvie, & Yianni, 2015), the concept is often presented as if the sole act of unpacking one's own biases is enough to resolve the power inequalities fundamentally embedded in dominant CIE research practices (Mignolo, 2011). Thus, while calls to engage in reflexivity have indeed become normative, this dominant form can serve as a reinforcement of a Western epistemological obsession with research validity, or to allow researchers to release themselves from serious engagement with 'the problematic of representation' (Pillow, 2003; Sriprakash & Mukhopadhyay, 2015). To draw a parallel to Tuck and Yang (2012)'s condemnation of casual references to 'decolonize' research methods, the appropriation of 'reflexivity' is akin to a "move to innocence" (p. 10) so that scholars can resolve any sense of guilt or responsibility to acknowledge the impact of colonialism undergirding the majority of countries where CIE research is conducted without having to concede land, power, or privilege. In other words, reflexivity can often function as an act of scholastic narcissism that serves to comfort the researcher rather than to unpack the dynamic repercussions of the research in which we are involved (Bourdieu, 1998).

For doctoral students, caught in the liminality of being a scholar-in-training, navigating reflexivity can be a process fraught with anxieties, tensions, and, in many cases, guilt over not fulfilling an ethical duty (Giampapa, 2011; Yarwood et al., 2015). Yet as our voices continue to be undervalued by the power structures of the academy, the angst, rage, uncertainties, guilt, and worry that we encounter is often left to non-traditional publication avenues such as blogs, social media, or conversations with our support networks. Only recently has it become acceptable for emerging scholars to publish more reflective pieces, especially within comparative and international education (Giabiconi, 2013; Naveed, Sakata, Kefallinou, Young, & Anand, 2017). While we do have a plethora of materials on methodology to consult, they tend to provide technical guidance rather than the lived experience of scholars struggling with these questions. Being left alone to ruminate on methodological dilemmas while still very much a novice researcher can sometimes turn into a question of *Has everyone figured out reflexivity but me?* thus reproducing the debilitating imposter syndrome (Posselt, 2018).

In this context, how do we as emerging researchers escape the superficial conceptualization of reflexivity as the positionality statement that turns it into just another checkbox to be ticked? When we say our unique positions have inevitably left an imprint on our analyses, do we just leave that as a hanging observation or delve specifically into the ways in which our readings of the data reflect something uniquely *us*? How do we get beyond the intellectual narcissism that treats reflexivity as an individual exercise of listing out our various identities and into a genuine conversation on accountability and ethics?

4   The Value of the Collective

For us, a way to more productively engage with these questions of reflexivity has been to do so as a group over a long period of time. Arguably, a key shortcoming of 'shallow' reflexivity is the fact that it often takes place as a personal, individualized, isolating endeavor that can easily turn into the narcissism critiqued above. Therefore, the key principle that guided our collective engagement was to see reflexivity as an ethical commitment in which "the reflexive practitioner or researcher is constantly engaged in the process of questioning (self-monitoring) their own knowledge claims and those of others as he/she engages in social interaction and the micro-practices of knowledge/power" (D'Cruz, et al., 2005, p. 83).

Furthermore, our steps support a culture of accountability, where we as emerging researchers seek not to call out one another, but rather construct what Bresler (2002) refers to as a zone of interpretation – a space where our different values, beliefs, and assumptions about our research can exist in tension and foment the establishment of new understandings and ideas. Through this collective critical reflection, the participants are forced to engage in 'rival thinking', which is not only the willingness but also the ethical responsibility for a researcher to subject their thoughts to critical scrutiny via systematic searching, evaluation, and exposure of individual and group biases (Amis & Silk, 2008). Because the participant has to explain and clarify their thought processes to others, this may tap into more taken-for-granted onto-epistemological assumptions.[1] In other words, through committing ourselves to reflexivity, through explaining oneself and listening to others' experiences, we are exercising a form of "epistemological vigilance" (Bourdieu & Nice, 2004, p. 89) to ensure that we continue to confront difficult questions and dive into discomfort rather than seek absolution from guilt.

As doctoral students, we acknowledge that these discussions can be extremely difficult due to the pressure to perform, to say certain things in order to 'look good' and 'sound intellectual'. But at some point, we began to trust one another enough to become vulnerable in our sharing. Our abilities to hear critiques of ourselves, to commit to difficult discussions, and avoid the pitfalls of performativity would not have been possible without trust. There is no linear path towards establishing this. Trust, for us, is a cultivated sentiment that comes with continued and persistent involvement, and above all, a commitment to support one another throughout the process of making sense of shared experiences and our relationships to them. Even though we come from disparate backgrounds and continue to have onto-epistemological and methodological clashes, our work together has created a space where we know our critiques come more from a place of empathy and not a desire to seem superior or to crush others' ideas.

Finally, we argue that there is no precise beginning or end point to this process; critically reflective inquiry and the cultivation of trust is an ongoing process that not only occurs prior and during research, but continues through sustained dialogue both among the research group *and with* the participants and institutions that contributed to the knowledge we produced (Moore, 2016). So frequently, one research project results in one conference presentation, and if we are lucky, a publication afterward. After this, we typically forge distance from that research and move hastily on to something else (Dillabough, 2008). The 'publish or perish' pressure to prioritize the quantity rather than the quality of our publications provides a further disincentive to engage in long, sustained inquiry. For us, the commitment to return as a group to this particular experience in Cuba is a move to detach ourselves from this compressed time, to answer Shahjahan's (2015) call to "move beyond Eurocentric notions of time that colonize our academic lives" (p. 489).

In the section below, we will lay out steps that we put together from our own experience, although as noted in the introduction, our actual collaboration did not unfold in such a neat and linear trajectory. What we hope to provide is a more systematic framework that can serve as an inspiration to other emerging researchers or short-term international program practitioners who wish to build this into their experience. Before continuing, we want to acknowledge that we ourselves were inspired by the program directors of our trip to Cuba, who openly centered the colonial dynamics of our Global North-Global South exchange and the constraints of this short-term program on our ability to conduct sustained research. They encouraged and implemented dialogical reflection sessions throughout our time abroad, which inspired us to continue to reflect together after the trip. In this sense, what we share in this chapter is less a critique of our experience in this short-term research program and more a willingness to expand and further imagine new possibilities.

5 The Process of Collective Critical Reflection

5.1 *Step 1. The Formation of the Group*

Ideally, the researchers that would form a working group for critical reflection would have been on the same international research program in the same year. Having a similar foundation would support the group's ability to dive into several nuances: how different people experience similar interactions and encounters, how research questions are formed, and how each member comes to a different goal for his/her research experience. Indeed, what allowed the four of us to continue our sustained engagement was our common experience in Cuba and being doctoral students from the same graduate program in the United States. Nevertheless, we are not a homogenous group. Each of us pursued a different research interest: values education through the natural sciences, teachers' self-perceptions, education for citizenship formation, and English pedagogy in higher education. Three of us are White cisgender men from the United States, and one of us is a cisgender woman from Vietnam. Some of us are fluent Spanish speakers; the others had to rely on interpreters throughout the trip. The combination of both commonality and differences allowed us to engage in more thought-provoking exchanges about our research and our relationship to Cuba.

In the absence of being involved in the same project, we believe the following points of commonality can still support the establishment of strong research reflection groups:
- Researchers who have participated in projects in the same country or region;
- Researchers whose sites of inquiry are similar (i.e. similar NGOs, school systems, governmental agencies, private organization, etc.);
- Researchers who conducted their research around the same time;
- Researchers whose work and programs are built around similar themes and disciplines.

5.2 *Step 2: Initial Analytical Session Prior to the Program*

Prior to going abroad, the group should meet at least once to discuss their expectations and the nature of their research projects. During this meeting, members should take time to reflect individually on what brought them to their research questions, given that the formation of the research topic itself is often deeply rooted in the researcher's life, and then share those with one another for feedback. The feedback should address concerns for any assumptions of the host community embedded in the initial research design, and support one another in constructing alternatives if necessary.

With this specific experience in Cuba, we had to come to term with the various privileges and 'baggage' we brought to Cuba. Although arguably most of the program participants did wish to play a part in improving the relations between the U.S. and Cuba, we were still situated as part of the U.S. academy. Our academic privileges are what allowed us to enter Cuba, conduct research, and leave. We need to acknowledge this power, since it is often all too easy to 'research and run', to extract what we feel we need for our growing careers in academia without considering the impact on the communities we would work with abroad.

Our national origin was also an issue of particular salience. For the three of us from the United States, the dominant narratives have always presented Cuba with suspicion and, frankly, as an enemy to U.S. sovereignty and democracy. Intertwined with this suspicion is also a fascination with Cuba as an exotified 'mystery success', especially for us in the field of education (Bell, 2013). On the other hand, from a Vietnamese perspective, Cuba is anything but exotic; it is still perceived to be the fraternal brother in socialist solidarity, although this does not mean that the Vietnamese perception of Cuba is unproblematic. Recognizing these identities also reflects different historical power dynamics in operation. As White U.S. men, we must name the legacy of Global North arrogance and colonialism, of which our country has and continues to be a part. For the other of us, as a Southeast Asian woman who is now being trained in the Global North, there was a different struggle with how country of citizenship cannot be automatic proof of innocence in neocolonial complicity. Unpacking these elements became part of our reflective process before, during, and after our time in Cuba.

5.3 *Step 3: In-Country Reflection Session(s)*

Step 3 is easiest for those researchers involved on the same program; however, through information and communication technologies, this meeting or meetings can also be held with a group that is operating in different geographical locations and time zones. Meetings should build off of established field notes and observations to create a dialogue in which each member assesses their progress and compares their expectations for their project with the realities they are encountering. Participants should use these sessions to adjust research questions, objectives, methods, and in general ways of engaging with the field.

For one of our group members, the in-country reflection sessions pushed him to re-evaluate his relationship to his home country, the United States. His research focused on Cuban English teachers' relationships with and values regarding the English language. During an interview with a female Cuban English teacher in her early 20s, he and his colleague asked how bringing in

English materials from places like the United States affected the dynamics of her class and whether it created tensions with her values. The Cuban teacher's response was powerful. She said that for her, there was a line – a line that maintains many of her core values as a Cuban woman while allowing her to learn and understand the viewpoints of others with different perspectives. It was here that the researcher felt the teacher's pride in her work, and how it reaffirmed her relationship to her country.

The experience had a profound impact on this group member, and he brought this to our reflection session. It made him wonder if he has this line in relation to the United States:

> I feel that I am always questioning the decisions and movements of my government – now more than ever under Trump – but I have not really asked myself if I have this line. I feel that I have certain values that feel true to who I am, but it is hard for me to see this as part of a sense of self – informed by my relationship to my country or not. (From reflection journal)

The teacher's response made him realize how much he still had to dissect about his relationship to his own country, and how this 'line' would potentially impact his research project and interpretations.

5.4 *Step 4: Post-Trip Reflection Sessions*

Once back in the researchers' home country, groups should meet biweekly for an extended period of time (one to two months at a minimum) to discuss their research. We found that it was helpful to set aside at least one hour for each dialogue to provide sufficient time to push each others' thinking. The first session should be about sharing the particular findings and analysis to provide context to the other group members, but the other sessions should be guided by the members' particular interests, issues, and questions raised. For example, as we started unpacking our limitations and positionalities during our initial meeting, we came to realize several fundamental issues in our research: the role of language and access to information, the problematic assertion that we were researching 'Cuba' when our data collection was limited to one or two cities, and whether natural sciences, which was one of our research foci, provided more of a universal language for sharing experiences with Cuban colleagues. Table 17.1 captures some of the aspects of our research that we discussed alongside related sample questions. In between the meetings, group members should return to their research and assess what may need to be reworked in all sections of the research (e.g., framework, literature, interpretation of findings, etc.).

TABLE 17.1 Potential themes and questions for reflection sessions

Theme of inquiry	Potential questions
Place	How have our perceptions of Cuba changed since the research program? What is our relationship to the country? What tensions remain?
Phenomenon/ phenomena	In reflecting, what do we feel led us to our research topic in Cuba? Were there other things we wanted to know that we realize now? What were our assumptions about the phenomenon/we wanted to study? Have these changed?
Participants	What led us to the participants we included for our study? Do we feel any biases we hold led us to those particular individuals? What does our relationship (or lack thereof) look like to our colleagues in Cuba?
Perceptions	What are the different elements of perception that informed the interpretation of our data? Do we have any interpretations that in retrospect we realize our research from Cuba does not support? What is the impact of our interpretations on how we understand Cuba, our colleagues, and our research focus?
Power	In what ways were power dynamics manifested throughout the research experience? Between participants and researchers? Among participants? Among researchers? How did the identities we hold and our affiliation with a U.S. program affect how we were treated and the conversations we had with participants? What are the existing dynamics of authority and knowledge production that confined our research in and about Cuba? How were they embedded and reproduced in our own work? How did we go about and how will we continue interrogating and challenging these dynamics?

5.5   Step 5: Reconnect with Participants (Member Check)

This is a critical step in not just reflexivity but any research endeavor in order to challenge the historical, colonial division of intellectual labor in which "global peripheries served as data mines for the accumulation of knowledge and the development of theory in the global North" rather than as legitimate producers of knowledge (Smith, 1999; Takayama, Sriprakash, & Connell, 2017).

This step can be challenging and was so in our process: we have struggled to include our Cuban colleagues in our collective reflection. In part this is due to communication challenges; the limited internet connectivity and surveillance mechanisms that our colleagues in Cuba face have made it difficult to maintain sustained contact. Moreover, upon returning to our lives in the United States, we prioritized other responsibilities and commitments above continuing the conversation. As mentioned, we do not feel there is ever a finite end point to the research process, and we are now taking steps to collaborate more with our Cuban colleagues. One of our members is working with a Cuban colleague on translating materials that another colleague working in the field of environmental science can review and reflect on. Another is finishing a manuscript on their work on English language education and will be in contact with Cuban counterparts for their review. If we wish to consider ourselves researchers who stand for equity, reciprocity, and ethics in research, reconnecting with our participants to discuss our work and its impact is essential.

Regarding our recommendations on this step, the member check process needs to be a conscious commitment from the moment we begin drafting our research plans. The members of a reflection group should design, discuss, and adjust their initial member check strategy prior to going abroad. While in country they should then talk to their participants and international colleagues about their proposed process. Through this conversation, emerging researchers can propose their vision for maintaining contact and collaboration (communication technologies like Skype, email correspondence, additional in-person meetings after the research project), and work with their colleagues to establish a plan that feels realistic and conducive to all parties. One venue that we are exploring for more in-person interaction is international conferences like the annual Comparative and International Education Society (CIES) meeting. Three of our members and one of our Cuban colleagues were able to use the most recent conference in Mexico City to discuss our collaborative, reflective process and seek their thoughts on the work we are doing. Whatever form member checks take, they should be repeated along with Step 4 as many times as would be productive for the members of the group (Green, 2007).

6   Reflecting on Our Reflections

In laying out these steps, we recognize that it is likely that doctoral students and emerging researchers globally are already engaging in some version of these practices; however, we still want to present our experience for two reasons. First of all, academia can be and has often been an individuating and isolating experience, especially for scholars who come from underrepresented and marginalized backgrounds (Posselt, 2018). Voicing the value of being in a group is not only about highlighting the professional and emotional support that belonging in a community can provide, but also to pose an explicit challenge to the individuating pressure that is rooted in Euro-centric structures of knowledge production and merit. Second of all, it is important for this collective reflexivity to be a systematic process, meaning that reflexivity is engaged with not as an occasional exercise of 'confession', but as a courageous commitment to continually throw oneself into discomfort.

Perhaps the process outlined above can give an impression of a harmonious collaboration of young scholars/friends who got together once in a while and chatted amicably about our research practices and experiences; it was not. Like we discussed above, although we share a lot of commonalities, we experienced and continue to experience tensions. As young scholars-in-training, we are still in the midst of grappling with our particular onto-epistemological assumptions and axiological commitments as future scholars, and there have been moments where it felt impossible to reconcile some of our philosophical differences. Some of us still value certainty, coherence, resolution, and the discovery of truths (even if they are multiple), while others wrestle with whether to still commit ourselves to these modern/Western ways of knowing and being. At times, it felt and feels like we are ships passing in the night.

But again, this is where the value of the collective shines. We made a commitment to each other, and so we continued explaining ourselves and, in so doing, came to understand the others' perspectives better. No matter the larger onto-political battles we were engaging in, we trusted each other enough to continue making ourselves vulnerable. This commitment to continue engaging with one another may already be, in itself, one small step towards the decolonization of research.

Acknowledgements

The authors wish to acknowledge equal participation of all listed authors. However, we also want to acknowledge the contributions of a fifth member of our group, Melanie Baker Robbins. She participated in all reflection sessions and presented with us at a conference where we first began drafting the ideas for this chapter. Due to personal commitments she was unable to be a part of this writing process; however, we would not be where we are without her.

Note

1   By 'onto-epistemological', we are drawing from Karen Barad's (2007) concept to indicate that questions of ontology and epistemology cannot be considered separately.

References

Amis, J., & Silk, M. (2008). The philosophy of politics of quality in qualitative organizational research. *Organizational Research Methods, 11*(3), 456–480. doi:10.1177/1094428107300341

Barad, K. (2007). *Meeting the universe halfway: Quantum physics and the entanglement of matter and meaning*. Durham, NC: Duke University Press.

Bell, K. (2013). Doing qualitative fieldwork in Cuba: Social research in politically sensitive locations. *International Journal of Social Research Methodology, 16*(2), 109–124. doi:10.1080/13645579.2011.653217

Bourdieu, P. (1998). *Practical reason: On the theory of action*. Stanford, CA: Stanford University Press.

Bourdieu, P., & Nice, R. (2004). *Science of science and reflexivity*. Chicago, IL: University of Chicago Press.

Bresler, L. (2002). The interpretive zone in international qualitative research. *Counterpoints: Research in international education: Experience, theory, & practice* (Vol. 180, pp. 39–81). New York, NY: Peter Lang.

Call-Cummings, M., Dennis, B., & Martinez, S. (2018). The role of researcher in participatory inquiry: Modeling intra-active reflexivity in conversational reflections. *Cultural Studies ↔ Critical Methodologies*. doi:10.1177/1532708617750677

D'Cruz, H., Gillingham, P., & Melendez, S. (2005). Reflexivity, its meanings and relevance for social work: A critical review of the literature. *British Journal of Social Work, 37*(1), 73–90. doi:10.1093/bjsw/bcl001

De Bellis, N. (2009). *Bibliometrics and citation analysis: From the Science Citation Index to cybermetrics*. Lanham, MD: The Scarecrow Press.

Dillabough, J. (2008). Exploring historicity and temporality in social science methodology: A case for methodological and analytical justice. In K. Gallagher (Ed.), *The methodological dilemma: Creative, critical and collaborative approaches to qualitative research* (pp. 185–218). New York, NY: Routledge.

Endres, D., & Gould, M. (2009). "I am also in the position to use my whiteness to help them out": The communication of whiteness in service learning. *Western Journal of Communication, 73*(4), 418–436. doi:10.1080/10570310903279083

Elliot, M. L. (2015). Critical ethnographic analysis of "doing good" on short-term international immersion experiences. *Occupational Therapy International, 22*(3), 121–130. doi:10.1002/oti.1390

Giabiconi, J. (2013). Serendipity ... *mon amour?* On discomfort as a prerequisite for anthropological knowledge. *Social Anthropology, 21*(2), 199–212. doi:10.1111/1469-8676.12013

Giampapa, F. (2011). The politics of "being and becoming" a researcher: Identity, power, and negotiating the field. *Journal of Language, Identity and Education, 10*(3), 132–144. doi:10.1080/15348458.2011.585304

Green, A. (2007). La lucha de los siete hermanos y su hermana Olowaili en defensa de la Madre Tierra: Hacia la pervivencia cultural del pueblo Kuna Tule [The struggle of the seven brothers and their sister Olowaili to defend Mother Earth: Towards the cultural survival of the Kuna Tule people]. *Revista Educación y Pedagogía, 19*(49), 227–237.

Hernández-Acosta, J. (2015). Designing cultural policy in a postcolonial colony: The case of Puerto Rico. *International Journal of Cultural Policy, 23*(3), 285–299. doi:10.1080/10286632.2015.1043288

Kortegast, C., & Boisfontaine, M. (2015). Beyond "It was good": Students' post-study abroad practices for negotiating meaning. *Journal of College Student Development, 56*(8), 812–828. doi:10.1353/csd.2015.0091

Martin, F., & Griffiths, H. (2012). Power and representation: A postcolonial reading of global partnerships and teacher development through North–South study visits. *British Educational Research Journal, 38*(6), 907–927. doi:10.1080/01411926.2011.600438

Mignolo, W. (2011). *The darker side of Western modernity: Global futures, decolonial options.* Durham, NC: Duke University Press.

Mitchell, T., Donahue, D., & Young-Law, C. (2012). Service learning as a pedagogy of whiteness. *Equity & Excellence in Education, 45*(4), 612–629. doi:10.1080/10665684.2012.715534

Moore, A. (2016). Doing and using educational research: Collaborative approaches in changing contexts. *Research in Education, 96*(1), 31–38. doi:10.1177/0034523716664575

Naveed, A., Sakata, N., Kefallinou, A., Young, S., & Anand, K. (2017). Understanding, embracing and reflecting upon the messiness of doctoral fieldwork. *Compare, 47*(5), 773–792. doi:10.1080/03057925.2017.1344031

Pillow, W. (2003). Confession, catharsis, or cure? Rethinking the uses of reflexivity as methodological power in qualitative research. *International Journal of Qualitative Studies in Education, 16*(2), 175–196. doi:10.1080/0951839032000060635

Posselt, J. (2018). Rigor and support in racialized learning environments: The case of graduate education. *New Directions for Higher Education, 181*, 59–70. doi:10.1002/he.20271

Rahman, S. (2009). Socio-economic vulnerability and neo-liberalism: Lessons from Bangladesh. *South Asia Research, 29*(3), 235–254. doi:10.1177/0262728009029000303

Schroeder, K., Wood, C., Galiardi, S., & Koehn, J. (2009). First, do no harm: Ideas for mitigating negative community impacts of short-term study abroad. *Journal of Geography, 108*(3), 141–147. doi:10.1080/00221340903120866

Shahjahan, R. A. (2015). Being 'lazy' and slowing down: Toward decolonizing time, our body, and pedagogy. *Educational Philosophy and Theory, 47*(5), 488–501. doi:10.1080/00131857.2014.880645

Shahjahan, R. A., Ramirez, G. B., & Andreotti, V. (2017). Attempting to imagine the unimaginable: A decolonial reading of global university rankings. *Comparative Education Review, 61*(S1), S51–S73. doi:10.1086/690457

Smith, L. T. (1999). *Decolonizing methodologies: Research and indigenous peoples.* New York, NY: Zed Books.

Sobe, N. W. (2017). Travelling researchers, colonial difference: Comparative education in an age of exploration. *Compare, 47*(3), 332–343. doi:10.1080/03057925.2016.1273760

Sriprakash, A., & Mukhopadhyay, R. (2015). Reflexivity and the politics of knowledge: Researchers as 'brokers' and 'translators' of educational development. *Comparative Education, 51*(2), 231–246. doi:10.4324/9781315114521-8

Takayama, K., Sriprakash, A., & Connell, R. (2017). Toward a postcolonial comparative and international education. *Comparative Education Review, 61*(S1), S1–S24. doi:10.1086/690455

Tuck, E., & Yang, K. W. (2012). Decolonization is not a metaphor. *Decolonization: Indigeneity, Education & Society, 1*(1), 1–40.

Yarwood, G., Ogilvie, H., & Yianni, C. (2015). Working in collaboration: Three PhD students trouble reflexivity. *Journal of Perspectives in Applied Academic Practice, 3*(2), 72–81. doi:10.14297/jpaap.v3i2

CHAPTER 18

New Directions for Consideration: Looking Forward and Ahead

Emily Anderson, Supriya Baily, Radhika Iyengar and Matthew A. Witenstein

Abstract

In this concluding chapter, the authors urge researchers to be open to many ways of thinking about their research questions and modes of analysis. The authors first revisit earlier chapters and summarize their work mainly focussing on the importance of voice in research, suggesting strategies to decolonize and innovate research and practice to amplify voices and participation. The objective of the chapter is to urge researchers and practitioners to continuously question their own research agendas to make them more inclusive. The authors conclude the chapters by recommending ideas that will enable researchers to approach crafting research ideas and their treatment with more caution.

Keywords

amplify voices – co-construction – methodological innovations – pre-fieldwork training – inclusive

1   Introduction

One of the goals of this book was to challenge the ways in which research is conceptualized and activated in comparative and international education (CIE). CIE is a dynamic field comprised of individuals trained across different academic disciplines and methodological traditions. While this diversity brings opportunities to incorporate practices from the social and behavioural sciences to the humanities, it does not yield consensus on how to engage comparison as a methodological approach (Baily, Shah, & Call-Cummings, 2014; Wiseman & Anderson, 2015). As we conclude this edited collection, we extend the recommendations posited by our contributors to identify practical approaches to learning, doing and using CIE research. We begin by revisiting each author's contributions in an effort to synthesize their conclusions. Next, with these conclusions in mind, we articulate the importance of voice in research, and finally, we introduce strategies to decolonize and innovate graduate-level research coursework, and to incorporate more inclusive practices to amplify voice, participation, and representation in knowledge creation across the research continuum. The core of the book illuminates diverse narratives and opportunities about engaging and involving less-heard voices more clearly and inclusively. Moreover, this combination of steps forward provides opportunities for advancing an inclusive intellectual agenda for decolonizing CIE research. In other words, the amplification of marginalized voices and availability of safe spaces can advance the field of CIE by acknowledging, applying and diligently working on these elements.

Reflecting on the symposium, the select statements from key plenary speakers offered a chance for us to recall the issues that were pressed upon in the dialogue of the event. Taking key elements of those statements, our chapters by plenary speakers (Leigh Patel, Gerardo Blanco, Patricia Parker and Ameena Ghaffar-Kucher) deepened the conversations around the need to seek reconciliation around methodological issues, provoke people to move outside of their methodological comfort zones, a reminder to research 'with' rather than 'on', and to reframe where we locate the centre.

These plenary speakers' voices opened space for other contributors to make their own calls for change. Alisha Braun explored the photo-voice method in the context of disabilities. D. Brent Edwards Jr. presented a critique of relying solely on quantitative methods to inform policy. He urged us to look at the underlying assumptions of using statistical procedures that provide the foundation of "what works", "best practices" and "evidence-based policy" in a global context. Kelly Grace and Sothy Eng took us to Cambodia to investigate the use of interviews and focus group discussions as tools to unravel the use of western paradigms used by INGOS and NGOS. Lê Minh Hằng, Brendan DeCoster, Jeremy Gombin-Sperling and Timothy Reedy engaged in self-reflection during workshops in Cuba to understand the impact of research on communities and stakeholders. The authors advocated for the inclusion of systematic collective critical reflective practice in all CIE work to make researchers more aware of their biases and to aim to make the research process more ethical. Karen Ross explored impact from insider and outsider viewpoints. She asked the question: who defines what impact is (or ought to be) in development work and what does this mean for organizational learning and reflection, as well as for research partnerships? Derrick Tu examined the pertinent and yet often-neglected topic of aesthetic knowledge in arts-based educational research and its potential application toward addressing inequalities. Huma Kidwai presented the voices of madrassa (Muslim education institutions) leaders in India, who are often frowned upon by mainstream formal education advocates. Erik Byker took us to Punjab, India, with motivated volunteers who use data to energize citizens. Byker helped us to understand the motivation of these foot-soldiers, the volunteers, who walk village after village to build awareness of the learning levels and learning issues of students. Radhika Iyengar and Matthew A. Witenstein's chapter questioned gender biases that are entrenched in culture and traditions in India, seeking to open the eyes of policy makers, researchers and practitioners alike to take a step forward in acknowledging the unlevel plane in terms of gender, and to proactively create educational outlets for life-long learning.

With this diverse repertoire of writers articulating wide-ranging interpretations of ontology, epistemology and method, the importance of voice in research has never been more meaningful or powerful. The ability for researchers to engage in a multitude of ways with how they consider their research questions, the data they collect and the modes of analysis they use, is exciting and ought to be strongly encouraged and advocated as a critical innovation in CIE research. Yet in all this, we must still worry as researchers about the co-option of voice and the fidelity of process, and in this way, we offer up some final thoughts about both the decolonization, intersectionality, and innovation of CIE research.

2   Considerations for Amplifying Voice

With the intent of the symposium and this volume to be able to navigate towards and for a better future for CIE research and educational change more generally, one of the critical tensions researchers and practitioners must navigate concerns their respective roles in this dynamic exchange space. Some questions one may ask include: Who has chosen this work and research endeavour? What types of methodologies are being used and are they really "alternative" (unpacking the notion of alternative methodologies is an important conversation to tackle in another forum) or are they socially just? How do intersectional identities play a role in the methodological process? Perhaps even more importantly are they local methodologies or at least co-developed between the researcher and members of the community? What words do we use when we articulate the ways in which we link with communities to hear and understand their voices and to make them more central in the research work done? Who decides how voice should be amplified and what should be shared? And why are we amplifying their voices (and who says they need to be)?

Perhaps through the exchange process between researcher and community members/participants, better approaches to making joint decisions about what should be amplified could be made. For example, Patel, Villarruel, and Wong (2013) worked through this tension between amplifying the voice of patients while also ensuring communities are meaningfully made aware of the opportunities available and how they can invest in their health. If part of this volume's focus is then on what can be known and how, we may want to ask ourselves, in what ways are we amplifying voice versus "giving voice"? Since the concept of giving voice may be viewed as hegemonically structured (with sensitivity to power) since it connotes someone bestowing something upon another (especially considering one has always had a voice), one might ask themselves how to move beyond this structure in a more dialogic manner. Perhaps researchers may consider grappling with concepts such as cultural curiosity and cultural humility in the work they are aiming to embark upon (Foronda, Baptiste, Reinholdt, & Ousman, 2016)? This volume promised to attend to the problem of the reproduction of unjust, rigidly structured hierarchies in and through CIE research processes. One way to unhinge this structure is through demonstrating interest and care (curiosity) while acknowledging to communities we are working in and with, that we have as much to learn in exchange and in partnership through the dialogic space (humility). This type of perspective and engagement may enable the opening up of opportunities for the dismantling of unjust hierarchies, in solidarity, and where educational change can be authored through careful, respectful, and mutual consideration.

Another important component still to resolve concerns how we, as CIE researchers, might create room in our research practice for voice amplification along with cultural curiosity and humility? What might this look like? Perhaps the language we use in our research work in concert with promising practices that are more collaborative and participatory, are meaningful and integral steps. As Mitra (2008) pointed out, collaborative and participatory practices can result in meaningful knowledge-building for those whose voices are amplified, while also cultivating enhanced relationships – a bedrock of ethical research practice. This synergy could ultimately lead to richer, more powerful research that effectively supports the needs of diverse communities.

One final opportunity to consider in our research practice is Seale's (2015) concept of an amplitude framework. She defined amplitude as "… the extent to which student voice has a transformative impact on the teaching and learning structures and spaces within a higher education institution" (Seale, 2015, p. 17).

Her explanation of amplitude is critical and clarifies that it is not necessarily the loudness of the voice but its power that is more crucial. Amplifying a voice in a powerful manner can therefore be leveraged into more equitable relationships without drowning out other communal voices. Finally, engaging an amplitude framework has the possibility of co-construction leading to new (or re-defined) spaces where community members' dignity and personhood is valued, and where the collective of voices may have enhanced power, tools and decision-making opportunities. But, how to do we provide a framework for this work for new scholars? How can we nurture courage in methodological work when we too often take the path of least resistance? How can we encourage students to "look, listen, learn … working with communities, whether they be households or schools … by spending non-contingent time with people and in their environments … to better understand the local context and to build relationships and trust" (Adukia, 2017)?

3   From Talk to Action

From the earliest stages of planning both the symposium and this book, as a team of colleagues we recognized that as researchers within CIE, we wanted to ensure that people were cognizant of the power of decolonizing research methods and the wide array of ways it was possible. As we navigate a more critical era, where the role of research is not just to show or tell, but also to promote transformation, the cases in this book seek to highlight the ways in which research can be a tool both of decolonization and enhanced and meaningful participation in the processes and practices of research. Part of our work was also to think about how to support novice researchers in these exercises. Conversations concerning ontological and epistemological philosophies can often feel like a distraction or diversion from picking a design and getting on with collecting the data. We have to reiterate as Pryor (2010) does that one's position on ontology and epistemology "inevitably shapes the research that you will do and the way you go about it" (p. 163). Awareness of our ontology and epistemology are especially important for students who find themselves struggling to approach the question of their choice, "cut off from their deepest proclivities for shaping questions to study, modes of enquiry, and forms of expression and representation" (Piantanida & Garman, 2010, p. 246). This constraint continues to arise, despite efforts at diversifying research, where the "hegemonic grip of postpositivist science" (Piantanida & Garman, 2010, p. 246) maintains control of funding and policy work. This book encourages us to think about research methodologies that are inclusive, procedures that take into account how they are received by those from whom we collect data, and topics that need to be given the space in academia to bridge the gaps among policy, research and practice. But this can be hard to implement, and the idea of both decolonization and decoupling the power of research with the researcher requires the courage to embrace uncertainty and change as well as the confidence that there is an audience receptive to your work. As such we seek to provide some tangible recommendations to support researchers who seek to feel more confident and supported as they work to shake off that "hegemonic grip" (Piantanida & Garman, 2010, p. 246).

One of the challenges in activating a research agenda is to learn and unlearn how to engage with research. Here, we refer to research as a systematic process of data collection and analysis intended for external dissemination. If we aim to innovate the ways in which research is taught in graduate-level CIE coursework, then we must also interrogate the ways in which research is produced, diffused, and received within CIE as an epistemic community. Citing Hass (1992), Schmidt (2009) defines an epistemic community as one that seeks to "coordinate agreement among themselves on policy ideas, which scholars have shown they may do in a variety of ways in a wide range of venues" (p. 310). The research continuum as discussed here, includes the processes through which research problems are articulated and investigated through data collection and analysis procedures; dissemination in peer-reviewed journals and books; and the ways in which consumers of research receive and make use of scientific knowledge.

The road from identifying a research question to the sharing of the results with your audience is often conceptualized as a cyclical process where new knowledge informs new questions (Pryor, 2010). While conceptualizing the process as a cycle suggests opportunities for reflection and innovation, it can also normalize a particular (dominant) system of knowledge production. This in turn can result in aversion to risk taking, privileging certain types of questions and methodologies over others, and legitimizes specific qualifications for expertise and review. Taken together, we argue, these factors can and do function to stagnate methodological innovation in the field of CIE.

Our introduction to research is shaped by our consumption of research via the scholarly literature. We suggest the following recommendations to support the continued exploration of decolonizing and innovating CIE research:

3.1   *Interrogate the Literature*
Our first engagements with literature require us to be able to navigate complex vocabularies, theories, and methodologies. In qualitative research, as referenced across many of the chapters in this book, it also requires the reader's ability to interrogate questions, assumptions, and procedures that are embedded

within research as the disseminated product of scholarship. Engagement with and interrogation of the literature – as a set of coordinated voices and perspectives within a field of study – is often relegated to the hidden curriculum of graduate coursework. As a result, students may not be offered the opportunity develop interrogatory reading skills which could enable their critical thinking and extension of the literature as part of their early academic training.

3.2 Integrate the Study of Methodology

The segmentation of methodology from other content-related coursework further normalizes the dislocation of research processes from outcomes. Instead, we imagine how research methods courses might be reconceptualized to promote graduate students' critical engagement with the literature and interrogation of research methods. Through this interrogatory framework, we posit that coursework and fieldwork could be better integrated to allow students to view the literature as people and ideas within an epistemic community, and to also provide opportunities to practice data collection and analysis procedures in real-word settings.

3.3 Support Greater Exposure to Field Work

As articulated by Grace and Eng (this collection), pre-fieldwork training is essential in order to orient graduate students to the realities of researching in and with communities that may represent different cultural identities than embodied by the researcher. Understanding the research site in terms of place and space may encourage graduate students to apply data collection and analysis procedures under the supervision of more experienced scholars, which in turn, may create spaces for methodological innovation.

3.4 Sit with the Discomfort

Knowing that methodologies are constantly evolving, we also recognize the power of gatekeepers in the research process who might feel most comfortable directing/curating research studies which are similar to their own methodological preferences. This methodological safe harbor does not encourage novice researchers to take risks and push forward methodological innovations they are ready to try. Definitions of the evidence of impact, whether we work in CIE arenas that are focused on practice or theory, could be opened up to broader, more innovative and creative ways to engage in the research process. Situating ourselves as experts requires a level of vulnerability to open ourselves up to methodological innovations we are unsure of, to speak out against unjust systems of power in knowledge creation that we are a part of, and to balance our willingness to take risks despite what we might see being demanded in venues such as funding, policy and publishing.

3.5 *Open up Publishing Venues*

Methodological innovations require editors willing to take risks and reviewers who are willing to be open to innovation. This volume has sought to highlight the ways in which methodology can be both rigorous and innovative, and seeking ways to ensure that such research is disseminated will be critical to the work of decolonizing research methods.

4   Concluding Thoughts

We end this book with the need to think about courage. Courage to take risks in our search for knowledge, courage to open up to multiple ways of knowing, and courage to lead a path forward to engage in this process of decolonization and innovation. This book emerged from a collaborative process in an environment with multiple scholars who represent a variety of methodological beliefs and academic values. We recognize that these beliefs are determined based on the experiences, knowledge and expertise a researcher brings to their work. We also situate these ideas within the context of our own academic values – what is the role of hierarchy? What constitutes 'evidence' in research? And who should benefit from research that is conducted, oftentimes in places that are far removed from the day-to-day work we do in CIE institutions, both academic and non-academic? Our work is both as teachers and scholars and in that regard, this reminder from Elizabeth Minnich can give us a moment to pause to think about our work as methodological guides:

> Knowledge gives us something we share that matters enough to have opinions about; opinions give us differing perspectives about the meanings as distinct from truth claims of knowledge. This is why, as teachers, we try both to convey knowledge and to encourage students to develop worthy opinions about it – to think about it, without submitting to it. In this we are recognizing that what is taken to be truth within a discourse of knowledge should not trump but remain in generative tension with our human plurality, our differences, our multiple perspectives, and our responsibilities. (Minnich, 2003, p. 22)

We end this book with many more questions than answers – but we also recognize that we are not seeking uniformity and agreement, but a space for many ways of knowing. What we do understand is that fidelity to philosophy, fidelity to methods and fidelity to the voices of the people we are working with and for, is of critical importance. Ensuring that we have these conversations as methodologists is something that we would encourage more, and look forward to the reception that these ideas get, with scholars and practitioners within the field of CIE.

References

Adukia, A. (2017, October). Symposium statement. In *Conference Proceedings of the 2nd Comparative and International Education Symposium: Interrogating and Innovating CIE Research*. George Mason University. Arlington, VA: GMU. Retrieved from https://cehd.gmu.edu/2017symposium/

Baily, S., Shah, P., & Call-Cummings, M. (2015). Reframing the center: New directions in qualitative methodology in international and comparative education. In A. W. Wiseman & E. Anderson (Eds.), *Annual review of comparative and international education* (pp. 139–164). Bingley: Emerald Publishing.

Ballantyne, E. F. (2014). Dechinta Bush University: Mobilizing a knowledge economy of reciprocity, resurgence and decolonization. *Decolonization: Indigeneity, Education & Society*, 3(3), 67–85.

Foronda, C., Baptiste, D. L., Reinholdt, M. M., & Ousman, K. (2016). Cultural humility: A concept analysis. *Journal of Transcultural Nursing*, 27(3), 210–217.

Haas, P. M. (1992). Introduction: Epistemic communities and international policy coordination. *International Organization*, 46(1), 1–35.

Minnich, E. (2003, September–October). Teaching thinking: Moral and political considerations. *Change*, 19–24.

Mitra, D. L. (2008). Amplifying student voice. *Educational Leadership*, 66(3), 20–25.

Patel, K. K., Villarruel, A., & Wong, W. (2013). *Amplifying the voice of the underserved in the implementation of the Affordable Care Act*. Institute of Medicine of the National Academies.

Piantanida, M., & Garman, N. B. (2010). Writing research. In P. Thomson & M. Walker (Eds.), *The Routledge doctoral student's companion* (pp. 244–255). Oxon: Routledge.

Pryor, J. (2010). Constructing research questions: Focus, methodology and theorization. In P. Thomson & M. Walker (Eds.), *The Routledge doctoral student's companion* (pp. 161–171). Oxon: Routledge.

Schmidt, V. A. (2008). Discursive institutionalism: The explanatory power of ideas and discourse. *Annual Review of Political Science*, 11, 303–326.

Seale, J. (2016). How can we confidently judge the extent to which student voice in higher education has been genuinely amplified? A proposal for a new evaluation framework. *Research Papers in Education*, 31(2), 212–233.

Wiseman, E., & Anderson, A. W. (2015). Introduction to part 3: Conceptual and methodological developments. In E. Anderson & A. W. Wiseman (Eds.), *Annual review of comparative and international education 2013* (pp. 85–90). Bingley: Emerald Group Publishing.

Index

Aajeevika Skill Development Programme (ASDP) 75
absenteeism 92, 93
academia 237
access 73, 74, 76, 83
activist 167
activity-based approach 78
administration 87, 90, 91, 96, 100, 102, 108
administrative language 91
administrative structure 75
aesthetic(s) 45–48
    cognitivism 10, 26
    qualities 45
affective economies 21
affirmation 78
Africa 99
African American teen girls 142
Akshay Mangla 87
altruism 121
American Evaluation Association 61
amplify voices, 167, 168, 244, 249
analysis
    qualitative 93
    quantitative 93
Anglicized Indians 91
Annual Status of Education Report (ASER) 70, 110–123
    Volunteer Questionnaire Survey 114
    Volunteer Survey 114, 115
answerability/answerable 22, 23, 187, 189
approval 81
Arabic 104
Architectural Assistantship 75
area vocational survey 75
arts 45–47
arts-based 46, 47
Arts-Based Educational Research (ABER), 10, 26, 45
arts-based research 46, 47
Asociación de Pedagogos de Cuba 226
assessment 52–55, 58–60, 89, 110–113, 115, 118–123
    tool 110
Association of Cuban Educators 226
assumption 78, 79, 82, 232, 242, 246

attendance 112
attitude 75, 79
authority 4, 5, 11
axiology/axiological 19, 20, 23, 24, 37
Azamgarh 89, 90, 95, 96, 101, 107

Barabanki 89, 91, 96, 107
Bareilly 88, 99, 100, 107
Barelvi 93
behavior of public officials 7
Beti Bachao initiative 74
Bhoomi Sena 87
Bhopal Gas disaster of 1984 73
Bhopal, India 73
bias 78
Black women 142
boarding 93
brave space 78
British colonial policy 91
brother 81
burden to reform 89
bureaucracy 87, 90, 92, 95, 98–103, 105–108
    analysis of 87
    communalization of 99
    structure 87, 91
bureaucrat 91, 94, 95

Cambodian 152, 155–157, 160
capitalism 142, 146, 226
capitalist 142, 202
case study 51, 62, 110, 111, 113–115, 120–122
change 5, 8, 9, 12, 17, 19, 23, 24
    social 53, 55, 57, 63
China 95
choice, lack of 105
CIES Symposium 3, 6, 12, 17
citation metrics 69
citizen 110, 111, 113, 116, 119, 120, 121
    assessor 111
    Indian 73, 74
    skills of 74
citizen-led assessment process 110
citizen-oriented engagement 113
citizenship 113–123
    global 95

INDEX

civil society organization 99
class 9
cleanliness standard 93
co-construction 149, 155, 157–159
co-creation 141, 142
cognitivism
    aesthetic 5
collaboration/collaborative 12, 50, 227
    relationship 149
colonial 18, 21, 22, 24, 26, 27, 31, 32, 141, 144, 146, 196
    dynamics 231
colonialism 8, 29, 30, 31, 77, 89, 90, 99
coloniality 1, 2, 7, 8, 10, 18, 20–22, 25, 26, 31, 32
colonialization 87
colonization 18, 23, 29, 30, 31, 67, 188
colonize 23, 30, 130, 134, 141, 143, 144, 151
communalism 95
communication
    gap 91
community 77, 78, 81–83, 88–90, 92, 93, 95, 97, 99–103, 107, 108, 141–147, 154, 167, 243–247, 249
Comparative and International Education (CIE) 67, 68, 70, 110, 120, 121, 130, 133, 135–139, 149, 167, 226, 241–249
    role of scholars 68
Computer Science 75
conflict 90, 91, 95, 99
conscience 92, 102
constant comparative method 115
constituency 97, 103
constitutional privilege 103
constructivist 22
Convention on the Rights of Persons with Disabilities (CRPD) 169
conversation 78
corruption 92, 96, 98
courage 245, 246, 248
critical 2–5, 7, 10, 12, 13
    framing, pedagogy 226
    reflection 229
    tension 243
    theory 8
critique 87, 94, 105–107
cross-language 149
    focus groups and interviews 150
cross-national comparison 50, 51
Crud Factor 212
Cuba 236

cultural
    hybridity 76
    knowledge 149
    needs 92
    practice 93
culture 76, 77, 79, 83, 87, 90, 91, 94, 95, 99, 100, 102, 105, 106, 108
    majoritarian 95
    national 95
curiosity 244
current affairs 77
curriculum 89, 91, 102
cyber security 83

data
    collection 110–115, 117–120
    collector 113
    conclusion from 115
    displaying of 115
    qualitative 113–115
    quantitative 113, 114
    reduction of 115
    transparency of 119
daughter 76, 81, 82
decision-making 78, 97, 142
decolonial 5, 7, 8, 13, 50, 141
decolonization 1, 2, 8, 18, 25, 32, 150
decolonize 1, 4, 9–11, 18, 25, 26, 30, 31, 90, 134, 137, 140–147, 149–153, 156, 196, 226
demand and supply 73, 83
demand side 73
democratic 4, 9
demographics 115
Deobandi 93
Department of Women and Child Development 74
descriptive statistics 114
destabilize 196
developing countries 72
development 29, 30, 87, 89, 94, 98, 102, 106, 108
dialogic/dialogical 231, 244
dialogue 1–4
difference 10, 20, 23, 27
    intergenerational 81
disability 11, 167–172, 174–176, 179–184
discipline 87, 93
discourse 167, 168
discussion 78, 79, 83, 96, 101
dismantling 149
disruption 132–134, 137

INDEX

distribution of data   218
District Institution of Education and Training (DIET)   111, 116
diverse   2, 4, 5
diversity   4, 167
doing good   228
domination   197
donor   154
dress code   93

economic depression   91
education   73–76, 78, 81–84, 87–90, 92–94, 102, 104–108, 111–113, 116–119, 121–123
   vocational   73, 75
educational institution   69
educational system   68
Education for All   169
education system   89, 90
effect size   208
electronics   75
empirical scientific   50
employment   74–76, 82, 93, 94, 97, 105
empowerment   61, 69, 84, 135, 154, 174, 175
engagement   4, 5, 7
English   91, 106
entanglement   198
epistemic
   blindness   21
   domination   21
   injustice   8, 21, 22, 27
   violence   21
epistemicide   207
epistemological   2, 4, 6, 8–10, 12, 13, 19–21, 24, 26, 45, 50, 55, 129, 133, 138, 141
   vigilance   230
epistemology   2, 4, 5, 12, 19, 23, 45, 47
equity   2, 5, 73, 236
ethical   6, 7, 244
ethics   7, 12, 167, 236
ethnicity   4, 210
ethnographic study   106
Eurocentric   2, 8, 30, 196
evaluation   52, 54, 58, 59, 61–63
evidence   52–54, 58
evidence-based   25, 53, 206
   action   111, 113, 119, 122
   policy   207
exclusion   5, 19, 21
experience   150–153, 155, 156, 158, 160, 164
external factor   79

extractive research   226
extremist   94, 99

facility   112
family   75, 77, 80, 81, 82
feedback   232
female participation   83
feminist   5, 8, 9, 14, 168, 182
field note observations   114
financial issues   81
first space   77
fixed identifications   76
focus group   95, 96, 148–152, 155, 159, 162, 164
   discussions   242
forms of knowledge   188
framework   231
free public school   92
Freire, Paulo   119
fundamentalist   94
funding agency   50, 52, 54, 60
funding model   73, 76

gatekeeper   154
Gayatri Spivak   67
gender   4, 9, 10, 67, 69, 73, 78–80, 82–84, 130, 133–136, 155, 156, 159
   equity   82
   norm   76
   role   78, 79
   stereotype   73, 83
   study   83
generational bias   82
Ghana   11, 167, 172
global education governance   206
global education policy   207
globalization   51, 70, 77, 82
Global North   50, 52, 53, 68, 196, 227
Global South   167, 196, 227
gold standard   209
governance   91
   political   90, 91
government-run school   110–112
government school   88, 92–94
Gujarat   102

handicraft   73
Haryana   114
healing   142
hegemony   8, 9, 12, 144, 167, 190
heteronormativity   146

hierarchy 3, 5, 6, 8, 11, 19, 69, 70, 76, 110, 120, 121, 146, 149, 150, 153–155, 162
hijab 93
Hindi
   spoken form 91
   written form 91
Hindu 88, 91–96, 99, 105, 107
Hindutva 95
Historically Black Colleges and Universities (HBCUS) 31
history 94, 96, 99, 105, 106, 108
home 74, 77, 80, 83
home and workspace, intersections of 77
Hoshiarpur 109
household 78, 80, 81
   survey 110, 112
housing 93
hukumat 96, 100
Hummel, Ralph 102
hygiene 93
hypothesis testing 208

ice-breaker 79
identity 6, 67, 68
   communitarian 95
   national 94, 95
   regional 91
   religious 91, 92
   researcher identity 153
ideological 2, 94, 100-101
ideology
   educational 89, 90
   nationalist 95
   religious 89
illiteracy 78, 91–93
impact
   assessment 50, 52–61
   evaluations 208
imperialism 90, 105
implementation 52
imposter syndrome 229
inclusion 167, 168, 172, 178, 180, 183
inclusive 79, 84, 167, 169, 170, 172, 173, 175, 176, 179, 181, 183, 184
inclusivity 1, 2, 7
inclusiveness 83
income 74, 80
India 68–70, 72–75, 77, 84, 86, 87, 90, 94–96, 99, 100, 102, 103, 105–123
Indigenous 18, 22, 23, 28, 30, 31, 142, 144, 146, 147, 149, 165

international non-governmental organizations (INGOS) 154
innovation 247, 248
inquiry 131, 133
institutional capacity 88
interdisciplinarity 145
international education 1, 2, 5, 7–9, 14
interpretation 149, 150, 152, 153, 155–161
interpreter 149–165
   training 149
interpretive approach 115
interpretive process 115
interpretivist 149–151
interrogation 247
intersectional 129, 135, 138, 141, 142
intersectionality 1, 2, 4, 5, 8, 9, 11, 130, 137, 141
intersection 9
interview 148–150, 152, 153, 155–162, 164, 242
   process 151
   semi-structured 93, 94
interviewing 49
Islam and Islamic history 93
Islamic
   calendar 93
   history 94
   learning 94
   studies 89, 91
Israel/Israeli 55–57, 59, 61, 62

Kaluram 78
Kenya 54, 121
knowledge 2–7, 9–11, 18–21, 23, 24, 26, 27, 30–32, 47, 48, 51–55, 58–61, 63, 129–131, 133–138, 141, 144–146, 149–163, 248
   aesthetic 45
   as a claim to power 68
   bottom-up 54
   decolonization of 68
   economy 72
   extraction 226
   hierarchy 6, 11, 150, 151, 153, 155
   legitimate 10, 20, 26, 50,157, 160
   production of 67–70, 141, 142, 235
   transformation of 69, 120, 121
   worker 69, 70

labor market 73, 74, 76
language 6, 7, 9, 89–91, 93, 94, 104, 107, 148, 150–154, 157–163, 165
   Hindi 90, 91, 94, 100, 107

language policy   90, 91
learning   51, 58–61
    level   109, 110
    opportunity   73, 74, 83
    outcome   93
legitimation
    process of   67, 68
legitimization   11
linguistic dominance   188
linguistic tradition   91
literacy   72, 104
literature   246, 247
local   4–6, 10, 50–52, 54, 55, 61, 62, 150, 154
    knowledge   160
Lucknow   86, 90, 97, 102, 104

maanyata   92
madrassa   1, 11, 69
    girl   90, 93
    manager   90, 92, 95, 101
    private   89, 90, 97, 103
    representative   90, 98, 99, 101, 102, 105
    state-funded   103
    resistance of   87
    teacher   95
    transformation of   87
Mahashakti women   76, 77
Mahashakti Seva Kendra (MSK)   73, 78, 79, 84
Majority South   191
male   81, 82, 160
Mali   121
map   112
marginalized   144
member check   236
mental model   74, 78, 79
methodological   2, 4, 6–8, 10, 12, 45, 50, 54, 55, 59
methodological pluralism   199
methodological practice   191
methodology   2, 4, 5, 9, 10, 13, 14, 20, 24, 79, 111, 121, 143
method   4, 5, 10, 12
metropole   190, 196
micro-level process   51
Millennium Development Goals   169
Minority North   191
mixed-methods   87, 114
    approach   113, 123
model of bureaucratic organizational structure   87

modern society   89
mother tongue   151
mulla   88
multigenerational   69
Muslim   89–95, 99, 100, 102, 105–108
    anti   93

narcissism   229, 230
Narendra Modi   103
narrative   167
National Curriculum Framework   102
nationalism/nationalistic   94, 95
National Service Scheme (NSS)   117
National Textile Ministry   73
neocolonial   2, 8, 18, 22, 45
neocolonialism   2, 91
neoliberal   168, 201, 226, 228
New Delhi   110, 114, 122, 123
Nigeria   121
non-formal education   55
non-governmental organizations (NGOS)   110, 52, 54, 55, 84, 154
normal curve   208, 209, 215, 218
normal distribution   217
Norwegian Agency for Development Cooperation (NORAD)   74
null hypothesis   212

observation protocol   114
observer   159
onto-epistemic   8, 17
onto-epistemological   4, 49, 187, 189, 231
onto-epistemology   2, 18, 22
ontology/ontological   9, 10, 12, 20–24, 141
opportunity   141, 241, 242, 244–247
    educational   73
oral material   91
organizational learning   50, 58, 59
organization   52, 55, 57, 60, 61
Others   2, 8
outsider perspective   10
outsider   30, 50, 51
ownership   54, 58

paathshaalas   95
paimaana   89
Pakistan   95, 100, 121
Palestine   95
paradigm   48

participant observation   114, 115
participant   78–84
participation   242, 245
participatory   50, 52, 61, 62, 141–143, 145, 147, 167
   framework   113
   methodology   143
   method   149
   research   110, 111, 145
participatory action research (PAR)   73, 74, 78, 82, 84, 111, 174
partnership   50, 55, 60
patriarchal
   legacy   76
   practice   73
   rules   83
   society   83
patriarchy   77, 142, 146, 188
peace-building   56, 57
pedagogy   2
people with disabilities   167–170, 172–175, 177, 179, 180, 182
perception   235
periphery   200
Persian   104
perspective   79
PhotoVoice   11, 167–169, 173–176, 178–180
pluralism   5
   philosophical   47
pluriversity   199
policy   83, 84
   executor   97
   influence on   86
   institution   72–74
   maker   89, 90, 94, 97, 101
   planning   97
   process   87, 105, 107
policy-making   95
   educational   89
political opinion   77
political party   96, 98–100
   loyalist   98
politicization
   infiltration of party representatives   98
polycentric   193
Polytechnic Education   75
polytechnics   74
poor educational background   92
population
   experiences of   69

positionality   5, 41, 133, 135, 137, 141, 146, 150, 160, 191, 227
positivist/positivistic   5, 45, 49, 50–52, 150–152, 162, 188, 220
postcolonialism/postcolonial   3, 5, 9, 14, 24, 50, 63, 68, 150, 227
postcolonialization   87, 99, 100, 101, 105–107
post-European   198
post-positivist   52
poststructural   8
poverty   92, 93, 107, 201
poverty line   75
power   1, 2, 4, 5, 8, 11, 12, 51, 52, 130, 133–135, 137, 138, 141, 142, 149, 150, 153–155, 159, 160, 162, 164, 165, 168, 172–175, 178, 229, 244, 245, 247, 249
   analysis   214
   calculation   214
   dynamics. See power
   knowledge   11, 141
practical   242
practitioner   2–5, 7, 9, 10
Pratham   110, 122, 123
Pratham Assessment Survey   110
praxis
   Freire   163
preparation of curriculum   75
privileges   233
probability test   218
problematics   141, 142
psycho-social   83
Punjab   109, 114
p value   208

qualitative   47, 48
   data   78
   method   148–150, 165
   research   47, 48
quantification
   power of   69
quantitative
   analysis   114
   method   207
quasi-experimental   53

racism   7, 31, 146
racist   32
Ramadan   94
randomization   210
randomized control trial (RCT)   210

INDEX

rapport   157, 161
reading material   112
reciprocity   236
reflection/reflect   42, 130, 135, 136, 151, 163, 226, 242, 246
   process   227
reflexivity   4, 12, 192
regression analysis   210
relatability   88
relational   23, 25
   accountability   23
relation
   in-country   95
relationship   55, 58–60, 155
religion   90, 91, 95, 96, 99, 100, 107
reparation   197
representation   131, 138, 242, 245
research
   data
      field-based   109
   design   111, 113
      mixed-methods vertical case study   87
   method   45
   methodology   19, 24, 69
      performativity of   68
   on communities   242
   practice   110, 120, 121
   producer of   69
   question   113, 117, 118
   validity   229
researcher   78
   identity   149
respondent   88, 90, 102, 104, 107
restorative justice   190
restory   198
result   82
rights   167, 179, 184
rival thinking   230
rural district   111, 112

Sadaka Reut   50, 55–61
safe space   30, 31, 157
safety   81, 83
sanskrit   90, 91, 107
Sarkar   90, 100
scapes   77, 83
school   88, 89, 91–96, 98, 104–108
   private   104
   public   97, 104

science   46, 90
scientific   51, 53
scientism   46
Secondary School Leaving Certificate (SSLC)   116
second space   77
secrecy   100
sectarian belief   93
secular   89, 91, 106
self-awareness   79
self-confidence   78, 79
self-reflection   226
Senegal   121
separatist   94
settler   18
   colonialism   226
Shia   93
silence   3
skill   72–76, 83, 84
   development   72–74, 82, 83
social
   action   113
   justice   5, 110, 111, 120, 121, 227
   location   23
   protection   74
   sciences   45
social network survey   7
socialization   22
socially desirable   79, 82
South Asia   3, 10, 68–70, 99, 110, 121–123
sovereignty   31
space   140–144, 146, 173
Spivak, Gayatri   67, 68, 71
stakeholder   9
standard deviation   213
standard error   213
standpoint   141
stereotype   69, 79
story   167
student   24, 25
subaltern   101, 102
Sub-Saharan Africa   121
Support to Training and Employment Programs (STEP)   74, 75
survey notebook   111, 112
sustainability   132, 134, 137, 141
Sustainable Development Goals   169
symposium   1, 3–7, 9–12, 17, 19, 27, 28, 32

taboo   77
Tanzania   121
teacher   90, 92, 93, 97, 103, 104
   madrassa   89, 99, 100
teacher training programs   75
team building
   prevention of   97
Technical and Vocational Education Training (TVET)   72–74, 76, 82–84
technology   112, 116, 123
temporality   21
tension   132, 136, 137, 155
textbook   4, 75, 96, 106
theme   78
theory/theoretical   3, 7–9
third space   76, 77, 82
tradition   76, 77, 79, 83, 90, 94
training
   manual   75
   program   74, 75
   vocational   73, 74
transformation   5, 8, 11, 141
transformative   2, 12
   ethos   110, 113, 115, 118–120, 122
transform   141
translation   149–154, 156–158, 162, 164, 165
trauma   42
trust
   lack of   93
trustworthiness   154
t-test   212
Tuhiwahi-Smith, Linda   144

Uganda   121
ummah   95
United Nations Educational, Scientific and Cultural Organization (UNESCO)   119, 123, 171
United Nations (UN) Sustainable Development Goal
   SDG4   73, 74, 83, 84
   SDG5   84
unity   95
universalism   20
university   141, 143–146
urban bias   100
Urdu   89, 91, 94, 100, 104, 108
United States Agency for International Development (USAID)   53, 54, 63

Uttar Pradesh (UP)   86, 87, 90, 91, 94, 97, 100, 103–105

value   50, 53, 54
   cultural   79
   positive   79
   system   74, 89
village leader   112
violence   8, 9, 30, 32, 99, 107, 142, 144
visibility   172
visual   131, 132, 136
vocational   73
   course   73
   education   10, 68, 69
   training   74–76
voice   1, 2, 7–10, 13, 134, 138, 149, 159, 161, 167, 242–244, 247, 248, 249
volunteer training   114

wages   74
Weber, Max   87
Western   20, 21, 29, 30
Western education   89
White savior   228
White supremacy   6, 7, 142
women   60, 72–84, 159
   economic participation of   69
   education for   68, 69
   environment for   73
   influence of   69
   in India   74
   in the workforce   72
   needs of   73
   perspectives of   69
   voices of   69, 73, 83
work book curriculum guide   75
workforce   72, 75
   female   74
   formal   72, 74
   informal   74
   population   74
working conditions   74
workplace   79
world culture   51
world systems   51

youth   54–56

zameer   102
zone of interpretation   230